# Ordering Pluralism

From the viewpoint of the constitutional crisis in Europe, slow UN reforms, difficulties implementing the Kyoto Protocol and the International Criminal Court, and tensions between human and rights and trade, Mireille Delmas-Marty's 'journey through the legal landscape' of the early years of the 21st century shows it to be dominated by imprecision, uncertainty and instability. The early 21st century appears to be the era of great disorder: in the silence of the market and the fracas of arms, a world overly fragmented by anarchical globalisation is being unified too quickly through hegemonic integration. How, she asks, can we move beyond the relative and the universal to build order without imposing it, to accept pluralism without giving up on a common law?

Neither utopian fusion nor illusory autonomy, *Ordering Pluralism* is Delmas-Marty's answer: both an epistemological revolution and an art, it means creating a common legal area by progressive adjustments that preserve diversity. Since an immutable world order is impossible, the imaginative forces of law must be called upon to invent a flexible process of harmonisation that leaves room for believing we can agree on—and protect—common values.

**Volume 1: French Studies in International Law**

# Ordering Pluralism

## A Conceptual Framework for Understanding the Transnational Legal World

Mireille Delmas-Marty

translated by

Naomi Norberg

·HART·
PUBLISHING

OXFORD AND PORTLAND, OREGON
2009

Published in North America (US and Canada) by
Hart Publishing
c/o International Specialized Book Services
920 NE 58th Avenue, Suite 300
Portland, OR 97213-3786
USA
Tel: +1 503 287 3093 or toll-free: (1) 800 944 6190
Fax: +1 503 280 8832
E-mail: orders@isbs.com
Website: http://www.isbs.com

Hart Publishing Ltd, 16C Worcester Place, Oxford, OX1 2JW
Telephone: +44 (0)1865 517530 Fax: +44 (0)1865 510710
E-mail: mail@hartpub.co.uk
Website: http://www.hartpub.co.uk

British Library Cataloguing in Publication Data
Data Available

ISBN: 978-1-84113-990-6

Typeset by Hope Services, Abingdon
Printed and bound in Great Britain by
TJ International Ltd, Padstow, Cornwall

# Series Editor's Preface

The CERDIN research centre of the University of Paris I (*Panthéon-Sorbonne*) is very pleased to inaugurate the Series 'French Studies in International Law', and we are grateful to Hart Publishing for agreeing to publish it. The Series aims to contribute to the dissemination in English of the works of the most eminent international law scholars writing in French. Because these works have not yet been published in English, this scholarship has been inaccessible to a great number of potential readers who, due to the language barrier, have not been able to become acquainted with or discuss it. This is highly regrettable, as it limits the debate on international law to works in English—the *lingua franca* of our contemporary world—and thus primarily to Anglophone scholars.

The publication of these works in English therefore seeks to create the conditions for genuine debate among Francophone and Anglophone international law scholars across the globe, a debate that should henceforth be based on the work of both. Learning of the others' theories through translation is in fact the first essential step towards acknowledging the contributions and differences of each. *Knowledge* and *acknowledgement* lead to understanding the irreducible core, as well as truth, in each legal culture's international law doctrine, its traditions and distinct ideas, as well as each author's way of thinking. They should make it possible to avoid the all-too-frequent misunderstanding of each other's position on international law that results from simple ignorance of each other's work. Between the Francophone and Anglophone worlds the rule has all too often been mutual, even courteous, indifference or ignorance, and dialogue the exception.

No book could better introduce this Series than Mireille Delmas-Marty's superb volume, *Ordering Pluralism*. Professor at the Collège de France, where she holds the chair in Comparative Legal Studies and Internationalisation of Law, Mireille Delmas-Marty is one of the most eminent and well-known of French legal scholars. Translated here for the first time into English, *Ordering Pluralism* provides a vision for the world and suggests a solution based on analyses so strong, illuminating and profound that they will leave no reader indifferent. It cannot help but stimulate a discussion that I hope is only just beginning.

Emmanuelle Jouannet
Professor, Sorbonne Law School (*University Paris 1*)

# Foreword

Mireille Delmas-Marty is a Member of the Institut de France, a professor at the College de France, a visiting professor at universities all over the world, the author of dozens of books and articles on legal subjects, particularly criminal and international law, and the recipient of many honors and awards. In a word, she is a great legal expert. She has specialized in international and transnational law. And that is the subject of this book.

Professor Delmas-Marty here writes about law that transcends national boundaries. That law is increasingly made in an ever-growing number of transnational legal bodies, including regional associations, such as the North American Free Trade Area, and more globally inclusive bodies, such as the International Criminal Court. Justice Sabino Cassese tells us, for example, that in 2004 there were around 2000 'global regulatory bodies, called international or intergovernmental organizations'.[1]

International and transnational law is made, not simply by those who write the treaties establishing these bodies, but also by the administrators and judges who work for them, including, for example, administrators at the European Union, judges at the Inter-American Human Rights Court, arbitrators at the Iran–US International Claims Tribunal, and adjudicators working at the World Trade Organization. The legal rules they create or interpret cover subjects of all kinds, ranging from commercial or trade law to criminal law. The content of that law relates ever more closely to the content of national legal systems, as each system draws inspiration from, and helps to shape, the others.

Those who work with law that reaches beyond the boundaries of a single nation work within an ever-expanding legal universe; and they understand the need to knit together the parts of that expanding legal

---

[1] Sabino Cassese, Administrative Law without the State? The Challenge of Global Regulation, 37 *NYUJ Int'l L & Pol* 663, 671 (2005).

universe into a more coherent whole. We know that law made outside
the United States can affect Americans. We know that sometimes it
does so by providing the applicable norm for deciding a specific
domestic case and sometimes by influencing the content of another
applicable domestic or transnational norm. We know that all the
while transnational law is itself subject to the influence of national law
as both kinds of law evolve through the work of both domestic and
transnational decision makers. But how are we to describe the content, the evolution, the direction of this ever more important expanding set of legal systems?

Just what is it that those who work with, and within, transnational
law have been dong? How successful have they been? What are their
failures? What are the consequences of what they have done? What
more should be done? We cannot even begin to think about such
questions until we have conceptual tools fitted for the job. We need
a framework and concepts that allow us to describe what this law is,
what it does, how it has grown, and how it fits together. We need an
initial description.

This book provides those tools and that description. It helps us
understand how law among nations and beyond single nations develops through cross-referencing, through efforts to harmonize, and
through the creation of hybrid rules of substance and procedure. It
helps us understand where this law develops, regionally or internationally. And it helps us understand the significance of the temporal
leads and lags created as this law develops over time. In a word, the
book helps us understand, talk about, and evaluate what is happening before our very eyes.

Why is this important to Americans? Consider how in recent years
the abstract considerations I have just mentioned have produced
concrete issues in the Supreme Court of the United States, the Court
on which I serve. Consider the practice of cross-referencing. Some
members of my own court (of which I am one), when writing an
opinion in a case involving American constitutional law, will sometimes refer to decisions handed down by judges of foreign constitutional courts. Two recent Supreme Court cases, *Lawrence v Texas*
and *Roper v Simmons*, illustrate the practice.[2] In *Lawrence* the court
struck down a state law criminalizing certain forms of homosexual
conduct, and it supported its decision in part by referring to a

---

[2] *Lawrence v Texas*, 539 US 558 (2003); *Roper v Simmons*, 543 US 551 (2005).

somewhat similar case from the European Court of Human Rights.[3] In *Roper* the court struck down state laws that would have applied the death penalty to 16- or 17-year-old defendants (convicted of capital murder), and it supported its decision in part by referring to the fact that no other nation applied a death penalty to offenders under the age of 18.

The practice has proved surprisingly controversial. Dissenting justices as well as several commentators have criticized the justices' practice of referring to foreign legal decisions. And 40 Members of Congress introduced legislation that would severely limit federal courts' use of foreign law in deciding constitutional issues. Since that time judges and commentators alike have engaged in debate. Indeed, my colleague Justice Scalia and I have debated the issue in opinions and at law school forums.

The terms of the debate run roughly as follows: those favoring the foreign-reference practice point to historical precedent. They add that the decisions of foreign courts do not bind us. And they argue that, in an ever more democratic world with ever more independent judicial systems faced with ever more similar problems, one nation's judges can and should learn from the experience of others. Those who oppose the use of foreign references distinguish historical practice, primarily on the ground that many of the foreign cases referenced came from nations with special jurisprudential ties to the United States, namely Britain or the British Commonwealth. They add that nothing prevents an American judge from learning about foreign case law by reading the work of others or corresponding with foreign colleagues. But, they say, an opinion's supporting citation wrongly smuggles a foreign view of a foreign law into a Constitution that is, and was meant to be, American in meaning and application. One distinguished judge wrote: 'To cite foreign law as authority is to flirt with the discredited . . . idea of a universal natural law; or to suppose fantastically that the world's judges constitute a single elite community of wisdom and conscience.'[4]

Note what is omitted from these arguments. Neither side says much about how the practice of cross-referencing within the United States takes place within a broader geographical context. Judges across the world make increasing use of each other's opinions. That may well be because of the increased use of written constitutions

---

[3] *Dudgeon v United Kingdom*, 45 ECtHR (1981) p 52.
[4] Judge Richard Posner, *Legal Affairs*, July/August 2004, at www.legalaffairs.org.

seeking to protect democratic institutions and individual human
rights and the increased reliance upon independent judiciaries to
help enforce those protections; it may reflect the increased similarity
of legal problems faced across the world. Regardless, the practice of
cross-referencing will have global, as well as local, effects. Before we
can evaluate those effects, we must know what they are. And we cannot know what they are without a vocabulary, a framework, and an
initial description of the transnational universe.

Consider the docket of our court. The number of cases involving
foreign or transnational law has been growing rapidly. Indeed, in the
year between *Lawrence* and *Roper* the court considered or referred to
foreign law in at least six 'bread-and-butter' cases, cases that are
important but do not involve such publicly controversial subject
matter as Lawrence's homosexual rights or Roper's death penalty.
The court's use of foreign law in these six cases provoked no adverse
comment. Everyone understood the need. The cases were unusual
only in that their number, six out of a total docket of 79, indicates the
increasingly routine nature of this kind of court business.

Consider the subject matter of those cases: (1) Does American
antitrust law authorize an Ecuadoran vitamin distributor to file suit
in America against a Dutch vitamin producer? (The distributor says
that the producer was a member of an unlawful vitamin price-fixing
cartel operating outside the United States.)[5] (2) Does American 'discovery' law permit one American firm to obtain documents from
another American firm in order to present them to the European
Union's anti-cartel Authority? (The Authority says it does not want
them.)[6] (3) Does the American Foreign Sovereign Immunities Act
bar Maria Altmann, an American citizen born in Austria, from
bringing a federal court lawsuit in 2001 against the Austrian
National Gallery to obtain possession of six Klimt paintings that she
says the Nazis took from her uncle in 1938?[7] (4) Does an environmental statute bar entry of trucks from Mexico—entry that the
North American Free Trade Agreement authorizes the President to
permit?[8] (5) To what kinds of contemporary injuries today does the
general language of the early-enacted (1789) American Alien Tort
Statute apply?[9] (The Statute permits compensation for injuries

---

[5]  *F Hoffmann-La Roche Ltd et al v Empagran SA et al*, 542 US 155 (2004).
[6]  *Intel Corp v Advanced Micro Devices, Inc*, 542 US 241 (2004).
[7]  *Republic of Austria v Altmann*, 541 US 677 (2004).
[8]  *Department of Transportation v Public Citizen*, 541 US 752 (2004).
[9]  *Sosa v Alvarez-Machain et al*, 542 US 692 (2004).

caused by actions 'in violation of the law of nations,' and its authors likely intended the statute primarily to authorize compensation for injuries caused by pirates.) (6) Does the Warsaw Convention, governing international airline accidents, authorize recovery for a death caused by an allergy to cigarette smoke?[10]

In all these cases the parties expected the court to look, and it did look, to international, transnational, or foreign legal sources. In the antitrust and discovery cases, for example, several foreign nations (Germany, Japan, Canada, and France) and the European Union filed briefs. In the airline accident case all participating judges agreed that the court must examine and treat as precedents Warsaw Convention cases decided in the courts of other nations. In applying the Alien Tort Statute, the court had to determine today's equivalent of 18th-century piracy, and in doing so it consulted both older and modern international legal practice.

In Mrs Altmann's case the decision of an intermediate Paris appeals court helped me better understand the 'sovereign immunity' to which the American statute referred.[11] Christian Dior had sued ex-King Farouk to collect a bill for dresses that the ex-King had bought for his wife before he lost his throne. The Paris court held that Farouk could no longer assert the sovereign immunity defense because he was no longer king. The decision thereby indicated that the Austrian National Gallery could no longer claim sovereign immunity, for (unlike the 1930s and 1940s) it was now engaged in commercial activities.

The growing number of these ordinary cases suggests a need for American judges better to understand the requirements of law that is not purely domestic. Two of the cases, the anti-trust case and the discovery case, required the court to understand how an administrative unit of a transnational regional organization, namely the European Union, does its work. One required an understanding of the legal relation of a different set of transnational rules, those of NAFTA, to American law. One required interpretation of a treaty, the Warsaw Convention. One required the application to a foreign entity of a legal concept, namely sovereign immunity, which draws content from international law. And one required the court to understand and to evaluate the likely the consequences of its interpretation of a domestic law, the American Alien Tort Statute, in a world where

---

[10] *Olympic Airways v Husain*, 540 US 644 (2004).

[11] *Ex-King Farouk of Egypt v Christian Dior*, 84 Clunet 717, 24 ILR 228 (CA Paris 1957).

many other countries may seek to apply somewhat similar law to the same or similar parties. The judges must know where to look to find the relevant transnational information; and they must know enough about its context to be able to evaluate what they find.

Again, to take this 'foreign law' into account properly demands some knowledge of the broader picture, that is, of the context in which that law is developing. If law professors and scholars understand that context, they can better inform us, directly or by informing the lawyers who practice in the area. And this book will help them do so.

Consider another recent case, *Medellin v Texas*.[12] The subject matter of the case before the court in that case involved the death penalty. The Vienna Convention on Consular Rights requires the police of a signatory nation to inform an arrested person from another signatory nation that he has a right to communicate with his own nation's consul. Texas state police had failed to inform a murder suspect from Mexico of this right; and the suspect was later convicted of murder and sentenced to death. The Vienna Convention also authorized the International Court of Justice (ICJ) to interpret that treaty. And the ICJ had held that the Convention required the United States to hold an additional hearing to see whether this communication failure was harmless. Texas refused to do so.

The American Constitution says that 'treaties' are 'supreme law' and 'Judges in every State shall be bound thereby.'[13] The question was whether this constitutional rule required Texas to follow the ICJ's ruling without more, that is, without any further domestic law enacted by Congress. The court answered that Texas need not comply; further action by Congress was needed; these provisions of the Vienna Convention were not self-executing. And, in so holding, the court set forth a legal rule that reaches well beyond cases involving the death penalty. It set forth criteria for determining when treaty provisions are self-executing. And those criteria, I fear, are so restrictive that few treaty provisions could satisfy them.

In my (dissenting) view, the circumstances present in Medellin satisfied traditional criteria long used (here and abroad) for determining whether a treaty provision is self-executing. The language of the treaty is specific and binding. The subject matter, criminal procedure, is judicial in nature (unlike, say, disposition of armed forces). It is easy for judges to fashion procedures to carry out the

---

[12] *Medellin v Texas*, 128 S Ct 1346 (2008).
[13] US Constitution, Art VI.

Convention's (and the ICJ's) mandate (unlike say, many highly generalized obligations). Judicial enforcement raises no constitutional issues (unlike, say, a treaty provision that deprived an individual of rights guaranteed by the American Constitution or which violated principles of separation of powers). In a word, the treaty and ICJ decision 'address' the 'judicial,' not the political, branches of government.[14]

My own view, however, did not carry the judicial day. And one might ask, now what is to be done? Because of the political difficulty of seeking individual laws from Congress provision by provision treaty by treaty, specifying whether an international obligation is self-executing, the court's contrary holding may threaten the enforcement of a range of treaty provisions, involving, for example, intellectual property, trade, and other subjects of commerce. Does that consequence warrant an effort to obtain a more general, criteria-specifying law, from Congress? What should any such law say?

Once again, to answer this question sensibly, we should know something about the likely contemporary significance of treaties and particularly treaties that create adjudicatory bodies. What is their likely subject matter? How important is it to ask Congress for what would be, in effect, a delegation to the treaty makers, to the President (who signs treaties) and to the Senate (which ratifies them), but not to the House of Representatives (which plays no role), of the authority to change domestic law? Once again I can point out that this book, by providing a description of what is happening in the transnational legal world as well as a conceptual framework for discussing it, can help us answer these very practical legal questions.

In providing these examples, I do not mean to suggest that this book will find its audience only among judges. To the contrary, the book is aimed at scholars, at specialists, and at those among the general public who take an interest in their work. I do mean to suggest, however, that even judges and even lawyers increasingly fall within the latter category. The subject is one that has practical implications for their work. The book is timely and relevant to the practical concerns of those who work with, and within, the legal system. We must thank Professor Delmas-Marty for her fine work. It will help us get started.

Stephen Breyer
Washington, DC

[14] *Medellin*, 128 S Ct 1392 (Breyer J dissenting).

# Contents

# List of Abbreviations

| | |
|---|---|
| ACHPR | African Commission on Human and Peoples' Rights |
| ACHR | American Convention on Human Rights |
| ACP | African, Caribbean and Pacific Group of States |
| AFDI | Annuaire français de droit international |
| *AJDI* | *Actualité juridique du droit international* |
| ALCA | Área de libre comercio de la Américas (see FTAA) |
| APC | Archives de politique criminelle |
| APEC | Asia-Pacific Economic Cooperation |
| ASEAN | Association of Southeast Asian Nations |
| ASIL | American Society of International Law |
| ATCA | Alien Tort Claims Act |
| BGB | Bürgerliches Gesetzbuch (German Civil Code) |
| CAN | Comunidad andina de naciones (Andean Community of Nations) |
| Caricom | The Caribbean Community and Common Market |
| CC | Conseil constitutionnel |
| CFSP | Common Foreign and Security Policy |
| Chr. | Chronique |
| CIA | Central Intelligence Agency |
| CoE | Council of Europe |
| CP | Penal Code |
| CPP | Code of Criminal Procedure |
| CT | Constitutional Treaty of the European Union |
| *D.* | *Recueil Dalloz* |
| *DC* | *Recueil des décisions du Conseil Constitutionnel* |
| DRB | Dispute Resolution Body (of the WTO) |
| EC | European Community |
| ECHR | European Convention on Human Rights |
| ECJ | European Court of Justice |
| ECO | Economic Cooperation Organization |
| ECOSOC | Economic and Social Council |

| | |
|---|---|
| ECSC | European Coal and Steel Community |
| ECtHR | European Court of Human Rights |
| EEC | European Economic Community |
| EHESS | Ecole des hautes études en sciences sociales |
| *EHRLR* | *European Human Rights Law Review* |
| *EJIL* | *European Journal of International Law* |
| EU | European Union |
| EUI | European University Institute |
| Euratom | European Atomic Energy Community |
| Europol | European Police Office |
| FAO | Food and Agriculture Organisation |
| FIDH | Fédération internationale des ligues des droits de l'homme |
| FTAA | Free Trade Area of the Americas |
| GATT | General Agreements on Tariffs and Trade |
| GG | Greenhouse gas |
| GMO | Genetically modified organisms |
| HRC | Human Rights Committee |
| HRLJ | Human Rights Law Journal |
| ICC | International Criminal Court |
| ICCPR | International Covenant on Civil and Political Rights |
| ICESCR | International Covenant on Economic, Social and Cultural Rights |
| ICHR | Inter-American Court of Human Rights |
| ICJ | International Court of Justice |
| ICRC | International Committee of the Red Cross |
| ICSID | International Centre for Settlement of Investment Disputes |
| ICT | International Criminal Tribunal |
| ICTR | International Criminal Tribunal for Rwanda |
| ICTY | International Criminal Tribunal for the former Yugoslavia |
| ILO | International Labor Organization |
| IMF | International Monetary Fund |
| ISO | International Organization for Standardization |
| *JCP* | *Juris-classeur périodique (Semaine juridique)* |
| *JICJ* | *Journal of International Criminal Justice* |
| LGDJ | Librairie générale de droit et de jurisprudence |
| MAE | Multilateral Agreement on the Environment |
| Mercosur | Mercado común del Sur (Southern Common Market) |
| NAFTA | North American Free Trade Agreement |

| | |
|---|---|
| NATO | North Atlantic Treaty Organization |
| NGO | Non-Governmental Organization |
| OECD | Organisation for Economic Cooperation and Development |
| OHADA | Organisation pour l'harmonisation du droit des affaires en Afrique |
| OLAF | European Antifraud Office |
| OXFAM | Oxford Committee for famine relief |
| PUF | Presses universitaires de France |
| *RCADI* | *Recueil des cours de l'Académie de droit international de La Haye* |
| *RCDIP* | *Revue critique de droit international privé* |
| *Rev dr aff* | *Revue Lamy droit des affaires* |
| *Rev dr internat.* | *Revue du droit international* |
| *Rev dr UE* | *Revue du droit de l'Union européenne* |
| *Rev dr unif* | *Revue du droit uniforme* |
| *Rev Marché unique* | *Revue du Marché unique européen* |
| *RGDIP* | *Revue générale de droit international public* |
| *RIDC* | *Revue internationale de droit comparé* |
| *RIEJ* | *Revue interdisciplinaire d'études juridiques* |
| *RSC* | *Revue de science criminelle et de droit pénal comparé* |
| *RTDH* | *Revue trimestrielle des droits de l'homme* |
| *RUDH* | *Revue universelle des droits de l'homme* |
| SCt. | Supreme Court (United States) |
| SEC | Securities and Exchange Commission |
| SLC | Société de législation comparée |
| SOX | Sarbanes–Oxley Act |
| TEC | Traity of the European Community |
| TEU | Treaty on European Union |
| TPICE | European Court of First Instance |
| US | United States Supreme Court Reports |
| UDHR | Universal Declaration of Human rights |
| UK | United Kingdom |
| UKHL | United Kingdom House of Lords |
| UMR | Mixed Research Unit |
| UN | United Nations |
| UNESCO | United Nations Educational, Scientific and Cultural Organization |
| UQAM | University of Quebec, Montreal |

US              United States
USC             United States Code
WHO             World Health Organization
WIPO            World Intellectual Property Organization
WISIS           World Summit on the Information Society
WTO             World Trade Organization

# Introduction

## The One and the Many: Pluralism in the Plural

NOW COMES THE hard part: to go beyond 'the relative and the universal'.[1] That book represents the first leg of a journey I will now continue, not to produce a never-ending description of the legal landscapes encountered, but to put them in order. Having exposed the weaknesses of legal universalism and the limits of relativism due to globalisation, I would now like to explore how to seek order without predetermining it.

At the dawn of the 21st century, the legal landscape's primary characteristics are imprecision, uncertainty and instability, or, as I put it when discussing their main manifestations, the fuzzy and the soft. And with the European Union's constitutional crisis and slow progress of UN reforms, the year 2005 did little to inspire optimism. Rather, it commanded modesty: instead of a legal order in the traditional sense, my journey through the legal landscape revealed the great disorder of a world both exceedingly fragmented, as if dismembered by an anarchical globalisation, and rashly unified, if not homogenised, by the hegemonic integration resulting as much from economic as military might. Ordering multiplicity without reducing it to sameness, admitting pluralism without giving up on building a common law with a common measure for fair and unfair, can therefore seem an unattainable goal.

But what some might call an entertaining but vain mental exercise, the poet Edouard Glissant calls 'tremorous thought': 'a tremendous insurrection of the imagination that would finally push humanities to

---

[1] See M Delmas-Marty, *Les Forces imaginantes du droit (I): Le Relatif et l'Universel* (Paris, Seuil, 2004).

see and invent themselves (notwithstanding any moral injunction) as they are in reality: never-ending change in perennial movement.'[2] To achieve this, one must no doubt distinguish between the various pluralisms that permeate legal discourse, and remember that the enigma of 'the one and the many' has haunted human civilisation throughout history. For example, the ancient Greeks wondered about what Empedocles called the 'double aspect of things: for at times the one rises alone from the many, yet at others, the many are born of one'.[3]

Empedocles seems to be echoing Lao Tzu's well-known passage, which has been quoted throughout history by Chinese and Western thinkers alike and which also associates two processes. First, division: 'The Tao begets the One, the One begets Two, Two begets Three, and Three begets the ten thousand things.' Then, fusion: 'The ten thousand things carry Yin on their backs and Yang in their arms; intertwining their breaths, they create harmony.' Applied to the legal field, the two processes seem to lead to a double deadlock: fusion signals a seemingly utopian and potentially worrisome legal unity, while separation presupposes complete autonomy, which no longer exists. Between the two, legal systems oscillate from an increasingly anarchical disorder to an increasingly open hegemony. To break the deadlock, jurists must abandon both utopian unity and illusory autonomy, and explore the possibility of reciprocal pro-creation between the one and the many. To convey the idea of movement, this process could be called 'ordering pluralism'.[4]

## Pluralism of Fusion and Utopia: The Great Legal Unity of the World

A quick trip through space and time will illustrate the concept of fusion in all its ambiguity.

### The Ambiguity of Fusion

In 1910, a year before an almost 2,000-year-old empire disappeared, Chinese jurists made a last attempt to convince the emperor of the

---

[2] E Glissant, *La Cohée du Lamentin* (Paris, Gallimard, 2005) pp 24–5.

[3] Empedocles, in Y Battisti, *Trois Présocratiques* (Paris, Gallimard, 'Idées,' 1968) p 57. Bilingual version: J Bollack, *Empédocle II. Les origines* (Paris, Gallimard, 'Tel', 1992) pp 18–19.

[4] Cf N Bobbio, 'Pluralismo' in Norberto Bobbio, N Matteucci, G Pasquino (eds), *Dizionario di politica* 2nd edn (Turin, Utet, 1983).

need for reform. The committee supervising the establishment of a constitutional government[5] put forth the idea of the 'Great Legal Unity of the world' to be attained through the 'fusion' of Chinese and western law. The suggested fusion was not reciprocal, however, so not at all pluralist, and the hoped-for unity would be illusory.

In fact, the goal was to westernise certain areas of Chinese law such as family law, which was scarcely egalitarian. The Great Legal Unity was an element of an evolutionary conception of humanity, which, after the era of 'decadence and chaos', would usher in the rising Peace and the Age of Great Peace. Borrowed from Confucius (who, like Empedocles and Lao Tzu, lived five centuries before the Christian era) and embellished by other classical Chinese philosophers, this phrase was reused by reformers such as Kang Youwei, author of *Book of the Great Unity*,[6] who tried to convince classical Chinese culturalists to embrace a universal ideal.

Kang's main disciple Liang Qichao took a more political approach. Like Kang, he was exiled to Japan in 1898 following the failed Hundred Days Reform movement that sought to institute a constitutional monarchy similar to Japan's during the Meiji era. In an essay entitled *Of the community*,[7] which resonates with meaning today, Liang suggested replacing 'citizen of the sky' with 'citizen of the world': 'There are citizens of nations and citizens of the world. Western countries have adopted a form of government by the nation; they have not yet attained government by world citizens . . . When the Age of the Great Peace arrives, all parts of the world, from the furthest to the nearest, the largest to the smallest, will be but one.' But Liang was not naïve, and exile turned this erudite jurist who cited the same classical sources as Kang Youwei into a realist who 'finally accepted that China could not survive without a definitive break with tradition'.[8]

Sharing this realism were other jurists, such as Shen Jiaben, who suggested to the emperor that Chinese and western law be fused.[9]

---

[5] See J Bourgon, 'Shen Jiaben et le droit chinois à la fin des Qing,' doctoral dissertation, EHESS, 1997, pp 767 *ff*.

[6] See A Cheng, *Histoire de la pensée chinoise* (Paris, Seuil, 1997) p 626 (noting that *Datong Shu (Book of the Great Unity)*, was published in its entirety only in 1935, eight years after Kang's death).

[7] Liang Qichao, Preface to *Shuoqun (Of the community)*, *Yinbinshi Wenji (Writings of Liang Qichao)*, Zhonghua Shuju, 1926 (cited by Cheng, *Histoire de la pensée chinoise*, above n 6, p 627).

[8] Cheng, *Histoire de la pensée chinoise*, above n 6, p 628.

[9] See Bourgon, *Shen Jiaben et le droit chinois à la fin des Qing*, above n 5.

Westernisation was the means to both convince the emperor to modernise political and legal institutions and to show western powers that semi-colonised China was ready to regain its sovereignty. Indeed, the commercial treaties imposed by the West promised that consular courts would be eliminated and the territoriality principle recognised when China modernised its law.

This mix of universalist idealism serving nationalist pragmatism is similar to the 'nationalist universalism' of the German historic school of the 19th century, which argued for a return to Roman-Germanic common law rather than accept the French civil code.[10] This similarity is not surprising, considering Liang Qichao knew of the German school and drew inspiration from it for his own works on the history of Chinese law.[11] Moreover, legal unity has been dreamed of across time and across cultures,[12] including in the West, from Vitoria's 16th-century *Civitas maxima*[13] to Giambattista Vico's 'Great city of nations' and Emmanuel Kant's cosmopolitism[14] in the 19th century. They weren't naïve, either. Vico emphasised that, though nations seem to follow the same path, 'isomorphism is not synonymous with synchrony: at any given moment in history, nations coexist at different stages of evolution'.[15] And Kant took care to exclude the possibility of a universal republic, which he believed could become the worst kind of tyranny. Instead, he

[10] See Delmas-Marty, *Le Relatif et l'Universel*, above n 1, pp 33 *ff*; JL Halpérin, *Entre nationalisme juridique et communauté de droit* (Paris, PUF, 1999); O Jouanjan, *L'Esprit de l'Ecole historique du droit* (Strasbourg, Presses universitaires de Strasbourg, 'Annales de la faculté de droit de Strasbourg', 7, 2004).

[11] See J Bourgon, 'La coutume et la norme en Chine et au Japon' (2001) *Extrême-Orient, Extrême-Occident* no 23; Liang Qichao, *La Conception du droit et les théories des légistes à la veille des Qing* (Escarra trans, Peking, 1926).

[12] See Delmas-Marty, *Le Relatif et l'Universel*, above n 1, pp 26 *ff*.

[13] F Vitoria, Leçon sur le pouvoir politique (M Barbier trans, Paris, Vrin, 1980); on Vitoria's 'cosmopolitan stoicism', see M Villey, *La Formation de la pensée juridique moderne*, text established, revised and presented by S Rials (Paris, PUF, 2003), pp 340 *ff*.

[14] See E Kant, *Idée d'une histoire universelle du point de vue cosmopolitique, Œuvres philosophiques* (Paris, Gallimard, 'Bibliothèque de la Pléiade,' 1984) vol II, pp 185 *ff*; *A la paix perpetuelle, vol III* (Paris, Gallimard, 'Bibliothèque de la Pléiade,' 1986) pp 333 *ff*; 'Le droit cosmopolitique', *Doctrine de droit*, 2nd part, 'Le droit public', vol III (Paris, Gallimard, 'Bibliothèque de la Pléiade', 1986) pp 625 *ff*. On Liang Qichao's translation of Kant, see J Thoraval, 'Sur l'appropriation du concept de « liberté » à la fin des Qing. En partant de l'interprétation de Kant par Liang Qichao' in M Delmas-Marty and PE Will (eds), *La Chine et la Démocratie. Tradition, Droit, Institutions* (Paris, Fayard, 2006).

[15] G Vico, *Principes d'une science nouvelle relative à la nature commune des nations* [*Principi di scienza nuova d'intorno alla commune natura delle nazioni, 1744*], A Pons (trans) (Paris, Fayard, 2001).

preferred independent nations and reserved his cosmopolitanism for civil society.

Kant is often cited, sometimes in opposition to Grotius, the father of *inter*national law, to support *supra*national legal unity founded on a pluralism of fusion. This tends to legitimate the universalist legal forms emerging above domestic law, from the Universal Declaration of Human Rights of 1948 (UDHR) to the 1998 statute of the International Criminal Court (ICC). But the weaknesses of a universalism that becomes legal in bits and pieces[16] indicate that it is not enough to take concepts from different traditions and stick them together to build worldwide legal unity. Pluralism cannot be decreed: imposed unity is most often synonymous with hegemonic domination, whereas pluralism concerns human rights, or crimes against humanity.

## Utopian Unity

Even when limited to a declaration such as the UDHR, which is not binding, 'cultural dialogue' is not easy.[17] In 1948, the Chinese diplomat and co-drafter of the Declaration Chang Pengchun ran into a linguistic obstacle when he urged his fellow committee members to complete the first article's reference to 'reason', which has strong western connotations, by adding *liangxin*, a concept closer to Confucianism. He succeeded ('All human beings are . . . endowed with reason *and conscience*'); but the word 'conscience' used in the English and French versions is a poor translation of the Chinese *liangxin*, which refers more to the respect due to others than to individual conscience. In fact, the French and English versions use the same word to designate human beings 'endowed with . . . conscience' and freedom 'of conscience', while the Chinese version uses two different terms, *liangxin* in Article 1 and *yishi*, which suggests intentionality and discernment, in Article 18.

Similarly, though it claims to say the same thing in every language, a comparison[18] of the various official versions of the ICC statute reveals numerous variations, some of which result from linguistic differences, some from the legal concepts themselves, which differ

16 See Delmas-Marty, *Le Relatif et l'Universel*, above n 1, pp 49 *ff.*
17 See Will, 'La contribution de la Chine à la DUDH,' in Delmas-Marty and Will, *La Chine et la Démocratie*, above n 14.
18 See E Fronza, E Malarino and C Sotis, 'Principe de précision et justice pénale internationale' in M Delmas-Marty, E Fronza and E Lambert-Abdelgawad (eds), *Les Sources du droit international pénal. L'expérience des tribunaux pénaux internationaux* (Paris, Société de Législation Comparée, 2005) pp 157–210.

among systems. The problem is therefore not simply language. As human rights progressively become legal principles, it becomes increasingly clear that 'human rights' does not mean the same thing to everyone. This is particularly clear with respect to the distinction between civil and political rights and economic, social and cultural rights—a distinction made, to the detriment of the principle of indivisibility, by adopting two distinct conventions (the UN covenants of 1966) that states could ratify together or separately, as they pleased. And even in a region as culturally homogeneous as Europe, the invention of the national margin of appreciation indicates that a fusion guaranteeing perfect legal unity is possible only in a few, rare areas,[19] as national judges pointed out with respect to the Treaty establishing a constitution for Europe and, now, the Lisbon Treaty.

For example, in 2004, the French *Conseil constitutionnel* underscored that the principles set out in the Charter of Fundamental Rights and Freedoms of the European Union, particularly the 'freedom, either alone or in community with others and in public or in private, to manifest religion or belief' (Article 11), do not require all member state practices to be the same: such rights may be restricted for reasons of 'public safety, order, health and morals, as well as to protect the rights and freedoms of others'.[20] From this, commentators have deduced that the 'French law on religious symbols at school is constitutionally valid and [that], from this perspective, the Treaty changes nothing'.[21] Even in Europe, then, fusion and a unified order are a long way off.

The issue of fusion has already been raised at the global level, however, with respect to crimes against humanity and international criminal justice. For example, the ICC statute imposes interpretational directives on the judges: in the absence of 'principles or rules of international law' (in other words, in the event of silence or ambiguity), judges must refer to 'general principles of law derived by the Court from national laws of legal systems of the world' (Article 21(1)(c)). That is, provided they respect international principles, judges are encouraged to fuse national criminal concepts. It remains to be seen how they will achieve such an objective, which, to be truly pluralist, would require access to all the sources of every nation's

---

[19] See Delmas-Marty, *Le Relatif et l'Universel*, above n 1, pp 64 *ff*.
[20] Conseil constitutionnel, 19 November 2004, decision 2004-505 DC.
[21] B Mathieu, 'La "Constitution" européenne ne menace pas la République', *Dalloz*, 2004, p 3075.

law.[22] Beyond that, as former First President of the International Criminal Tribunal for the former Yugoslavia (ICTY) Antonio Cassese wrote in a dissenting opinion, different systems must be 'combine[d] and fuse[d]'.[23] But true legal hybridisation requires working at a deeper level, not simply accumulating data, and is therefore probably not possible. Indeed, a study of the unwritten sources of international criminal law—general principles and custom—shows that there is still quite a way to go. Far from representing the various legal systems of the world, the case law of the *ad hoc* international criminal tribunals (ICTY and ICTR, the International Criminal Tribunal for Rwanda) indicates strong western hegemony[24]: the five countries cited by far the most are the United States, Germany, the United Kingdom, France and Italy.

If fusion carries the risk of reducing the utopian Great Unity to hegemony, is the pluralism of separation, which assumes states are perfectly autonomous, also an illusion in the age of globalisation? As the 2004 report to the UN Secretary General pointed out, 'No state, no matter how powerful, can by its own efforts alone make itself invulnerable to today's threats'.[25] This assertion was echoed in the World Summit document submitted to the General Assembly in 2005: 'No State can stand wholly alone.'[26]

## Pluralism of Separation and the Illusion of Perfect Autonomy

Separation refers to the inevitable and necessary division of human societies: 'Oh indeed, humans can unite only in division! They maintain their union only through incessant division! It is thus. It cannot be otherwise.'[27] Written by Gotthold Lessing during the Enlightenment,

---

[22] In 2005, the Max-Planck Institute for Foreign and International Criminal Law began compiling the first worldwide criminal law database. Methodological issues remain unresolved.

[23] *Erdemovic*, ICTY, Appeal Chamber, 7 October 1997 (Cassese dissent para 4).

[24] See L Gradoni, 'Nullum crimen sine consuetudine' in M Delmas-Marty, E Fronza and E Lambert-Abdelgawad, *Les Sources du droit international pénal*, above n 18, pp 25–74.

[25] High Level Panel on Threats, Challenges and Change, *A More Secure World, Our Shared Responsibility*, UN, 2 December 2004, para 36.

[26] Draft outcome document of the high-level plenary meeting of the General Assembly of September 2005 submitted by the President of the General Assembly, A/59/HLPM/CRP.1, para 5, 8 June 2005.

[27] GE Lessing, 'Dialogue entre Ernst et Folk', *Nathan le sage* [1779] (Paris, Flammarion, 1997) p 37.

the dialogue between Ernst and Folk is still current. To borrow the Italian philosopher Salvatore Veca's expression, there is now an 'art of separation', which Veca presents as a fundamental element of political pluralism: fundamental not only in how pluralism is described, but in prescribing it as a value.[28]

## The Art of Separation

This expression easily applies to the legal field: part of the contemporary legal doctrine, which has progressed from describing pluralism as a simple fact to prescribing it as a value,[29] bases the principle of separation on strictly *inter*national law, which is limited to distributing jurisdiction among equal and autonomous systems. But plurality and pluralism must not be confused.

Separation enables plurality, but it does not guarantee pluralism. It does not link systems together, but juxtaposes different legal orders without building a common order. For example, when the American philosopher Michael Walzer describes multiple 'spheres of justice', he sets out a principle of 'complex equality',[30] which he links to distributive justice. But he explains neither how to guarantee it, nor how juxtaposing autonomous spheres leads to a shared normativity (moral or legal) that is anything more than minimal.[31]

As Emmanuel Levinas has written, plurality, which he calls 'numerical' to distinguish it from pluralism, 'is defenseless against totalisation'.[32] To resist totalisation and become pluralism, plurality needs subjectivity—the face of the other—as proof of what Levinas calls 'multiple existing'. But Paul Ricœur wants to know whose face it is, and imagines it is the face of a 'master of justice'[33] whose injunction is the only thing that interrupts the perfectly symmetrical and reciprocal exchange.

Such a master exists only if law becomes *supra*national. Whether simply recognising the fact of pluralism or prescribing it as a value, *inter*national law postulates recognition of the other (other state or other legal system), but does not guarantee it. In other words, it

---

[28] See S Veca, *Ethique et Politique* [*Etica e Politica*] (Paris, PUF, 1999) p 99.

[29] See Delmas-Marty, *Le Relatif et l'Universel*, above n 1, pp 222 *ff*.

[30] M Walzer, *Spheres of Justice*, P Engel (trans) (Paris, Seuil, 1997) p 23.

[31] See generally M Walzer, *Thick and Thin, Moral Argument at Home and Abroad* (Notre Dame, University of Notre Dame Press, 1994).

[32] E Levinas, *Totalité et Infini* (Leiden, Martinus Nijhoff, 1961), Reedn Le Livre de poche, 'Biblio essais' no 4120, pp 242–50.

[33] P Ricœur, *Soi-même comme un autre* (Paris, Seuil, 1990) p 221.

is silent in the face of totalisation, whether totalisation stems from globalisation-related phenomena or from one system's hegemonic extension.

My analysis of the limits of legal relativism faced with globalisation (of crime, flow of intangibles, and risk) includes several examples of how the pluralism of separation has failed. This failure is confirmed by the UN report *A More Secure World*'s[34] analysis of the six major threats to collective security (poverty, interstate and internal conflicts, the proliferation of weapons of mass destruction, terrorism and organised crime): free circulation—of persons, goods, services and capital, to which technological progress has added information—has shown that when it comes to states protecting their territory and populations, legal autonomy is an illusion.

## Illusory Autonomy

Confronted with the global strategies of the most powerful private actors, be they corporations or criminal organisations, national legal systems seem singularly defenceless and more and more dependent on each other. It is no accident that so-called *inter*state co-operation has been replaced by the harmonisation of procedures and substantive rules, as is the case with the 2002 framework decision on the European arrest warrant: from a desire to facilitate extradition by simplifying the procedures and eliminating the diplomatic phase, European states succeeded in agreeing on common definitions for 32 offences and minimal procedural rules.

Nor is it an accident that, in the struggle first against bribery, then against money laundering, protecting national public interests is placed second behind protecting transnational trade interests (free competition on the world market). This order of priorities expresses another type of interdependence, between public and private interests.[35] In fact, private actors' strategies are facilitated by information technology. The internet's ubiquity and instantaneousness defies the concept of national territory and weakens national legal systems by multiplying possible conflicts of jurisdiction,[36] unless trade law no longer directly neutralises domestic norms to protect freedom of

---

[34] See http://www.wwan.cn/secureworld/.

[35] See Delmas-Marty, *Le Relatif et l'Universel*, above n 1, pp 257 *ff*, 277 *ff*. See also N Capus, 'Le droit pénal et la souveraineté partagée' (2005) *Revue de science criminelle* 251.

[36] See *ibid.*, pp 337 *ff*.

services, as did a decision on electronic commerce by the Dispute Resolution Body (DRB) of the World Trade Organization (WTO).[37]

But the purposeful strategies of globalisation's actors are not the only cause of lost autonomy. Technological advances literally globalise (or make more visible) biotechnological, ecological and sanitary risks. Here again, the autonomy of national systems seems weakened: in theory, each state chooses the degree of protection it intends to guarantee, but it is clear that the issue of climate change due to human activities, for example, cannot be resolved at the national, or even regional, level alone.[38] While identical constraints cannot be imposed immediately on every country, a reasonable balance must be found. Within the WTO framework, states may restrict imports to protect the national public interest from ecological, sanitary or phyto-sanitary risks, but only to the extent that such restrictions are not manifestly disproportionate to the risk.[39] In theory, the WTO does not evaluate the risk's magnitude, only the proportionality of the restrictions to the risk. In practice, the difference is so subtle that it may be clearer to simply say that states enjoy a 'national margin of appreciation, [but it] is not unlimited and may vary depending on the interests concerned'.[40]

In addition, the hegemonic expansion of certain systems must be taken into account. As I discussed in *Le relatif et l'universel*, American law influences every area of law. For example, the Sarbanes–Oxley Act of 2002 applies American rules of corporate governance, with their attendant civil and criminal penalties, to all companies subject to Security and Exchange Commission (SEC) reporting requirements.[41] A more recent example of both the global strategies of corporations and the hegemony of American law over what is openly becoming a 'market of laws' is the Russian oil company Ioukos's

---

[37] See C Manara, 'Commerce électronique: première décision de l'Organe de règlement des différends de l'OMC', *Dalloz*, 2004, p 3122. This decision, which is based on the general agreement on the service trade, sets aside the American legislation on providing gaming and betting services challenged by Antigua.

[38] See B Collomb and G Dollé, 'Kyoto? Oui! La directive européenne? Non!' *Le Monde* (Paris, 11 December 2004). See also the response by Y Jadot and P Quirion, 'Kyoto? Oui! Le leadership européen? Maintenant!' *Le Monde* (Paris, 21 December 2004).

[39] See, eg, WTO Dispute Resolution Body, Measures Affecting the Importation of Apples, AB-2003-4, 26 Nov 2003.

[40] H Ruiz Fabri and P Monnier, 'Chronique' (2004) *Journal de droit international* 1022, 1025.

[41] See Delmas-Marty, *Le Relatif et l'Universel*, above n 1, pp 321–3.

attempt to file bankruptcy under American law.[42] The attempt failed, but not for legal reasons alone. The determining factor was neither international law, which is clearly unsuited to the situation, nor national law, though the argument of national autonomy was raised, but Russia's economic and political power.[43] A weaker and more democratic state would probably have been disarmed.

Finally, the pluralism of separation is not only of little help in combating the hegemonic expansion of national law, it is also insufficient to overcome the risk of legal disorder when a powerful state rejects an international norm, believing it to run counter to national interests. Disorder thus stems from the appearance of zones of resistance, or even 'legal black holes', an expression used with respect to Guantánamo, but applicable elsewhere. Even in Europe, restrictions on the rights of men and women based on morality or religion generally escape European, and a fortiori international, judicial review.

National judicial review does of course exist in the United States,[44] as well as in Europe. For example, the British Anti-terrorism, Crime and Security Act 2001 created a legal void by authorising the Home Secretary to order the long-term administrative detention, without judicial review, of aliens suspected of terrorism. The Act was censured by the House of Lords on the grounds that it violated the prohibition on discrimination contained in the European Convention on Human Rights (ECHR).[45] Parliament then filled the legal void, but allowed the administration to maintain its policy: the Prevention of Terrorism Act 2005 authorises imposing various control measures on 'individuals involved in terrorism-related activity' (Preamble). This Act requires that a judge approve the measures, but it also allows for extra-judicial emergency

---

[42] See N Nougayrède, 'Ioukos tente de se placer sous protection juridique américaine', Le Monde (Paris, 17 December 2004).

[43] See Le Monde (Paris, 18 and 23 December 2004): the Russian Federal Property Fund challenged the American judgment and President Putin approved the disputed sale of Ioukos's subsidiary.

[44] See, eg, the decisions of the United States Supreme Court discussed in Delmas-Marty, Le Relatif et l'Universel, above n 1, pp 208 and 236; G Fletcher, 'Citoyenneté et dignité de la personne dans la jurisprudence du droit de la guerre: Hamdi, Padilla et les détenus de Guantanamo Bay' (2005) Revue trimestrielle des droits de l'homme 841; DM Amann, 'Abu Ghraib' (2005) 153 University of Pennsylvania Review 2085.

[45] See A(FC) v. Secretary? of State for the Home Department [2004] UKHL 56. The Convention was made directly applicable in the United Kingdom by the Human Rights Act 1998, which was presented by the British government as the means to avoid censure by the European Court and to bring human rights home (the draft bill was entitled 'Rights Brought Home'). This may seem paradoxical, since judges at home can censure certain choices of the administration.

measures and expands the exceptional regime and suspension of defence rights to citizens.[46] Conscious of the risk of incompatibility with the ECHR, the British government went so far as to question its adherence to a text that it considers unsuited to combating terrorism as it has evolved.[47]

Nevertheless, when the very principle of the international norm is rejected, ideas circulate through cross-references between various courts and create a 'judicial dialogue' that expresses a certain systemic permeability. For example, Chile has not ratified the Rome Statute creating the International Criminal Court (ICC), nor did it create a mixed tribunal to try General Pinochet, but the Chilean Supreme Court confirmed the lifting of the latter's immunity and the issuance of a warrant for his arrest.[48]

Better still, though the United States opposes the ICC and wouldn't consider for an instant creating an *ad hoc* tribunal to judge the events of 11 September, the United States Supreme Court held that persons detained as 'enemy combatants' (that is, having the rights of neither combatants nor criminals), whether they be citizens or aliens, have the right to petition the court to challenge their detention.[49] Some judges of the Supreme Court have even cited the International Covenant on Civil and Political Rights (ICCPR) even though it is not directly applicable before American courts.[50] They also sometimes cite foreign case law or that of the European and Inter-American Courts of Human Rights, and, as I will discuss, have even gone so far as to refer to world public opinion. In response, two members of Congress proposed a bill to prohibit judges from basing their decisions on foreign law that has not been incorporated into American law by legislation and does not help better determine the original meaning of the laws of the United States.[51]

These multiform interactions show the world has gone from complicated (multiple and heterogeneous) to complex (interactive and

---

[46] See JC Paye, 'The Prevention Security Act britannique du 11 mars 2005' (2005) *Revue trimestrielle des droits de l'homme* p 635.

[47] See the indignant reaction of the president of the Parliamentary Assembly of the Council of Europe, *Le Monde* (Paris, 15 September 2005).

[48] See 'La Cour suprême du Chili donne son feu vert au jugement de Pinochet', *Le Monde* (Paris, 5 January 2005).

[49] See the decision of 28 June 2004 discussed in Delmas-Marty, *Le Relatif et l'Universel*, above n 1, p 236 and n 57.

[50] See L Condorelli and P de Sena, 'The Relevance of the Obligations Flowing from the UN Covenant on Civil and Political Rights to US Courts Dealing with Guantanamo Detainees' (2004) 2 *Journal of International Criminal Justice* 107.

[51] See H RES 568, 108th Congress, 17 March 2005.

unstable)[52] and have encouraged me to suggest that 'ordered pluralism' is possible: 'pluralism' because differences are tolerated; 'ordered' if global law succeeds in overcoming the contradiction between the one and the many.

## 'Ordered Pluralism'

### The Challenge of 'the Great Legal Complexity of the World'

One response to the world's legal complexity is to maintain separation and, without imposing fusion, build something like a legal order, or an ordered legal area. The challenge of 'the Great Legal Complexity of the world', a response to the utopian 'Great Unity', lies in human society's capacity for resistance. In Europe, for example, national systems resist integration into an international legal order that would impose uniformity, but they have nonetheless lost a large part of their autonomy: major choices are made at the international level,[53] not only by state representatives, but by private actors as well, particularly multinational or transnational[54] corporations. Indeed, private economic actors now compete with states by developing their own norms. Though states remain the 'fundamental' subject of international law and the primary producers of norms, they are no longer the only actors and their territories are no longer the only normative areas.

From these tensions between public and private, or local, national and global, fragments of a common law have emerged, blurring the categories that separated universalism from relativism. As I mentioned above, relativism is related to the pluralism of separation; it implies systemic autonomy, while increasing interdependence is in fact reducing autonomy. Universalism, however, is related to the pluralism of fusion, in that it would grant primacy to international norms. While international texts sometimes affirm such primacy, it is rarely upheld.

Though otherwise very useful, terms commonly found in the ordinary legal vocabulary—terms such as 'order', 'system', 'hierarchy' or 'autonomy'—are inadequate when it comes to translating

---

[52] See C Godin, *La Totalité vol 6: La Totalité réalisée* (Paris, Champ Vallon, 2003) p 455.

[53] See PM Dupuy, *L'Unité de l'ordre juridique international. Cours général de l'Académie de droit international public* [2000] (Leiden, Martinus Nijhoff, 2003); Delmas-Marty, *Le Relatif et l'Universel*, above n 1, p 10 *ff*.

[54] So called because their strategies openly cross borders, the transnational becoming 'the fallen mask of the multinational'. Godin, above n 51.

the phenomena of interdeterminacy, inconsistency and instability that accompany the internationalisation of law. Indeterminacy results from the processes of integration which, in becoming inter- active, have diversified and freed themselves from the principle of hierarchy. Inconsistencies arise when organisational levels become fragmented as international organisations multiply and become more and more sectorial (human rights, trade, environment, etc). Instability is a consequence of differences in speeds of integration, which produce dysfunctions both between and within legal ensem- bles, as well as between actors (as the debate surrounding the European directive anticipating the implementation of the Kyoto Protocol on greenhouse gases shows).

To avoid the extremes of world disorder (radical separation and absolute relativism) and an order imposed by the mightiest nation in the name of universalism (total hegemonic fusion), we need to move beyond the universal/relative dichotomy and explore the possibility of a law that would order complexity without eliminating it, trans- forming it into 'ordered pluralism'.

## The How-to of Ordering Pluralism

At first glance, the answer to the challenge of the Great Legal Complexity of the world seems to constitute a sort of bricolage that attempts, through multiple interactions (judicial and normative, spontaneous and imposed, direct and indirect) to link together legal ensembles (national and international) that history has separated and that will not accept hegemonic fusion.

In this game of interactions, separation does not entirely preclude integration. On the contrary, as is the case with living organisms, the separation and integration of tasks is coordinated.[55] But integrating tasks requires overcoming the political and legal obstacle of national sovereignty, which is insurmountable only when conceived in absolute terms. In fact, we are not moving towards a world 'without sovereignty',[56] but towards a 'dilution of sovereignty'.[57] But this 'diluted' sovereignty has yet to be transformed into the shared sover-

---

[55] See H Atlan, *Entre le cristal et la fumée* (Paris, Seuil, 1989); JC Ameisen, *La Sculpture du vivant* (Paris, Seuil, 2003).

[56] H Badie, *Un monde sans souveraineté. Les Etats entre ruse et responsabilité* (Paris, Fayard, 1999).

[57] H Ruiz Fabri, 'Droits de l'homme et souveraineté de l'Etat: les frontières ont- elles été substantiellement redéfinies?' in O Jouanjan and C Grewe (eds), *Les Droits individuels et le juge en Europe. Mélanges Fromont* (Strasbourg, Presses universitaires de Strasbourg, 2001) pp 371 *ff.*

eignty at the heart of the both the European Constitutional Treaty and the Lisbon Treaty and, implicitly, the UN report on threats to security, the title of which refers to 'our shared responsibility', thus sovereignty. Either way, sharing requires imagining new legal techniques to make norms less rigid and enable practices to evolve.

This is where the difficulty lies: the interactions already occurring between multiple and heterogeneous legal systems do not offer the same image of legal certainty as that which results from the principle of hierarchy in the standard representation of legal systems. And yet, these are indeed legal, and therefore normative, interactions: they define an 'ought to be' (normativity), rather than simply an 'is' (normality), though of course one influences the other. This is why human willpower, beliefs and ideologies limit the analogy with biological organisms or machines, however instructive it may be. Legal interactions guarantee neither the organic continuity of biological processes of self-regulation, nor the mechanical foreseeability (except accidents or failures) of physical phenomena, but organise themselves without pretension by successive adjustments that are always partial, always imperfect. Metaphors inadequately describe these processes, which are begun anew again and again without ever evoking the pyramid's domination, the network's continuity, or the machine's automaticity.

Turning this bricolage into a legal order will require 'the assurance that it's possible to approach this chaos, to last and grow in the unforeseeable, to go against certainties cemented into their intolerances'.[58] But certainties are part of legal culture, and it is difficult to consider the transformations of various components of law in their ambivalence, at once negative and positive. Difficult to admit that the indeterminacy of integrative processes, which may weaken the legal order by reducing foreseeability and fostering arbitrariness, can also contribute to preserving diversity. Difficult, as well, to accept that the fragmentation of the normative area, which dissociates the legal area from national territory, can help overcome obstacles (as in the area of bribery, for example, in which repressive mechanisms began at the UN then switched to the Organization for Economic Cooperation and Development (OECD), to Inter-American and European conventions, and finally, to the European Union). Difficult, at last, to consider that the differing speeds at which legal systems evolve, which destabilise normative time and lead to

[58] Glissant, *La Cohée du Lamentin* above n 2, pp 25–6.

perverse effects when the differences are too great (between global trade law and human rights, for example), can also serve to correct mistakes.

An epistemological mutation is just beginning: a veritable cultural revolution affecting the very concepts of legal order and legal systems. The hypothesis of ordered pluralism may show the way at least toward harmony—or rather, harmonisation in the broad sense—if not a future world order. This hypothesis emphasises movements and ongoing processes rather than the models they produce, as harmonisation is neither unity nor plurality, but generation: movement from one to the other. As Empedocles wrote, '[c]hange never ceases its perpetual becoming: either Love joins everything in unity, or Hate disperses and dissociates what Love has reunited. Thus, to the extent one is always born of the many and where, unity dispersed, the many is always constituted . . . change never ceases its perpetual becoming.'

To illustrate this perpetual movement from the one to the many and vice versa, I will begin with the processes of normative and judicial interaction, as they govern the establishment of an order that will be pluralist only if it accommodates differences yet produces consistent results. In the second part of the book, I will treat the normative area directly, stressing the shift in organisational levels from the national to the regional and global levels. Lastly, I will present a study of normative time from the perspective of speeds of transformation to show how better synchronisation might be achieved between trade law and human rights, for example, and how different speeds of integration might coexist in a single legal area, such as the 'European area' or the 'Kyoto area'.

In the end, what I am suggesting is that jurists, whose art consists in qualifying facts by putting them into pre-established categories, should instead adapt categories to shifting realities. The change would be considerable, but I believe it is inevitable.

# Part 1
## Processes of Interaction

Law can be internationalised without any pluralism whatsoever, through the simple extension of a hegemonic system. By its very simplicity, such a process could, in fact, seem the most probable hypothesis in light of the omnipresence of American law. But despite its status as a 'superpower', the United States is not the only candidate for global hegemony and the competitors are so numerous that I feel confident in betting they will neutralise each other and in daring to propose another hypothesis (the subject of this book): a pluralist internationalisation that favours interactions between different legal systems, or ensembles (a more neutral term that takes into account currently forming ensembles that are too changing and unstable to constitute true legal systems).

My hypothesis of ordered pluralism involves renouncing the binary opposition between hierarchical relationships (by subordination of one order to another) and non-hierarchical relationships (by coordination) and considering the process of interaction in a more nuanced fashion, a bit like the reflection of diverse pluralisms.

The pluralism of separation, built on the autonomy of each ensemble, limits interactions to horizontal processes, such as the reciprocal influence of one ensemble, institution, or even supreme court, on another. But reciprocity, which literally conditions coordination, is rarely sufficient to 'ordering', which implies ensemble-wide consistency.

To better guarantee consistency, interactions must be 'verticalised', a term I use to indicate a return toward hierarchy, but a flexible one that accepts a national margin of appreciation. By enabling the rapprochement of systems around higher, shared principles that are sufficiently 'fuzzy' to preserve the national margin, this second type of interaction, called harmonisation, is pluralist by definition:

accepting a national margin of appreciation avoids completely eliminating any and all differences. This is what distinguishes harmonisation from the third process, which is unification.

Unification allows for no margin whatsoever, but fuses systems or, more modestly, legal concepts, in order to protect a norm that may be imposed to respect a strict normative hierarchy. Unification bears traces of pluralism, however, when it results from an interactive process of hybridising various ensembles, rather than from the hegemonic extension of a single system. As I will show below, unifying criminal procedure on a single model (inquisitory or accusatory) is not the same thing as inventing a unified, mixed procedure through hybridisation, such as the procedures currently employed before the various international criminal tribunals.

Though I put coordination through cross-references, harmonisation by rapprochement, and unification through hybridisation in three categories, this is merely descriptive, and does not preclude slippage from one process to another, which is facilitated by the instability of practices. Between purely horizontal and purely vertical interactions, there are countless intermediary practices, such that harmonisation could become the predominant and emblematic process of ordered pluralism. Categorisation is, however, useful for illustrating the various processes of interaction and underscoring the heterogeneity inherent in pluralism, even when it is ordered.

# 1
# Coordination through Cross-references

SEPARATION DOES NOT necessarily mean isolation. Distinguishing pluralism from numerical pluralism, Emmanuel Levinas writes that the former 'does not isolate the terms constituting the plurality: while protecting them from a totality that would absorb them, it leaves them to trade or war among themselves'.[1] It is no accident, then, that law was first internationalised through trade and war, but as a strictly inter-state legal matter. The novelty today is that situations of interdependence are multiplying. Despite discontinuities stemming from the autonomy of legal ensembles, interdependency renders isolation impossible and fosters multiple exchanges. No matter the area, national law is surrounded on all sides, so to speak: neither 'independent' state governments, nor legislators in 'sovereign' parliaments, nor judges on 'supreme' courts can totally ignore the existence of other national, regional and international legal ensembles. And the regional (European and Inter-American) and global (WTO, UN, WHO, ICC, etc.) ensembles are themselves vulnerable to the permeability and porosity of law.

But how can simple horizontal exchanges devoid of hierarchy lead to coordination? The dialogue undeniably begun by judges[2] cannot by itself guarantee the consistency underlying the notion of order. To do so, cross-references must become a mechanism for ordering pluralism.

---

[1] E Levinas, *Totalité et Infini* (Leiden, Martinus Nijhoff, 1961), Reedn Le Livre de poche, 'Biblio essais' no 4120, pp 242–50.
[2] See J Allard and A Garapon, *Les juges dans la mondialisation* (Paris, Seuil, La République des idées, 2005).

## Impossible Isolation

The 'modern' concept that identifies law with the state tends to lead to isolation, as the limited place given to comparative studies shows. And the first jurists who showed an interest in internormative phenomena, such as Jean Carbonnier, saw them more as sociological than legal: '[b]etween law and other normative systems, bonds are formed and broken, movements, conjunctions, and conflicts are produced; these are autonomous phenomena . . . the phenomena of internormativity'.[3] Carbonnier could just as easily have been describing the relationships, movements, conjunctions and conflicts between different legal ensembles. But he was wary of comparative law, which he not entirely incorrectly suspected of devastating panjuridism: '[t]he more laws there are in conflict, the more the passion of law . . . is inebriating, just as the currency exchange trade flourishes with the multiplication of currencies'.[4]

Whatever the inflationary risks of the legal exchange trade, exchange is inevitable because isolation has become impossible. This impossibility was not immediately apparent because legal reasoning did not give it an official place. Exchange occurs in the interstices, fostering a *de facto* internormativity that legal scholars are only just beginning to notice within the European Union,[5] and which they distinguish from internationality, which still needs states.[6] But it is above all revealed by the interpretational cross-references among various judicial or quasi-judicial bodies tasked with applying norms to concrete cases.

### De facto *Internormativity*

*De facto* internormativity presupposes relationships between non-hierarchical normative ensembles, at whatever level in the normative area. Such relationships can be established between levels, as a way to fill in discontinuities in the hierarchical chain,[7] but the phenom-

---

[3] J Carbonnier, *Sociologie du droit* (Paris, PUF, 1978; coll. Quadrige, 1994) p 317.

[4] J Carbonnier, *Droit et Passion du droit sous la Vè République* (Paris, Flammarion, 1996) p 45.

[5] See generally L Idot and S Poillot-Peruzzetto (eds), 'Internormativité et réseaux d'autorité. L'ordre communautaire et les nouvelles formes de relation' (2004) *LPA* nos 199–200.

[6] See H Gaudemet-Tallon, 'L'internationalité, bilan et perspective' (2002) *Revue du droit des affaires* 73.

[7] For example, between international human rights instruments and domestic law in countries that do not accept direct applicability, or between the international criminal tribunals (ICTs) and regional human rights instruments.

enon is particularly visible between ensembles at the same level (national, regional or global): first they imitate each other, then begin to refer more or less explicitly to each other depending on the case.

Well known to comparative scholars, the idea of imitating, or borrowing from one another, was explained by Rodolfo Sacco, who qualifies the effects by showing that the common law produced by imitation is far from unified, because imitation does not change the conceptual moulds forged by history and reaches only the superficial strata of legal systems.[8] But this assessment also needs to be qualified with respect to international law, where the weight of history is less restrictive and the experts who draft texts, like the international judges who apply them, belong to different legal cultures. And the faster evolution occurs, the less history plays its moderating role, as the international criminal tribunals attest.

Borrowing between international (or supranational) ensembles can therefore be facilitated, and its effects strengthened, by the novelty of legal construction. But borrowing can be difficult to spot, except in flagrant cases, such as in the Council of Europe and the European Union, where texts are often copied with very little variation. For example, the 1997 EU Convention on the Fight Against Corruption foreshadows the Council of Europe conventions signed in 1999.[9] An even clearer example is the EU framework decision of 2003 on the criminal protection of the environment, which reproduces almost entirely the mechanism provided for in the Council of Europe convention of 1998.[10] Though some differences subsist, there is almost perfect convergence on the definition of the offences.

---

[8] See R Sacco, 'L'idée de droit commun par circulation de modèles et par stratification' in M Delmas-Marty, H Muir Watt and H Ruiz Fabri (eds), *Variations autour d'un droit commun* (Paris, Société de Législation Comparée, 2002) 195.

[9] M Delmas-Marty, *Les Forces imaginantes du droit (I): Le Relatif et l'Universel* (Paris, Seuil, 2004) p 252. By recognising the criminal jurisdiction of the European Community in its decision of 13 September 2005, the European Court of Justice (ECJ) may encourage the Commission to develop a community criminal law that would be imposed directly on the member states. See S Manacorda, '*Judicial activism* dans le cadre de l'espace de liberté, de justice et de sécurité de l'Union européenne' (2005) *Revue de science criminelle* 940.

[10] See G Giudicelli-Delage, 'Le droit pénal de l'environnement. L'exception européenne' (2005) *Revue de science criminelle* 767. Owing to a conflict of jurisdiction between the European Union Council and the Community institutions (Commission and Parliament), the framework decision was invalidated by the ECJ (decision of 13 September 2005). Subsequent to a complaint filed against the Council by the EC Commission and the European Parliament, the Court declared the framework decision void for having 'encroached on the jurisdiction of the Commission' by imposing a harmonisation of criminal law having the primary objective of protecting the environment, which falls within the Community's jurisdiction. The substantive contents

But imitation also occurs at the global level (the procedural rules contained in the ICTY Statute are directly inspired by the fair trial provisions of Article 14 of the ICCPR), and models circulate freely from one level to another. For example, anticipating the creation of a European prosecutor who would lead criminal investigations under the control of member-state judges, a group of experts tasked with drafting the so-called *Corpus juris* borrowed from the then newly adopted ICC Statute and suggested creating a 'preliminary European chamber' that would control investigations and refer cases for trial.

Such borrowing may not always be traceable to its source, but references are becoming more and more explicit, and thus traceable, between the European Union and the Council of Europe. Though European construction began by separating trade law from human rights, the latter have been incorporated into EU treaties over time. The 1997 Treaty of Amsterdam put the case law of the European Court of Human Rights on an equal footing with the constitutional traditions of the member states as a source of inspiration and orientation for the new Union (Article 6). The Treaty of Nice of 2000 then provided specific definitions in the EU Charter of Fundamental Rights and the 2007 Lisbon Treaty would, if ratified by all member states, give the Charter binding legal force (Article 6(1) Treaty on European Union (TEU)). In this way, human rights would be 'communitised' while waiting for the European Union to ratify the European Convention on Human Rights (Lisbon Treaty, Article 6(2) TEU), which would subordinate one ensemble to the other.

At the global level, cross-references are increasing as international instruments multiply under the influence of human rights and economic globalisation. In the absence of hierarchy, some cross-references at least have the merit of avoiding isolation of the WTO: the preamble to the WTO agreements sets out the 'goal of sustainable development to protect and preserve the environment', thereby admitting an exception to protect the environment (as did Article XX of the GATT).[11] But this is a generalised text that does not specify the formal relationship between commercial norms and the

were reproduced in the 13 March 2001 proposal for a Directive on the protection of the environment through criminal law, which has been confirmed by the European Parliament and is awaiting Council confirmation.

[11]   See Delmas-Marty, *Le Relatif et l'Universel*, above n 9, p 392.

roughly 200 multilateral agreements on the environment (MAE) at the global level. Since the jurisdiction of the Dispute Resolution Body (DRB) is limited to commercial agreements, though the DRB occasionally takes MAEs into account, it does so solely to clarify the debate on trade, not to protect the environment.[12] Free trade is still the rule, and environmental preoccupations, like those with health, are considered 'externalities'—exceptions of an external origin—and are therefore interpreted restrictively.

In short, internormativity creates a dialogue, but does not provide a solution in the event of conflict and each judge decides on a case-by-case basis. Interpretation is therefore of utmost importance.

### Interpretation by Cross-reference

But interpretation requires interpreters. That is, each normative ensemble must have a judicial or quasi-judicial body, which is very rarely the case. Despite the progressive judicialisation of the UN Human Rights Committee (called an 'international judicial authority' by the ICTs), there is no true world court for human rights. As for the environment, there is neither a global organisation nor a judicial body. And all judges, national and international alike, must be involved, even if the idea of interpretation has a different meaning for the former than for the latter, who are subject to the provisions of the Vienna Convention on the Law of Treaties.

To be sure, their functions are similar: national judges are becoming 'internationalised', as much by the direct applicability of international law as by the extension of national jurisdiction[13]; and international judges are becoming both commonplace, as their jurisdiction extends to private actors (victims of human rights violations or perpetrators of international crimes), and independent, as they adopt interpretational methods that break with those of general international law. Exchanges among all judges are developing to such an extent that, though no legal principle dictates reciprocal reception of case law, 'it is . . . current practice'.[14]

---

[12] See MP Lanfranchi, *L'Outil économique en droit international et européen de l'environnement* (Paris, La Documentation française, 2002) p 127.

[13] See generally A Cassese and M Delmas-Marty (eds), *Juridictions nationales et Crimes internationaux* (Paris, PUF, 2002).

[14] G Canivet, 'Les influences croisées entre juridictions nationales et internationales. Eloge de la bénévolence des juges,' seminar presentation at the Collège de France, May 2005, revised version published (2005) *Revue de science criminelle* 799.

In the competition that is setting in between and across national and international case law,[15] belonging to the same legal tradition (important particularly among common law courts) is not the only factor: reasoned decisions may be even more important. 'The advantage obviously goes to those who produce convincing, carefully reasoned decisions that refer to social, economic, cultural or ethical criteria going beyond pure legal reasoning and mobilizing values of universal reach.'[16] The concept of 'benevolence' highlighted by Guy Canivet, former First President of the French *Cour de cassation*, allows for reconciling competition and coordination and gives content to the conception of the authority of decisions that the Italian jurist Massimo Vogliotti developed by distinguishing *potestas*, the extrinsic authority stemming from the status of judge, and *autorevolezza*, the intrinsic authority resulting more from a particular judge's prestige, stature, and the quality of her decisions.[17] But the stature, if not the status, of a judge can be heightened by horizontal processes of coordination and the quality, and therefore authority, of decisions can be strengthened through cross-references from one court to another.

But such 'reciprocal integration',[18] to use Alessandro Bernardi's expression, may not always be possible. There is no obstacle to such cross-references among national courts, and indeed more or less formal networks between supreme courts have sprung up along regional or linguistic lines, or even according to legal specialty, such as competition or environmental law.[19] Exchanges are more delicate, however, between international courts specialising in different fields. In this respect Europe, with its bipolar legal structure, provides an excellent example. It was only after the EU member states had all ratified the ECHR (the last of the then nine members being France, in 1974) that it became possible for the European Court of

---

[15] See M Kamto, 'Les interactions des jurisprudences internationales et des jurisprudences nationales' in Société française du droit international, *La Juridictionnalisation du droit international* (Paris, Pedone, 2003); JF Flauss, 'La présence de la jurisprudence de la Cour suprême des Etats-Unis d'Amérique dans le contexte européen des droits de l'homme' (2005) *Revue trimestrielle de droits de l'homme* 313.

[16] Canivet, 'Les influences croisées', above n 14.

[17] M Vogliotti, 'La 'rhapsodie': fécondité d'une métaphore littéraire pour repenser l'écriture juridique contemporaine. Une hypothèse de travail pour le champ pénal' (2001) *Revue interdisciplinaire d'études juridiques* 141.

[18] A Bernardi, 'L'européanisation de la science pénale' (2004) *Archives de politiques criminelles* 5.

[19] See G Canivet, 'Protection de l'environnement par le droit pénal: l'exigence de formation et de spécialisation des magistrats' (2004) *Dalloz* 2728.

Justice (ECJ) judges to take the Convention into account, and vice versa. Beyond informal encounters and exchanges between judges to harmonise their points of view and avoid decisional conflicts, cross-references from one body of case law to the other then began to develop.[20] Though there is a tendency, as with national judges, to cite cases according to subjective preferences,[21] the method can nonetheless foster reciprocal cross-fertilisation.

But Europe is exceptional compared to other regions and the world. Very few members of the WTO have ratified both UN covenants on human rights and granted individuals the right to petition the UN Human Rights Committee in the event of a violation. And the continued lack (despite the creation of a Human Rights Council that is a bit more independent than the former Commission[22]) of a world court of human rights to counterbalance the increasing power of the WTO's Dispute Resolution Body deepens the divide.

The creation of international criminal tribunals and then the ICC, however, fosters more complex cross-references,[23] not only with the UN Human Rights Committee and the ICJ, but also between international criminal courts and regional human rights courts. The levels are not the same (regional/global) and the areas are different (human rights/criminal law), but the judges nonetheless engage in dialogue. The ECtHR has begun to cite international criminal tribunal case law,[24] while these tribunals refer to human rights instruments and the case law of the regional courts. While most of these latter references concern procedure, they also serve to clarify fundamental issues[25]: the definition of the crime of inciting to commit genocide, for example, was broadened in the so-called

---

[20] See G Cohen-Jonathan, 'La CESDH et la Communauté européenne' in *Mélanges Fernand Dehousse*, vol 1: *Les progrès du droit des gens* (Paris/Brussels, Fernand Nathan/Labor, 1979) 157; M Delmas-Marty, *Pour un droit commun* (Paris, Seuil, 1994) pp 240 *ff* (English version: *Towards a Truly Common Law*, N Norberg (trans) (Cambridge, CUP, 2002) pp 184–95).

[21] See D Spielmann, 'Un autre regard: la Cour de Strasbourg et le droit de la Communauté européenne' in *Mélanges en hommage au doyen Gérard Cohen-Jonathan* (Brussels, Bruylant, 2004) 1447.

[22] United Nations General Assembly, A/Res/60/251, 15 March 2006.

[23] See S Zappalà, *Human Rights and International Criminal Procedure* (Oxford, OUP, 2003).

[24] See *MC v Bulgaria* (2003) 2003-XII EHRR 646 (referring to the criminal definition of rape).

[25] See *Kunarac*, ICTY, 22 Feb 2001, Appeals Chamber 12 June 2002 (including, conversely, the ECtHR case law in the criminal definition of rape).

Rwandan media case by reference to case law on the freedom of expression.[26]

This is clearly a case of cross-referencing, since the ICTs consider themselves autonomous. They reject any hierarchy not only between themselves and the regional human rights courts or the Human Rights Committee, but also with respect to the ICJ: even though the ICJ 'is the principal judicial organ within the United Nations system . . ., there is no hierarchical relationship between the two courts'.[27] The consequences are laid out in convoluted terms: 'Although the Appeals Chamber will necessarily take into consideration other decisions of international courts, it may, after careful consideration, come to a different conclusion.'[28]

Such an attitude is liable to provoke criticism from all sides. On the human rights side, there lies the danger of an autonomy that fosters what Françoise Tulkens has called using human rights 'à la carte',[29] such that judges will be suspected of having 'instrumentalized international human rights law', transforming it into a simple interpretative tool such as for 'statutory or regulatory rules, particularly with respect to procedural guarantees'.[30] But the ICT judges underscore the specificity of international criminal justice and note that, while the state is the guarantor of human rights, it plays only a marginal role in international criminal law.[31] On the general international law side, commentators are calling for 'banalising' sources in order to limit interpretational references to international law alone, 'because these tribunals are international'.[32] But they are also

---

[26] See P Weckel and A Balguy-Gallois, 'L'affaire du procès des médias, TPIR, 2 Dec 2003' (2004) *Revue générale de droit international public* 507; D Boyle, 'Droits de l'homme et crimes internationaux. Les enjeux du procès des médias devant le TPIR' in *Mélanges en hommage au doyen Gérard Cohen-Jonathan*, above n 21, pp 303 ff.

[27] *Mucic et al* (Celibici case), ICTY Appeals Chamber 20 February 2001 para 24 (internal citations omitted).

[28] *Ibid.*

[29] See A Cassese and M Delmas-Marty (eds), *Crimes internationaux et Juridictions internationales* (Paris, PUF, 2002), pp 144–88; Delmas-Marty, Muir Watt and Ruiz Fabri, *Variations autour d'un droit commun*, above n 8.

[30] E Lambert-Abdelgawad, 'Les TPIY et TPIR et l'appel aux sources du droit international des droits de l'homme' in M Delmas-Marty, E Fronza and E Lambert-Abdelgawad (eds), *Les Sources du droit international pénal. L'expérience des tribunaux pénaux internationaux* (Paris, Société de Législation Comparée, 2005) pp 135–55.

[31] See A Cassese, 'L'influence de la CESDH sur l'activité des TPI' in Cassese and M Delmas-Marty, *Crimes internationaux et Juridictions internationales*, above n 29, pp 143 ff. See also *Kunarac*, above n 25 paras 470 and 478.

[32] H Ascencio, 'La banalité des sources par rapport aux sources du droit international général' in Delmas-Marty, Fronza and Lambert-Abdelgawad, *Les Sources du droit international pénal*, above n 30.

'criminal' tribunals, and the problem lies precisely in reconciling the two, because the subjects of criminal justice are not states, but individual victims and perpetrators. Unless individuals are likened to states and the concept of punishment and imprisonment to economic sanctions, it seems impossible to give up, as referring to general international law only would require, the criteria of independence and impartiality, as well as due process principles—especially since the ICC Statute requires that the law be applied and interpreted 'consistent[ly] with internationally recognized human rights' (Article 21(3)).

Finally, there is a more delicate question that divides criminal law specialists, who defend the principles of legality (no crime or punishment without prior law) and strict construction,[33] and those who support a broad interpretation in the interests of combating impunity and due to the specificity of an international criminal justice that is still forming, in an uncertain and fragile context where there are neither global police nor a legislature independent of states. International judges seem to share the 'realism' of general international law and the 'militancy' of human rights,[34] but a third variant must be added: the legality principle of criminal law.

Cross-referencing has the merit of clarifying the debate in its ideological (realist or militant) and legality-oriented aspects, but it does not provide the means for deciding between them. Justice without hierarchy is being built by trial and error, a sort of porosity between various ensembles, a co-penetration by capillarity. But this is a transitional phase in the construction of a true world legal order: a phase during which internormativity and cross-referencing lead to developing a community of judges, at least, if not a community of values, as death penalty case law shows.

## Judicial Dialogue on the Death Penalty

This is a significant example, because criminal law is traditionally considered the domain par excellence of national sovereignty, and the power over life and death the emblem of the sovereign.

---

[33] See E Fronza, E Malarino, C Sotis, 'Principe de précision et justice pénale internationale' in Delmas-Marty, Fronza and Lambert-Abdelgawad, *Les Sources du droit international pénal*, above n 30.

[34] P Weckel, 'Les confines du droit européen des droits de l'homme et les progrès du droit' in *Mélanges en hommage au doyen Gérard Cohen-Jonathan*, above n 21. See also G Cohen-Jonathan and JF Flauss, 'La CEDH et le droit international général' (2003) *Annuaire français du droit international* 661.

This is in fact why the death penalty, as well as its abolition, is an issue for each national legislature. For a long time, judges simply applied the law and dialogue was limited to a few, very isolated authors, such as Cesare Beccaria, who suggested abolishing the death penalty as early as 1764.[35] Leopold II followed this suggestion, at least for a few years, in Tuscany, where his penal code abolished the penalty in 1786.[36] But everywhere else, the young Beccaria (he was twenty-five in 1764) was taken as a provocateur or a fool. Immanuel Kant, for example, supported the death penalty and mocked 'the sympathizing sentimentality of affected humanity'.[37] Criticising this penchant for *compassibilitas* and Beccaria's thesis basing 'the illegitimacy of the death penalty on the fact that it cannot be contained in the social contract', Kant concludes, without further discussion, that 'all that is nothing but sophistry and chicanery'. In the nineteenth century, Victor Hugo was another very isolated abolitionist, and the abolitionist movement picked up again—cautiously—in the twentieth century only after the Second World War. The tide began to turn in 1945 with the Italian and German constitutions, but none of the more recent human rights instruments, such as the UDHR (1948), the ECHR (1950), the ICCPR (1966), the American Convention on Human Rights (ACHR, 1969), and the African Charter (1981), prohibit the death penalty, which is considered a legitimate exception to the right to life.

And yet, human rights form the basis for the dialogue on the death penalty that international judges began with their brethren on other international courts and national supreme courts. Since the European Court of Human Rights' audacious interpretation of the ECHR in *Soering v United Kingdom*,[38] there have been a number of surprising cross-references spreading out from Europe and coming back again from the United States, after the issue of the procedural rights of aliens condemned to death came before the ICJ and the Inter-American Court of Human Rights (IACHR).

[35] See C Beccaria, 'De la question de la peine de mort' in C Beccaria, *Des délits et des peines*, XVI (Paris, Editions d'aujourd'hui, 1980).

[36] See S Manacorda, 'Restraints on Death Penalty in Europe' (2003) 1 *Journal of International Criminal Justice* 263.

[37] E Kant, 'Doctrine du droit' VI, 335, *Métaphysique des mœurs* vol 3 (Paris, Gallimard, 1986) p 605.

[38] *Soering v UK* Series A, no 16 (1989) (holding that extraditing a person sentenced to death to the United States constitutes a violation of Article 3's prohibition of torture).

## The Extradition Dialogue

Dialogue on the death penalty may be considered inherent to extradition, which requires the state competent to try a case or execute a condemned person to ask another state to transfer the suspect or prisoner to it. Judges in the state receiving the extradition request must therefore authorise the transfer, in application of extradition treaties. But *Soering* requires the criminal judge in a receiving state to verify the conformity, with the ECHR, of the criminal law of the requesting state.

In 1989, the ECtHR showed a certain audacity in condemning the United Kingdom for having authorised (but not yet carried out) the extradition to the United States of a person condemned to death. Though the United Kingdom had abolished the death penalty, it hadn't yet ratified the additional protocol on abolition (protocol 6). It could therefore invoke in its defence Article 2 (right to life) of the ECHR, which makes a very explicit exception for the death penalty. The Court therefore based its decision on Article 3, which prohibits torture and other inhuman or degrading treatment, considering that the conditions in which the state of Virginia organised executions—that is, after a wait on death row that may last many years—constitute such treatment. Without a guarantee that the death penalty will not be sought at trial or carried out if already pronounced, extradition to the United States is therefore a violation of the ECHR.

*Soering*'s application with respect to other countries[39] may increase its influence considerably, not only in Europe,[40] but throughout the world. In fact, it seems to have been decisive in the Canadian Supreme Court's reversal of prior case law: in 1991, fearing Canada would be overrun with American fugitives, that Court authorised (by five votes to four) the extradition of a condemned person to the United States, despite the fact that the Canadian Charter of Rights and Freedoms limits the death penalty to 'exceptional cases' (Article 7). Ten years later in *Burns*, the Canadian Court borrowed heavily from *Soering*, which has no legal authority

---

[39] For examples concerning Iran and China, see *Aspichi Dehwari v Netherlands* (1999) and *Yang Chun Jin v Hungary* (2001), both of which were struck from the role after extradition was refused.

[40] See Italian Constitutional Court, 26 June 1996, Cassazione penale 1996, p 3258, note Dionatellevi.

in Canada, direct or indirect, and abandoned this 'dusty'[41] doctrine, holding that extradition in similar circumstances is prohibited. ECtHR case law has no authority in South Africa, either, but it was nonetheless cited to support the South African Supreme Court's 1995 decision holding the death penalty contrary to the prohibition of cruel, inhuman and degrading treatment.[42]

And the dialogue continues among the law lords on the Judicial Committee of the Privy Council, a *sui generis* judicial body that takes appeals from death penalty decisions handed down in certain Commonwealth states (namely Belize or the Caribbean states, while waiting for an autonomous supreme court to be created). In a decision concerning the death penalty pronounced by the Court of Appeal of Belize (which became independent in 1981), the Privy Council cites *Soering* extensively, as well as the Supreme Court of South Africa's decision, to conclude that the case must be retried.[43]

But the cross-references go on and on, because the Canadian Supreme Court's reversal led to an evolution in the UN Human Rights Committee's case law: having upheld the first extradition decision referred to it in 1991 (*Kindler*), the Committee held in *Judge* in 2003 that Canada had violated the ICCPR by extraditing Judge, who had been sentenced to death, to the United States. The HRC did not directly criticise its previous assertion that extradition does not in itself constitute a violation of the right to life guaranteed by Article 6 (paragraph 10.2), but held that the violation stems not only from the Canadian Court's reversal, but also from the remarkable changes, in fact and in law, in international opinion and the growing consensus in favour of abolition (paragraph 10.3). More precisely, the Committee bases the violation on the issue of remedies, thus indicating the importance of another dialogue, which addresses the death penalty through the issue of procedure.

---

[41] W Schabas, 'From *Kindler* to *Burns*: International Law is Nourishing the Constitutional Living Tree' in G Cohen-Jonathan and W Schabas (eds), *La Peine capitale et le Droit international des droits de l'homme* (Paris, Panthéon-Assas, 2003) pp 143 *ff*.

[42] *State v Makwanyane*, 1995 (3), South Africa, 391.

[43] See *Reyes v R* (Belize) [2002] UKPC 11 (11 March 2002). See also *Roodal v The State* (Trinidad and Tobago) [2003] UKPC 78 (20 November 2003); *Khan v The State* (Trinidad and Tobago) [2003] UKPC 79 (20 November 2003); *Matthew v The State* (Trinidad and Tobago) [2004] UKPC 33 (7 July 2004); S Lehrfreund, 'International Legal Trends and the Death Penalty in the Commonwealth Caribbean' in Cohen-Jonathan and Schabas, *La Peine capitale et le Droit international des droits de l'homme*, above n 41, pp 231 *ff*.

*The Procedural Dialogue*

The dialogue on procedure began on the American continent, moving from the IACHR to the ICJ and then Europe. Numerous death sentences pronounced in the United States concern aliens, to whom the Vienna Convention on Consular Relations grants certain benefits, such as the right to be informed of the possibility of consular assistance. Several cases have arisen involving aliens condemned to death in the United States who were not informed of their consular rights. Paraguay was the first to lodge a complaint with the ICJ, which ordered, to no avail, the suspension of the execution in question.[44] Germany followed suit, trying to protect two of its nationals who were minors at the time of the crime.[45] In the meantime, Mexico had asked the IACHR for an advisory opinion; then it, too, petitioned the ICJ on behalf of 50 of its nationals sentenced to death in 10 different states.[46] A dialogue was thus engaged among judges from every level at once: national, regional and international.

A dialogue of the deaf, apparently: despite the emergency procedure used in *Lagrand*, neither of the ICJ's orders convinced the United States Supreme Court to change its case law, nor the Arizona authorities to suspend the execution, which took place the day after the order was issued. In its decision of 27 June 2001, the ICJ notes that its conservatory measures were not respected and, asserting their obligatory nature, finds the United States to be in violation of its obligations. But it does not directly address the issue of the death penalty, which it merely qualifies as a 'severe penalty', without taking up the debate on its inhuman and degrading nature or on procedural guarantees. The IACHR, however, much more explicitly considered in its advisory opinion[47] that the right to be informed of consular assistance is an element of due process. Issued while the *Lagrand* case was pending before the ICJ, this opinion seems to have been implicitly taken into account and to have influenced that

---

[44] See *Breard (Paraguay v United States)*, International Court of Justice, 9 April 1998.

[45] See *Lagrand (Germany v United States)*, International Court of Justice, order 3 March 1999, decision 27 June 2001. See also P Weckel, 'L'affaire Lagrand et la condamnation à mort des ressortissants étrangers aux Etats-Unis' in Cohen-Jonathan and Schabas, *La Peine capitale et le Droit international des droits de l'homme*, above n 41, 103.

[46] See *Avena (Mexico v United States)*, International Court of Justice, order 5 February 2003, decision 31 March 2004.

[47] Inter-American Court of Human Rights AO no 16/99, 1 October 1999, reprinted in (2000) *Revue générale de droit international public* 788.

court's decision. And though the ICJ made no direct reference to it, it also seems to have influenced that court's decision of March 2004 against the United States in the *Avena* case brought by Mexico.

Meanwhile, the issue of due process came back around to the European continent in *Öcalan v Turkey*.[48] Before his death sentence was commuted to life in prison in 2002, the Kurdish opposition leader alleged a number of violations of the ECHR stemming from his 1999 transfer to Turkey and trial. The ECtHR carefully analysed the evolution of rights in Europe and underscored that, of 47 member states of the Council of Europe, 43, including Turkey after 2002, had abolished the death penalty. It therefore concluded that 'the death penalty exception in Article 2 has been significantly modified' and 'capital punishment in peacetime has come to be regarded as an unacceptable, if not inhuman, form of punishment which is no longer permissible under Article 2' (paragraph 196, decision of 12 March 2003). But the Court adds this rather obscure statement: 'it cannot now be excluded, in the light of the developments that have taken place in this area, that the States have agreed through their practice to modify the second sentence in Article 2 § 1 in so far as it permits capital punishment in peacetime' (paragraph 198).

The Grand Chamber did not confirm this statement, cautiously limiting itself to judging 'that it is not necessary for the Court to reach any firm conclusion on these points . . .' (paragraph 165), preferring instead to resolve the case on procedural grounds. Subscribing to the reasoning of the Court, which had cited the Human Rights Committee, the IACHR's advisory opinion and a later IACHR decision,[49] the Grand Chamber repeats that 'the implementation of the death penalty in respect of a person who has not had a fair trial would not be permissible' (paragraph 166).

It is to be hoped that the dialogue continues. After its Supreme Court reversed itself in 1976,[50] the United States became one of the four nations (along with China, Saudi Arabia and Iran) responsible for more than 80 per cent of executions worldwide.[51] But American

---

[48] *Öcalan v Turkey* (Grand Chamber) (2005) 2005-IV. See, eg, A Clapham, 'Symbiosis in International Human Rights Law: the Öcalan Case' (2003) 1 *Journal of International Criminal Justice* 475.

[49] Inter-American Court of Human Rights *Hilaire, Constantine & Benjamin et al v Trinidad* Series C no 94 (2002).

[50] Compare *Furman v Georgia*, 408 US 238 (1972) with *Gregg v Georgia*, 428 US 153 (1976).

[51] See G Cohen-Jonathan, 'Avant propos' in Cohen-Jonathan and Schabas, *La Peine capitale et le Droit international des droits de l'homme*, above n 41, p 13.

judges have not given up on international dialogue. Justice Breyer, for example, referred extensively in a dissenting opinion to the growing number of courts, including the ECtHR, that have found the death penalty to be inhuman or degrading.[52] Sometimes presented as the 'Court's leading advocate of the idea that the Supreme Court needs to take greater notice of the legal opinions abroad',[53] Breyer found himself in the majority when the Court, citing world opinion,[54] held in 2002 that executing the mentally ill was an 'excessive' punishment, then followed a similar reasoning with respect to minors in 2005.[55]

Still, the dialogue is subject to judicial goodwill. The Supreme Court chooses the criteria on which references to comparative law are based, such as the similarity of the issues raised or their transnational nature, and any acknowledgement of foreign norms is strictly optional.[56] And the lower-court judges who hear the cases on remand have their own discretionary powers. Following the ICJ's decision in *Avena*, for example, the Oklahoma Court of Criminal Appeals suspended the execution[57] and the governor commuted the sentence to life imprisonment; but under the same circumstances in the *Medellín* case, the federal court of appeals in Texas refused to take *Avena* into account, despite numerous Latin American and European *amicus curiae* submissions.[58] This wariness of international law can be

---

[52] See *Knight v Florida*, 528 US 990 (1999).

[53] C Lane, 'Thinking outside the US', *The Washington Post*, 4 August 2003.

[54] See *Atkins v Virginia*, 536 US 304 (2002). See also N Norberg, 'La Cour suprême des Etats-Unis et la peine de mort' (2002) *Revue de science criminelle* 917.

[55] See *Roper v Simmons*, 543 US 551 (2005).

[56] See S Breyer, 'La place des normes étrangères dans la jurisprudence de la Cour suprême des Etats-Unis', unpublished lecture given at the Collège de France, 14 June 2005. See also DM Amann, 'Raise the Flag and Let it Talk: on the Use of External Norms in Constitutional Decision-Making' (2004) 2 *International Journal of Constitutional Law* 597.

[57] See *Torres v Oklahoma*, No PCD-04-442, Oklahoma Ct Crim App, 13 May 2004. See also SD Murphy, 'Contemporary Practice of the United States Relating to International Law' (2004) 98 *American Journal of International Law* 581.

[58] See *Medellín v Dretke*, 371 F 3d 270 (5th Cir, 2004). The Supreme Court granted certiorari in 2004, but dismissed the writ as improvidently granted in 2005 (*Medellín v Dretke*, 544 US 660) after President Bush announced that the United States would comply with the *Avena* decision. Medellín returned to the Texas Court of Criminal Appeals, which held, inter alia, that the President does not have the power to enforce an ICJ ruling in state courts. The Supreme Court agreed, also ruling that the Convention is not self-executing and therefore not binding on Texas without further action by Congress. See *Medellín v Texas*, 06-984, 26 March 2008. Texas executed Medellín on 8 August 2008, notwithstanding Mexico's 5 June 2008 urgent request for ICJ interpretation of its *Avena* judgment and indication of provisional measures.

explained by the American conception of the rule of law: judicial power to interpret international norms is strictly limited by the political branches (legislative and executive). After the Supreme Court heard the *Medellin* case on appeal, the Bush administration withdrew the United States from the additional protocol to the Vienna Convention on Consular Rights (by letter of 7 March 2005). This abrupt end to such interpretational cross-references indicates that it is time to determine the conditions under which cross-referencing may lead to ordering pluralism.

## Conditions for Ordering Pluralism

The process of normative and judicial cross-referencing essentially creates a dynamic that, under certain conditions, will enable the integration and reconciliation of the multiple constraints of national and international ensembles, which were conceived according to different models from the very beginning. It is a necessary, but insufficient, phase of ordering pluralism. To achieve an overall consistency that would overcome contradictions, a phase of stabilisation is needed.

### The Dynamic Phase

For interaction among dissimilar legal ensembles to create a dynamic, several conditions must exist. The first is reciprocity, which implies symmetry between both institutions and judicial bodies. Symmetry exists, for example, between the two main European legal ensembles (EU treaties and ECHR), but not between the DRB of the WTO and the UN Human Rights Committee. And even when symmetry exists between legal instruments, state ratification poses a problem, as reciprocity requires that states ratify the same instruments. Between the EU and the ECHR, or Mercosur and the ACHR, there is at least partial symmetry with respect to ratification; but there is none in North America, as the United States, a member of NAFTA along with Canada and Mexico, has not ratified the American Convention. Nor is there such symmetry in Africa between the Organization for the Harmonisation of Business Law in Africa (OHADA) and the African Charter on Human Rights, or at the global level between the UN covenants of 1966 and the WTO agreements.

The second condition concerns judicial dialogue more directly and refers to judicial status, because only independence and life tenure provide the freedom necessary to enter into the dialogue. The adoption by the United States of a resolution such as the above-mentioned Feeney–Goodlatte resolution, which would prohibit judges from basing their reasoning on foreign law, would provide a counter-example of both the innovative, even subversive, force of cross-references and the conservative, even regressive, resistance of a nation when it closes in on itself.

In this respect, Chinese resistance also constitutes a counter-example, despite the Constitution's incorporation of the principle of the rule of law, since judicial nominations and careers are still under the Communist Party's control. Receptivity of international law is, however, becoming apparent: the Penal Code now contains a principle of 'internationalisation'; the issue of ratifying the ICC Statute is openly debated; and while there may not yet be an abolitionist movement, the debate on death penalty includes proposals, partially inspired by comparative and international law, of laws strengthening defence rights and shortening the list of capital crimes. And, though judicial dialogue has not yet been established, Chinese judges, particularly Supreme Court judges, are becoming more familiar with foreign case law. For example, in its highly discussed decision of 2 August 2002 recognising the direct applicability of the Constitution to a private dispute, the Court took into account a decision of the United States Supreme Court.[59]

Cross-references thus seem to be characterised by the judges' desire to not feel tied to one legal area or another. They therefore refer in a disorganised manner to multiple sources chosen without rigour and sometimes without objectivity. In other words, the dynamic thus created fosters reciprocal information and enables differences to be taken into account to a certain extent, but it does not resolve conflicts, particularly since it does not even guarantee that obligatory norms will be respected. Though some United States Supreme Court judges cite UN HRC case law (and even that of the European Court of Human Rights[60]), the Supreme Court does not recognise the direct applicability of the ICCPR, even though it was ratified in 1992. And, as I discussed above, American judges resist applying measures ordered by the ICJ, even though they are obligatory.[61]

---

[59] See S Balme, 'Juridicisation du politique et politisation du juridique dans la Chine des réformes (1978–2004)' in M Delmas-Marty and PE Will (eds), *La Chine et la Démocratie. Tradition, Droit, Institutions* (Paris, Fayard, 2006).

[60] In addition to the examples cited with respect to the death penalty, see, with respect to adult homosexuality, *Lawrence v Texas*, 539 US 123 (2003).

[61] For a comparison of American and British case law, see C Booth and M du Plessis, 'Home alone?—The US Supreme Court and International and Transnational Judicial Learning' (2005) *European Human Rights Law Review* 127.

Of course, the issue is largely political, but it also involves improving legal methods, as ordering pluralism will not be possible without stabilisation.

## The Stabilisation Phase

Between human rights and criminal law, just as between human rights and trade law or between trade law and social, environmental or health law, the danger of dialogue and internormativity is continuing a discussion that has no end or synthesis, but is instead subject to the uncertainties of constantly renewed competition. Such a discussion may stimulate judges' imagination, but it may also foster forum shopping.[62] Only synthesis can bring the stabilisation on which ordering pluralism depends. To achieve it, once dialogue has been established, there are several interpretive techniques available. For example, various courts and international law authorities have already recognised more or less explicitly the imperative nature of certain norms, particularly in the area of human rights, through the qualification of *jus cogens*.[63] But the ICJ cautiously avoids this term, preferring the more vague terms 'customary obligations' and '*erga omnes* obligations'.[64] And the idea of custom allows for surreptitiously reintroducing a certain hierarchy. In fact, it implicitly underlies numerous decisions of the European Court of Human Rights, including *Öcalan*, in which the Court laid the foundations for a customary abrogation of the death penalty exception in Article 2 of the ECHR.

Beyond interpretive techniques, the inevitable issue of the hierarchy between inter-related international ensembles arises only indirectly, through national law. It has already done so in Europe, where stabilisation occurs in two steps. The first is indirect: the ECtHR reviews violations of the ECHR by incorporating Community norms[65] or

---

[62] G Guillaume, 'Advantages and Risks of Proliferation: a Blueprint for Action' (2004) 2 *Journal of International Criminal Justice* 300.

[63] See PM Dupuy, 'Le *jus cogens*, une révolution?' in PM Dupuy, *L'Unité de l'ordre juridique international. Cours général de l'Académie de droit international public* [2000] (Leiden, Martinus Nijhoff, 2003).

[64] G Cohen-Jonathan, 'Rapport introductif' in G Cohen-Jonathan and JF Flauss (eds), *Droit international, Droits de l'homme et Juridictions internationals* (Brussels, Bruylant, 2004).

[65] See *Cantoni v France* (1996) 1996-V; *Matthews v UK* (1999) 1999-I; *Bosphorus Hava Yollari Turizm v Ireland* (Grand Chamber) (2005) 2005-VI (where the Community rule at issue authorised the seizure of goods in application of a UN Security Council resolution).

other international norms[66] into national law. But direct control requires hierarchy, which will be established in a second step leading to vertical integration, namely, the ratification of the ECHR by the European Union, as provided by the Lisbon Treaty.

The global level is less stabilised, but scholars foresee the possibility of instituting an interlocutory appeal to the ICJ such as exists in the regional courts (namely in the form of interlocutory appeals to the ECJ).[67] In other words, the issue of contradictions between various normative ensembles, and therefore that of hierarchy, cannot be avoided much longer.

In short, cross-references seem necessary but insufficient. They are necessary to help avoid conflicts, reduce some contradictions and thus enable spontaneous coordination, but they cannot guarantee overall consistency in the event of a conflict. In this way, coordination makes way for transition by acclimating the various legal ensembles to internormativity, but it can only lead to ordering pluralism if horizontal processes, counterbalanced by imperative *jus cogens* norms or custom, eventually become 'verticalised'.

Moving from co-ordination to sub-ordination does not necessarily require instituting a strict hierarchy, the rigidity of which might lead to its being rejected to protect national specificities. This is why harmonisation processes are so important: they enable the rapprochement of different systems which, without striving for uniformity, may be characterised precisely by its less rigid hierarchy due to the recognition of national margins of appreciation.

---

[66] See *Bankovic v Belgium and others* (2001) 2001-XII; *Behrami v France,* judged admissible in 2003 but struck from the list in 2007, discussed by G Cohen-Jonathan, above n 64.

[67] See Guillaume, 'Advantages and Risks of Proliferation,' above n 62.

# 2
# Harmonisation by Approximation

THE WORD 'HARMONISATION' is rife with musical connotations and sends us back to ancient times, when law was associated with song and music: 'The first laws were poems that, before writing was invented, were more easily remembered because they were sung.'[1] In fact, the Greek word *nomos* ('norm') is translated as both *lex* (law) and *cantus* (song) in Latin. In Chinese as well, the character *lü* means the 'measure of measures',[2] in the area of laws as well as sounds. Indeed, the aim of the first treatises of Chinese law was to combine legal science, music and poetry: 'to harmonize sounds to compose a text, place terms in parallel categories, make rhymes where the measure means both music and law'.[3]

While legislators today seem to have lost touch with poetry and music, music can still help understand how diversity contributes to, rather than detracts from, harmonisation. In his *Symposium*, Plato attributes the explanation to the doctor Eryximachus: 'From contrary elements, such as sharps and flats, the art of music, by making them agree with each other, produces harmony. Because of course, if the sharp and the flat maintain their differences until the end, there will be no harmony at all'; thus, '[h]armony is a "resonating together" and to "resonate together" is to "speak together"'.[4] But to harmonise legal ensembles, 'resonating together' must also lead to 'reasoning together', that is, basing a common measure on reason.

---

[1] Cicero, *De legibus*, II, 23, 59, cited in G Vico, *Principes d'une science nouvelle relative à la nature commune des nations* [*Principi di scienza nuova d'intorno alla commune natura delle nazioni, 1744*], A Pons (trans), (Paris, Fayard, 2001), book II, para 469.

[2] PE Will, 'La réglementation administrative et le code pénal mis en tableaux' (2003) XXII *Etudes chinoises* 93; J Bourgon, 'Shen Jiaben et le droit chinois à la fin des Qing', doctoral dissertation, EHESS, 1997, p 523.

[3] J Bourgon, 'Shen Jiaben et le droit chinois à la fin des Qing', above n 2, p 290 and the examples cited pp 300 *ff*.

[4] Plato, *Le Banquet*, with 39 drawings by Vieira da Silva (P Boutang (trans), Paris, Hermann, 1972), p 46.

Law is not music, however, and legislators rarely succeed in making agree national legal traditions they perceive to be in conflict. As compared to the splendour of the bicentennial celebrations of the French Civil Code (1804–2004), symbol of all the virtues,[5] the violence of French opposition to the proposed European Civil Code, accused of harbouring every vice,[6] indicates the impossibility of supranational codification, even limited to Europe.

Harmonisation thus stands as an alternative to codification: a new and original process that aims at integration (normative and/or legal), but without insisting on perfect integration or imposing unification.

To get to the core of ordered pluralism and explain more concretely how preserving national margins of appreciation allows shared guiding principles to be applied without leading to uniformity, I will take an example from moral and religious diversity. Within Europe, and *a fortiori* at the global level, by revealing the practical problems in implementing diversity, this example highlights the need to identify the specific conditions under which pluralism can be ordered through either codes or guiding principles.

## Imperfect Integration: Impossible Codification

The movement towards harmonisation must no doubt be situated between the two impossible extremes of isolation and codification. Unlike cross-references, which are limited to horizontally coordinating different legal ensembles, harmonisation instils a somewhat vertical relationship, which implies hierarchy between the top (regional or global) and the bottom (national). But this hierarchy is not fixed and unchanging: sometimes domestic law is superior to international law. This is the raison d'être of principles such as subsidiarity in European Community law and complementarity in the ICC Statute, which encourages finding solutions at the national level. To express this inversion, I have used the phrase 'tangled hierarchies'[7] to indi-

---

[5] See namely G Cornu, 'Un code civil n'est pas un instrument communautaire' in B Fauvarque-Cosson and D Mazeaud (eds), *Pensée juridique française et Harmonisation européenne du droit* (Paris, Société de Législation Comparée, 2003); Y Lequette, 'A propos du projet de code civil européen' in *ibid*.

[6] See *Le Bicentenaire du code civil, Dalloz*, special edition, 8 April 2004.

[7] M Delmas-Marty, *Pour un droit commun* (Paris, Seuil, 1994) p 101 (*Towards a Truly Common Law*, N Norberg (trans) (Cambridge, CUP, 2002) p 65). See also A Bernardi, 'Entre la pyramide et le réseau: les effets de l'européanisation du droit sur le système pénal' (2004) *Revue interdisciplinaire d'études juridiques* 1.

cate that harmonisation moves both up from domestic law towards a common supranational law, and down from supranational to national law.

In short, it does not seem possible to determine the articulation between the one and the many once and for all, from top to bottom or bottom to top; successive adjustments must be made in both directions. These ad-justments, meaning movement towards the just, are based on trust and distrust. But if *inter-* and *supra*national law are represented as the centre of a circle with spokes radiating out to the states, these adjustments can also be envisaged dynamically, moving with either centripetal (supranational primacy) or centrifugal (supranational subsidiarity) force.

This indicates the complexity of the interactions that drive the process of harmonization and the importance of the 'national margin', which manifests both the rejection of unification and the desire to agree on a common measure, a common law.

## Complex Dynamics

By successive adjustments and readjustments, harmonisation calls up the image of a billiard player, 'with an apparently hesitant, yet typically adroit stroke'.[8] Such apparent clumsiness and dexterity by oscillation, by 'vibrational energy', in Roland Barthes' words, are particularly apparent in the European Lisbon Treaty. Consistent with existing law, the Treaty institutes an oscillation between two dynamics: first, seemingly to reassure the member states, a centrifugal dynamic is expressed through the principles of subsidiarity and proportionality (Article 5(1) TEU), which is clarified in an additional protocol (Protocol No 2) and strengthened by another that allows for ceding power to national parliaments (Protocol No 1). Though seemingly more discreet on a first reading, the centripetal dynamic is nonetheless there in the 17th Declaration concerning provisions of the Treaty, which sets out, consistent with ECJ case law, the primacy of European Union law. This primacy is not qualified as a 'fundamental principle', but it determines a dynamic that is largely stimulated by the creation of an 'area of freedom, security and justice' based on mutual recognition (Article 67(3) TFEU), which adopts the phrase coined at the 1999 Tampere Summit).[9]

---

[8] R Barthes, *Le Neutre. Cours au Collège de France (1977–1978)* (Paris, Seuil, 2002), p 174.

[9] See AM Leroyer and E Jeuland (eds), *Quelle cohérence pour l'espace judiciaire européen?* (Paris, Dalloz, 2004).

To be sure, pluralism seems to be reaffirmed in the phrase indicating that this area will be constituted 'with respect for fundamental rights and the different legal systems and traditions of the Member States' (Article 67(1) TFEU), as well as by the chapters that follow, prudently entitled 'judicial co-operation', first in civil, then criminal, matters. But even if the term 'co-operation' seems to favour horizontal interaction, current practices reveal an inevitable slide towards harmonising to foster 'mutual recognition' (Article 81 TFEU in civil matters and Article 82 TFEU for co-operation in criminal matters). As illustrated by the concept of 'minimum rules', referred to several times in both Articles 82 and 83 TFEU, the text explicitly provides for this movement: mutual recognition includes 'approximation' of laws, that is, harmonisation, 'when it proves essential to ensure the effective implementation of a Union policy in an area which has been subject to harmonisation measures' (Article 83(2) TFEU).

The European arrest warrant mentioned above provides a concrete example of this movement, which has been called 'forced',[10] from interstate co-operation to supra-state harmonisation. The goal is to improve co-operation by facilitating extradition between member states. To do so, both the procedure and the substantive conditions had to be simplified, so the diplomatic phase and the requirement of double incrimination were both eliminated. But the member states do not trust each other enough to apply these simplified procedures across the board: the arrest warrant is available for only a limited list of offences, the establishment of which presupposes identical definitions and a minimum of similar procedural guarantees.

States are thus pulled deeper and deeper into the system as each such instrument inevitably calls for another. Co-operation's initial focus on procedure has thus shifted in practice to the approximation of substantive definitions (elements of the offence, conditions for guilt, penalties), which may in turn lead to greater repression for the sake of efficiency. The process of interaction is therefore becoming one of true harmonisation, whether through framework decisions

---

[10]  G Giudicelli-Delage, 'Remarques conclusives' (2005) *Revue de science criminelle* 15. See also S Manacorda and G Giudicelli-Delage (eds), *L'Intégration pénale indirecte. Interactions entre droit pénal et coopération judiciaire au sein de l'Union européenne* (Paris, Société de Législation Comparée, 2005), pp 375–83; A Bernardi, 'Stratégies pour une harmonisation des systèmes pénaux européens' (2002) *Archives de politique criminelle* 195; A Bernardi, 'L'européanisation du droit pénal' (2004) *Archives de politique criminelle* 5.

(such as those of 2002 on terrorism or human trafficking, or of 2003 on protecting the environment through criminal law, or on the sexual exploitation of children), conventions (such as the 1995 convention on protecting the Community's financial interests or its additional protocols), or even directives (such as the directive of 29 April 2004 concerning indemnities for crime victims).

Moreover, harmonisation is not limited to criminal law. With respect to contracts,[11] for example, it has been shown that harmonisation results from several movements: first, regionalisation, as when European contract law takes over for global law; second, generalisation, moving from very specific and exceptional European instruments (such as on abusive clauses or automobile sales) to the broader reflection on European contract law suggested by the European Commission in its communications of 13 July 2001 and 12 February 2003; and finally, privatisation, which I use here to indicate the resurgence of a 'scholars' law', such as the *jus commune* of the Middle Ages, initiated by legal commentators within private organisations such as Unidroit, the Lando Commission or the 'study group on a European Civil Code'[12] created by the German jurist Christian von Bar.

One need not review every area concerned by European construction[13] to see that the complex dynamics accompanying the process of harmonisation raise the issue of consistency, not only between sources of Community law and domestic law, but also, more broadly, with other sources of harmonisation: regional, such as the ECHR; global, such as the Vienna Convention on Contracts for the International Sales of Goods; or, in the area of criminal law, the various conventions of larger scope (UN, OECD).[14]

Indeed, the process of harmonisation is developing at the global level as well. Even when it is not explicitly provided for, the 'harmonising

[11] See L Fin-Langer, 'L'intégration du droit du contrat en Europe' in M Delmas-Marty (ed), *Critique de l'intégration normative* (Paris, PUF, 2004), pp 37–111.

[12] See C von Bar, 'Le groupe d'études sur un code civil européen' (2001) *Revue internationale de droit comparé* 127; 'Vers un code civil européen' (2002) *Les Annonces de la Seine* no 33. See also Y Lequette, 'A propos du projet de code civil européen', above n 5.

[13] See JS Bergé, 'Le droit d'une communauté de lois: le front européen' in *Le Droit international privé : esprit et méthode. Mélanges Paul Lagarde*, special edition of the *Revue critique de droit international privé* (Paris, Dalloz, 2004) pp 113–36; S Poillot-Peruzetto, 'La diversification des méthodes de coordination de normes nationales' in *Internormativités et Réseaux d'autorités: l'ordre communautaire et les nouvelles formes de relations, Les Petites Affiches*, 5 October 2004, pp 17–31.

[14] See J Normand, 'Conclusion' in Leroyer and Jeuland, *Quelle cohérence pour l'espace judiciaire européen?*, above n 9, pp 167 *ff*.

effect' must still be taken into account, as it can produce international instruments such as the Rome Statute of the International Criminal Court.[15] By encouraging states that want to assert their jurisdiction to adopt norms sufficiently close to the international standard to be determined capable of prosecuting a case (Article 17(1)(a)), the Statute can be considered an instrument of indirect harmonisation, the implementation of which will depend on the criteria used by the Court to determine whether or not a state's domestic law is compatible with international requirements.

But compatibility does not require strict conformity with the international standard. For harmonisation to be accepted in countries with different legal traditions, a model that is too directly inspired by the state order cannot be imposed. Explicitly or implicitly, a 'national margin of appreciation' must be recognised to facilitate the adjustments and readjustments that characterise the harmonisation process.

### Margins of Variable Widths

Providing for a national margin of appreciation is the key to ordering pluralism. On the one hand, it expresses the centrifugal dynamic of national resistance to integration. On the other, since the margin is not unlimited but bounded by shared principles, it sets a limit, a threshold of compatibility that leads back to the centre (centripetal dynamic). By adjusting the width of the acceptable margin, oscillations between national resistance and harmonisation enable judges to determine this threshold.[16]

As with harmonisation, the national margin of appreciation is not just a European phenomenon: commentators are increasingly referring to the concept of a margin in highly diverse contexts. In the area of international criminal law, for example, the concept has been used to describe an application contrary to that in Europe: rather than

---

[15] See E Fronza and E Malarino, 'L'effet harmonisateur du statut de la cour pénale internationale' in M Delmas-Marty, M Pieth and U Sieber (eds), *Les Chemins de l'harmonisation pénale/Harmonising Criminal Law* (Paris, Société de Législation Comparée, 2008).

[16] See namely HC Yourow, *The Margin of Appreciation Doctrine in the Dynamics of European Human Rights Jurisprudence* (Leiden, Martinus Nijhoff, 1996); P Mahoney, 'Marvellous Richness of Diversity or Invidious Cultural Relativism' (1998) 19 *Human Rights Law Journal* 1; J Sweeney, 'Margins of Appreciation: Cultural Relativity and the ECHR' (2005) 54 *ICLQ* 459. For more general thoughts on the formal validity of a pluralist common law, see M Delmas-Marty and ML Izorche, 'Marge nationale d'appréciation et internationalisation du droit' (2000) *Revue international de droit comparé* 753 (English version: (2001) 46 *McGill Law Journal* 923).

invoking the national margin of appreciation to defend their repressive measures against claims of incompatibility with international human rights norms, states may invoke the margin to restrict domestic application of repressive measures imposed internationally to protect the world order, claiming that they are incompatible with domestically protected fundamental rights.[17] In addition, the OHADA Treaty has been criticised for insufficient reference to the margin,[18] while implicit inclusion of the margin in WTO law has led to asking whether it 'would not be clearer to say that states enjoy, in the [area of sanitary and phytosanitary risks], a "national margin of appreciation" that is not unlimited, but may vary depending on the interests concerned'.[19]

Indeed, its variability makes the national margin a preferred instrument that constitutes in some ways the legal complement to the political principle of subsidiarity and makes it possible to conceive of harmonisation as the result of a set of dynamics that can be centrifugal or centripetal, ascending or descending. In fact, upward harmonisation, which characterises normative integration within the EU, refers explicitly to the subsidiarity principle. In its communication concerning the European law of contracts, the European Commission of Human Rights recalls that 'the principle of subsidiarity serves as a guide as to how the Community powers are to be exercised at Community level', adding that '[s]ubsidiarity is a dynamic concept and should be applied in the light of the objectives set out in the Treaty', and pertinently underscoring that the concept 'allows Community action within the limits of its powers to be expanded where circumstances so require, and conversely, to be restricted or discontinued where it is no longer justified'.[20] The duality inherent in a dynamic that is both centripetal (expanding the Community's

---

[17] See Fronza and Malarino, 'L'effet harmonisateur', above n 15.

[18] See P Dima Ehongo, 'L'intégration juridique des économies africaines à l'échelle régionale ou mondiale' in Delmas-Marty, *Critique de l'intégration normative*, above n 11, pp 194 *ff*.

[19] H Ruiz Fabri and P Monnier, 'A propos des mesures sanitaires et phytosanitaires' (2004) *Journal du droit international* 1025 (discussing Japan—Measures Affecting the Importation of Apples, Appellate Body Report, WT/DS245/AB/R, adopted 26 November 2003).

[20] Commission of the European Communities, *Communication from the Commission to the Council and the European Parliament on European Contract Law* (COM)2001 398 final, 11 November 2001 (available at: http://ec.europa.eu/consumers/ cons_int/safe_shop/fair_bus_pract/cont_law/cont_law_02_en.pdf). See also Fauvarque-Cosson and Mazeaud, *Pensée juridique française et Harmonisation européenne du droit*, above n 5, annexe 1, point 43, pp 265 *ff*.

action) and centrifugal (restricting or discontinuing it when it is no longer justified) is clearly set out in the Protocol on the application of the principles of subsidiarity and proportionality, and the ECJ reviews the use of the margin of appreciation.

But subsidiarity introduces the same duality with respect to the processes of downward harmonisation resulting from the European Convention on Human Rights, through the concept of a national margin of appreciation. This concept does not appear in the Convention; European judges (first at the European Commission of Human Rights, then the Court itself ) granted it very early on, in cases in which they upheld restrictive or even derogatory measures taken to protect public order. Considering that 'the subsidiary nature of the international machinery of collective enforcement established by the Convention'[21] stems primarily from the principle of 'double jurisdictional competence' subordinating the admissibility of complaints to the exhaustion of domestic remedies, the European Court of Human Rights esteems that the national courts are better situated than it is to determine the meaning of restrictions based on public order. It does not, however, give up its right to review, but limits its review according to the threshold of compatibility.

Between the classical alternatives (obligation of conformity and sovereign appreciation), the lighter alternative of 'compatibility' is thus interposed. Conformity requires identity: that is, national practices must conform strictly to the conduct prescribed by the international norm. Compatibility, however, requires only a certain minimum proximity between state practices and the international norm. Whether it limits international court review (relative European primacy) or expands it (relative national sovereignty), the national margin shows that harmonisation can be conceived as a process of 'arrang[ing] partially distinct legal orders'.[22] This process and the problems related to implementing the margin are revealed more concretely in the cases involving moral and religious diversity discussed below.

[21] *Belgian Linguistic Case* [1968] Series A, No 6, para 10.

[22] Delmas-Marty, *Pour un droit commun*, above n 7, p 113 (*Towards a Truly Common Law*, above n 7, p 73). On the related concept of functional equivalence, see M Delmas-Marty, *Les Forces imaginantes du droit (I): Le Relatif et l'Universel* (Paris, Seuil, 2004), pp 253, 257 and 412.

# Moral and Religious Diversity: International Principles and the National Margin

If there is an area that seems to have resisted all attempts at unification, in Europe and *a fortiori* at the global level, it is that of morals and religion. Does this mean that without unification, the harmonisation process has already been engaged, indirectly descending under the influence of human rights instruments, or ascending directly from the construction of the European Union (first, the Charter of Fundamental Rights, then the Constitutional and now the Lisbon Treaty)? I will have to qualify my answer. '[A] true European law of religions'[23] does not yet exist, but Europe constitutes the first laboratory for observing, analysing and testing the processes involved in ordering pluralism and for understanding both why moral and religious diversity requires a national margin, and what the practical difficulties in implementing harmonisation are.

## *The Need for a National Margin*

During the 50 or more years between the drafting of the European Convention on Human Rights (1950), the EU Charter of Fundamental Rights (2000) and the Constitutional Treaty (2004), the need for a national margin was obscured. The Convention merely sets out the principles of freedom of thought, conscience and religion (Article 9) and of expression (Article 10), complemented by non-discrimination (Article 14, which targets religious discrimination in particular) and the right of parents to educate their children 'in conformity with their own religions and philosophical convictions' (Protocol 1, Article 2).

All these principles appear in the EU Charter as well (Articles 10, 11 and 14), and at the request of the European Parliament, they were supplemented by an article affirming that the Union would respect cultural and religious diversity (Article 22). But owing to disagreement as to whether the Preamble should contain a reference to the principle of separation of church and state or to the Union's 'religious heritage', these preliminary paragraphs merely contain a very general reference to the common values of the 'peoples of Europe' and to the Union's 'spiritual and moral heritage'. With respect to the

---

[23] Against, see JF Flauss (2000) *Actualité juridique du droit international* 1014. But the author was more reserved in 2004: see 'Les signes religieux', in T Massis and C Pettiti (eds), *La Liberté religieuse et la CESDH* (Brussels, Bruylant, 2004) pp 99 *ff*.

Preamble to the TEU, consolidated by the Lisbon Treaty, however, raucous debate ended with the assertion that the Union draws 'inspiration from the cultural, religious and humanist inheritance of Europe'.

Since the Treaty has not been ratified, there is no way to test whether this assertion simply means that states can draw on the past, or whether 'religious norms are not entirely dissociated from civil norms',[24] as Jean Baubérot suggests, referring to Article 17 TFEU's promise that '[t]he Union respects and does not prejudice the status under national law of churches and religious associations or communities in the Member States'. According to Baubérot, this means they will take precedence over civil society.

The hardest thing will be to combine common principles with diversity, which is not only recognised, but prescribed in the interests of pluralism by Article 21 of the Charter, which is incorporated into the European Treaties. But the Lisbon Treaty does not clearly explain how the Charter is to be interpreted or applied: it recalls the principle of subsidiarity, imposes limits along the lines of those expressed in the ECHR, and concludes that rights must be interpreted 'in harmony' with national traditions (Lisbon Treaty, Article 6(2) TEU), but does not explain how to harmonise these traditions among themselves and makes no reference to the national margin.

The reference to the European Convention on Human Rights in Article 6(3) TEU would no doubt allow ECtHR case law to be taken into account, but it is abundant and at times inconsistent on the issues of morals (as opposed to freedom of expression or to privacy) and religious freedom (which can be restricted in the interests of public order or the rights of others).

The difficulty was first noticed in a case pitting the protection of morals against freedom of expression via the censorship of a 'little red book' of sexual education aimed at schools.[25] The ECtHR remarks that the member states' domestic laws do not have a uniform conception of morals, then moves from describing to prescribing by asserting that without pluralism, tolerance and open mindedness, 'there is no democratic society', and that freedom of expression must apply even to ideas 'that offend, shock or disturb the State or any sector of the population'.[26] It concludes, however,

---

[24] J Baubérot, *Laïcitié 1905–2005, entre passion et raison* (Paris, Seuil, 2004), p 183.
[25] *Handyside v United Kingdom* Series A no 24 (1973).
[26] *Ibid.*, para 49.

that censoring the book does not constitute a violation of the freedom of expression because the very diversity of domestic laws indicates that the Court must recognise a national margin of appreciation.

Twenty years later, the pluralism 'dearly won over the centuries'[27] was cited to support religious freedom. Finding the arrest and imprisonment of a Jehovah's Witness for proselytising to be a violation of the Convention, the Court asserted that freedom of thought, conscience and religion 'is one of the foundations of a "democratic society"[:] one of the most vital elements that go to make up the identity of believers and their conception of life, but it is also a precious asset for atheists, agnostics, sceptics and the unconcerned'.[28] Later, religious freedom would be examined in various aspects related to the freedom to have convictions and to act on them (education of children, conscientious objection to military service, and fiscal status).[29]

The analysis is more delicate when freedom of expression conflicts with religious liberty, as was first shown in the area of blasphemy. Because of the national margin of appreciation, once again founded on the diversity of member states' laws, the ECtHR upheld the conviction for blasphemy of the Otto-Preminger-Institut resulting from the Innsbruck diocese's complaint following the release of Werner Schroeter's film *Das Libeskonzil*. In light of the national margin of appreciation, the restriction on freedom of expression was justified by the fact that 'respect for the religious feelings of believers as guaranteed in Article 9 [could] legitimately be thought to have been violated by provocative portrayals of objects of religious veneration'.[30]

Criticised as 'a deplorable encouragement of religious fanaticism',[31] the decision might seem isolated, particularly since the Inter-American Court of Human Rights held Chile's banning of the film *The Last Temptation of Christ* to violate freedom of expression.[32] However, the *Otto-Preminger* decision implicitly touched off a

---

[27] *Kokkinakis v Greece* A260-A (1993), para 31.

[28] *Ibid.*

[29] See *La Liberté religieuse et la CESDH*, above n 23.

[30] See *Otto-Preminger-Institut v Austria* A295-A (1994), para 47. See also P Wachsmann, 'La religion contre la liberté d'expression, sur un arrêt regrettable de la CEDH, *Otto Preminger Institute c. Autriche*' (1994) *Revue universelle des droits de l'homme* 441; G Haarscher, 'La blasphémateur et le raciste' (1995) *Revue trimestrielle des droits de l'homme* 417.

[31] Philippe Wachsmann, 'La religion contre la liberté d'expression', above n 30.

[32] See Inter-American Court of Human Rights, *Olmedo Bustos v Chili* Series C no 73 (2001).

debate that has continued in more radical terms with respect to the so-called 'Islamic headscarf', the prohibition of which has not yet been censured by the ECtHR.[33]

To be sure, the issue is first and foremost a domestic one. As did the texts that preceded it, the French law of 15 March 2004[34] shows that tensions are strong between freedom of expression and freedom of thought, conscience and religion, as well as between the right to manifest one's religion or conviction and the principle of equality or non-discrimination between men and women. But domestic law cannot ignore international principles. In fact, the Vice-President of the ECtHR was heard (in every sense of the word, as he was clearly favourable to France's adopting legislation) by the Stasi commission on the application of the principle of *laïcité* (separation of church and state).

Jean Baubérot, a member of the commission whose report largely influenced the law, worried that reality was being reduced to 'mediatized current events': 'Islam is an amplifying mirror, not a decisive element of the problems encountered today by *laïcité*; however, it 'is at the heart of secular life today in an almost obsessive way'.[35] François Ost went even further in his rewrite of Sophocles' *Antigone*: in the scene in which the heroine (renamed Aïcha) avenges her brother's death, she confronts her principal at the entrance to school wearing a veil.[36]

The real issue lies deeper than wearing religious symbols and is not limited to Islam, as the *Otto-Preminger* decision and the legal commentaries that followed indicate. It was made explicit in a later case concerning Turkey's ban on wearing the Islamic headscarf. Challenged by a university student claiming her right to religious freedom, the Turkish government argued 'that religious duty and freedom were two different concepts that were not easily reconciled. The former notion required, by definition, submission to divine, immutable laws, while the notion of freedom presupposed that the

---

[33] See *Karaduman v Turkey* (1993) UN Human Rights Committee DR 74 p 73; *Dahlab v Switzerland* (2001) 2001-V; *Leyla Sahin v Turkey* (2004) (not reported).

[34] 'Loi encadrant, en application du principe de laïcité, le port de signes ou de tenues manifestant une appartenance religieuse dans les écoles, collèges et lycées publics.' See P Malaurie, 'Laïcité, voile islamique et réforme legislative' (2004) *Jurisclasseur périodique*, I, 124; V Fabre-Albert, 'La loi française du 15 mars 2004' (2004) Revue trimestrielle des droits de l'homme 575 (both authors discussing the three commissions that rendered opinions in December 2003 (Stasi and Debré commissions) and February 2004 (Conseil national consultative des droits de l'homme).

[35] Baubérot, *Laïcité 1905–2005*, above n 24, p 268.

[36] François Ost, *Antigone voilé*, Larcier, 2004.

individual enjoyed the widest possible range of opportunities and choices.'[37]

I, myself, had occasion to enter into the debate on the tensions between divine truth and reasoned truth during a conference in Iran, where I gave a presentation on the European Convention on Human Rights and the harmonisation resulting from the European Court of Human Rights' case law. Transposing my remarks to the global level, an Iranian cleric asked me about the metaphysical assumptions he believed must precede any harmonisation. He felt the road was closed due to the apparent incompatibility between the postulate of a divine truth that governs social and political life and a secular and reasoned approach to human rights. But at least he was willing to enter into dialogue. Similarly, the European Constitutional Treaty urges the Union to recognise the identity and specific contribution of churches and non-confessional organisations, and to maintain 'an open, transparent and regular dialogue' with them (Article 17(3) TFEU).

The problem is that dialogue isn't enough. It can pave the way towards legal approximation, but cannot build it, and it doesn't resolve the issue of pluralism's limits. In the Turkish case, the plaintiff had very astutely pleaded that the tensions are the inevitable consequence of pluralism and that 'the authorities' role in such circumstances was not to eliminate the cause of the tensions by doing away with pluralism, but to ensure that the competing groups were tolerant of each other'.[38]

The Court chose not to answer either the plaintiff or the Turkish government on this point; it merely examined the regulation on wearing religious symbols in teaching establishments, thus taking the risk of reducing reality to current events. It therefore once again upheld a state restriction on religious freedom because diversity required it to grant a margin of appreciation. In doing so, the Court called attention to the margin's problematic implementation.

## Implementation Difficulties

Well understood, a national margin of appreciation is no doubt the best way to avoid simply juxtaposing differences and, instead, progressively rendering practices compatible. Citing the preamble to the ECHR (which tasks the Council of Europe with the protection 'and development' of human rights), the European Court of Human

---

[37] *Leyla Sahin v Turkey*, above n 33, para 92.
[38] *Ibid.*, para 88.

Rights recognises the evolutionary nature of these rights and reserves to itself the right to progressively raise the threshold of compatibility (and thus to narrow the margin over time). But this variability raises the spectre of judicial subjectivity[39] and calls into question the foreseeability of decisions, and thus of the formal validity of the system.

The instructions for using the margin must therefore be laid out. The margin's width can evolve, to borrow the Court's terms, according to three series of criteria, the combination of which seems random given the different nature of the criteria: first, the circumstances, demands and context; second, the legitimate aim claimed by the state to support the restriction (protection of order, morals, or the rights of others); and third, a criterion of comparative law (convergence or divergence of national laws).

Applied to moral or religious diversity, it is not at all clear what determines the width of the margin. Sometimes, as in a case concerning homosexuality, the Court prefers the first criterion, asserting that national practices must occasionally be reviewed, particularly with 'regard . . . to scientific and societal developments'.[40] Other times, it finds that the legitimate aims cited by the states to support their restrictive measures (in the areas of national security, protection of judicial impartiality and independence, health, morals, religion, economic well being, etc.) are decisive: 'the scope of the domestic power of appreciation is not identical as regards each of the aims listed in Article 10(2).'[41] The margin is therefore narrower when judicial authority is at stake (judgment against the British government for contempt of court upheld), and wider when aims such as protecting morals or religion are involved (such as in the blasphemy and headscarf cases).

At yet other times, such as in the *Leyla Sahin* case, the diversity of national practices seems to be decisive: asserting that 'there is no uniform European conception of the requirements of "the protection of the rights of others" and of "public order"' (paragraph 102), the

[39] See O de Schutter, 'L'interprétation de la Convention européenne des droits de l'homme, un essai de démolition' (1992) *Revue de droit international des sciences diplomatiques et politiques* 83. Cf WJ Ganshof van der Meersch, 'Le caractère autonome des termes et la marge d'appréciation des gouvernements dans l'interprétation de la CESDH' in *Mélanges Wiarda* (Cologne, Carl Heymanns Verlag, 1988), pp 201 *ff.*
[40] See *Rees v United Kingdom* Series A no 106 (1986), para 47. See also M Delmas-Marty (ed), *Raisonner la raison d'Etat. Vers une Europe des droits de l'homme* (Paris, PUF, 1989), pp 491 *ff.*
[41] *Sunday Times v United Kingdom* Series A no 30 (1979).

Court deduces that it must grant the states a margin of appreciation. Though limited to a rapid survey (paragraphs 53–57) that seems insufficient to me given the reality of practices,[42] the Court finds its comparative study extensive enough to enable it to situate the debate occurring in Turkey, where 'there are extremist political movements . . . which seek to impose on society as a whole their religious symbols and conception of a society founded on religious precepts' (paragraph 109).

In an earlier decision, the Court had found that in this context of political and religious struggles, the ban on the Muslim party Refah Partisi did not violate the right to freedom of association.[43] In the headscarf case, it recalls the efforts of the competent authorities to teach and apply 'the values of pluralism, respect for the rights of others and, in particular, equality before the law of men and women' and concludes: [i]t is understandable in such a context . . . that the relevant authorities would consider that it ran counter to the furtherance of such values to accept the wearing of religious insignia, including as in the present case, that women students cover their heads with a headscarf while on university premises' (paragraph 110).

The Court's reasoning on the substantive issue is understandable as well, but it is weakened by the Court's moving from one criterion to another without explaining why, as if it were legitimating its decision *post hoc*. And in a case involving the prosecution of a man for the crime of homosexual conduct between adults,[44] even though it was an issue of morals and despite the differences in member states' laws, the Court recognised that societal evolution led to decriminalisation. In that case, the national margin was so narrow that some called it 'extinct'.[45]

Similarly, the Court held that by not authorising marriage between transsexuals, the United Kingdom violated the rights to privacy and dignity.[46] This reversal,[47] despite scientific uncertainty and the

---

[42] For a much more precise and reasoned comparative analysis, see E. Bribosia and I Rorrive, 'Le voile à l'école: une Europe divisée' (2004) *Revue trimestrielle des droits de l'homme* 951.

[43] See *Refah Partisi v Turkey* (Grand Chamber) (2003) 2003-II.

[44] See *Dudgeon v United Kingdom* Series A no 45 (1981). See also *Norris v Ireland*, Series A no 142 (1988).

[45] See C Picheral and AD Olinga, 'La théorie de la marge d'appréciation dans la jurisprudence de la CEDH' (1995) *Revue trimestrielle des droits de l'homme* 567.

[46] See *I v United Kingdom* (2002) (not reported). Cf *Jersild v Denmark* Series A no 298 (1994).

[47] See L Burgogue-Larsen, 'De l'art de changer de cap' in *Mélanges en hommage au doyen Gérard Cohen-Jonathan* (Brussels, Bruylant, 2004), pp 335 *ff*.

absence of any European consensus, led the Court to abandon the criteria previously mentioned and eliminate the margin altogether, considering that the United Kingdom's position created a situation of distress that was intolerable. In the three headscarf cases, however, the Court grants a wide margin and finds no violation of the Convention.[48] Comparing these cases reveals unexplained—and inexplicable—differences. Legal pluralism would seem to depend on a social pluralism that is more words than deeds, the variations of which are difficult to foresee.

But it does not follow that the national margin must be eliminated. Rather, its use must be rationalised by specifying the conditions that will enable it to order pluralism around shared guiding principles.

## Conditions for Ordering Pluralism: From Codes to Guiding Principles

My task now, therefore, is to explain how fuzzy guiding principles, as opposed to precise codes, can contribute to ordering pluralism. That is, how they can overcome the contradiction that seems inherent in the two words: 'pluralism' refers to dispersion or free movement, while 'ordering' evokes structure, even constraints. In fact, the Latin root of the word 'order', *ordo*, means line or row. Ordering pluralism therefore means making pluralism 'toe the line', or lining up its component parts. But on the contrary, the goal of pluralist harmonisation is to respect each part and enable their harmonious expression: 'to compose a mosaic, which is not done by throwing the various pieces haphazardly, but by combining them such that they create as harmonious a design together as possible.'[49]

In other words, the process of harmonisation cannot guarantee the harmony of the legal forms it produces without institutional and formal organisation.

---

[48] The court has also cited the national margin of appreciation to protect anonymous births (*l'accouchement sous X*). See *Odièvre v France* (2003) 2003-III. See also A Gouttenoire-Cornut and F Sudre, '*Odièvre v France*' (13 February 2003) *Juris-classeur périodique*, II, 10049. Cf P Malaurie: La Cour européenne des droits de l'homme et le « droit » de connaître ses origines. L'affaire Odièvre' (2003) *Juris-classeur périodique*, I, 120 (defending the decision as 'calming').

[49] Delmas-Marty and Izorche, 'Marge nationale d'appréciation et internationalisation du droit', above n 16, p 83.

## Institutional Organisation

More than the application of precise rules that tend towards unification, the application of guiding principles requires a clear framework and independent review.

Whether the guiding principles arise from directives, regulations, framework decisions, model laws, international conventions or *sui generis* ensembles, the national margin gains by being clarified. As Judge Françoise Tulkens of the European Court of Human Rights has shown, the Court has steadily increased its use of the national margin over the last few years, even in areas well beyond those of its 'natural'[50] application, namely Articles 8–11 and Article 1 of Protocol 1. This expansion calls into doubt the public-order-related basis for limiting the margin to restrictive and derogatory measures, and tends to create an 'atomic' or 'solar' system with varying degrees of protection.[51] The danger is that the concept of the margin, which was initially a legal instrument designed to preserve national diversity, will become a political instrument expressing the respective power of each state vis-à-vis the ECtHR.

But it is not enough to clarify the legal framework. There must be an independent and impartial review of the width of the margin, which depends on several factors at once: the initial 'transmitters' of the norm, that is, legislatures, broadly understood; and the 'receivers' responsible for transposing international norms into domestic law. I am referring here to national legislatures, who receive international norms and transmit domestic ones; to national judges, who become receivers of international norms when these are directly applicable[52]; and to legislatures and judges, when the former incorporate principles into domestic law and the latter apply them, thus becoming secondary receivers.

---

[50] F Tulkens and L Donnay, 'L'usage de la marge d'appréciation par la Cour européenne des droits de l'homme. Paravent juridique superflu ou mécanisme indispensable par nature?' (2006) *Revue de science criminelle* 3.

[51] See Yourow, 'Findings and Conclusions' in *The Margin of Appreciation Doctrine*, above n 16, pp 185 *ff* (and his diagram of 'atomic' or 'solar' systems, p 190). See also Delmas-Marty, *Le Relatif et l'Universel*, above n 22, pp 126 *ff*.

[52] For two examples of the direct applicability of the ECHR in France, see the decision of the *Conseil constitutionnel* with respect to the Treaty establishing a constitution for Europe (decision 2004-505 DC of 19 November 2004) and, in the United Kingdom, the House of Lords' decision on the Anti-terrorism, Crime and Security Act 2001, *A(FC) v Sec of State for Home Dep't* [2004] UKHL 56.

At each step and in each configuration, the process of harmonisation may be denatured and legal disorder may result, because an excessive margin leads to the fragmentation of international law, while too narrow a margin can destabilise the domestic legal order. Each step therefore requires a different type of review. To avoid the international transmitter's abusing its position to impose, rather than a guiding principle, a rule that is too precise and precludes any margin whatsoever, thus transforming harmonisation into forced unification,[53] national parliaments should be able to base a challenge on principles such as subsidiarity and proportionality, as provided by the Lisbon Treaty. And to avoid renationalisation of international principles by the receivers, supranational review must be available, such as that exercised by international judges (ECtHR, ECJ, DRB) or oversight committees (UN Human Rights Committee, OECD working group on bribery).

But even when it exists, review is insufficient: as the example of moral and religious diversity shows, the logical structure is quite complex, namely with respect to combining the various criteria that govern the decision.

## Logical Organisation

Logic must not be confused with rigidity, however, nor consistency with cohesion. Marie-Laure Mathieu-Izorche has shown that consistency is necessary, but insufficient on its own: '[t]he consistency of the complex system represented by [ECtHR] case law would serve no purpose if it were not supported by the cohesion of its recipients, that is, the states. However, as with a house, it is clear that even if the façade is built in a consistent manner, it may crumble with the first earthquake if no give or flexibility was provided for.'[54] She therefore concludes that 'consistency requires logic, but cohesion needs fuzziness, flexibility, and respect for diversity'.[55]

While the national margin of appreciation is in this sense conceived as a margin for manoeuvring rather than as a margin of error, it is nonetheless also a margin of uncertainty, which leads to a certain transfer of power to the reviewing body. Even if it is expressed in terms of compatible/incompatible, rather than

---

[53] See the examples cited in Delmas-Marty, *Critique de l'intégration normative*, above n 11.

[54] ML Mathieu-Izorche, 'La marge nationale d'appréciation, enjeu de savoir et de pouvoir, ou jeu de construction?' (2006) *Revue de science criminelle* 25.

[55] *Ibid.*

conform/not conform, the judge's decision is necessarily binary. Her reasoning, however, is based not on binary logic, but on a logic of gradation, or fuzzy logic, which leads to concluding that the state practice in question is proximate to, rather than the same as, the reference principle. As I have underscored numerous times, the concept of the margin is in no way incompatible with logic, but it rejects the separation (true/false or legal/illegal) proper to binary reasoning. In fuzzy logic, a proposition may be true to varying degrees.

The judge thus varies the degree of normative truth, as it were, following the observable data as closely as possible. In this way, the European Court of Human Rights, for example, contributes to the stability of the structure despite, or perhaps due to, its complexity. However, for complexity to contribute, by adjustments and readjustments, to the stability proper to harmonisation processes, international judges must respect two methodological conditions: transparency, which requires them to elaborate on the criteria serving as filters; and discipline, which implies that they respect these filters.

Elaborating criteria is not so easy, since harmonisation cannot come from the top. It necessarily lies at the intersection of 'two planes of friction': between the states, and between state authorities and international judges. It is therefore time 'to understand that the margin represents an opportunity, and seize it; to understand that what is supposedly marginal is in fact transversal[.] [A]ll actors benefit from the margin of freedom that uncertainty brings: states, of course, who find room in it to exercise their power; but also judges, who find themselves in a position to help the global rule evolve, while letting the players contribute to its perfection.'[56]

It is therefore not surprising that, according to this vision of law that is transversal rather than marginal or pyramidal, the criteria governing the variability of the national margin, and thus the final decision, are so difficult to establish. An open system built through interaction with its environment may be more durable than a closed system, but it requires more energy to maintain. The three criteria cited by the ECtHR and discussed above are therefore clarified by numerous 'pertinent factors', of which Judge Tulkens has identified eight. These factors help clarify very vague circumstantial and contextual criteria by introducing the 'gravity of the disputed limitation', the 'degree of complexity of the issue raised before the Court', and, a possibility raised more and more frequently as former Eastern-bloc

[56] *Ibid.*

countries join the Council of Europe, the 'situation of crisis existing in the defendant state'.[57] At the same time, the variety of these factors and the complexity of such a method may, she emphasises, make the use of the margin 'opaque, arbitrary and unforeseeable'.

Clearly, then, it is not enough to establish a list of criteria. Once established, the criteria must be respected. When the judges stop applying the highly refined combinations of criteria they themselves developed, as with respect to the variations in the national margin in the areas of moral and religious diversity, they devalue the extremely sensitive system they created, at the risk of reducing the foreseeability of their judgments and thus weakening the formal validity of the entire system.

It therefore seems to me that judicial transparency and discipline, reasoning and self-limitation are the ingredients for realising the European Union's motto, 'united in diversity'. The method is exacting, but to preserve ordered pluralism, there is only this subtle game of shared, guiding principles applied in a differentiated way. Committing to playing this game with determination and discipline is a way of showing that the union of peoples, including in other regions and at other levels, is not necessarily synonymous with uniformity, and that the universalism of values can adapt to the curves in space and time.

But something is still incomplete in this harmonisation conceived as a process of approximation of legal systems that remain different. The Preamble of the Constitutional Treaty called on peoples 'united ever more closely, to forge a common destiny', while the Lisbon Treaty is supposed to mark 'a new stage in the process of creating an ever closer union among the peoples of Europe'. The underlying suggestion is that there is an even more ambitious process: unification.

---

[57] Tulkens and Donnay, 'L'usage de la marge d'appréciation par la Cour européenne des droits de l'homme', above n 50, p 7.

# 3

# Unification by Hybridisation

IGHT UNIFICATION BE the royal road to the internationalisation of law? After all, normative and judicial cross-references merely establish a relationship without integration, and harmonisation reveals the complexity and imperfections of a compatibility that is sometimes synonymous with arbitrariness. Unification seems to be the only process capable of producing perfect integration.

'Perfect' in a formal sense, that is: by not recognising a national margin of appreciation and eliminating differences, it would produce regional and even world legal orders organised according to the hierarchical and coherent model of the traditional national legal order. But perfection would not be guaranteed from an empirical point of view because unification is so hard to implement that it may be largely ineffective. And it would be even further from perfect from an axiological standpoint, even on the relatively limited scale of Europe, as its seeming negation of pluralism calls its legitimacy severely into question.

To be sure, the Lisbon Treaty associates unification with pluralism, but without saying how 'the process of creating an ever closer union' will respect the diversity and pluralism it is supposed to protect. And at the global level, unification seems to have been almost unanimously rejected: it is no longer seen as a far-off and unreal utopia, but as a nightmare we fear will come true in the form of Kant's imagined tyranny of a global state. That fear is even stronger now that one law seems to be being created outside the regional framework, in areas as diverse as international criminal justice and international contracts.

But unique and hegemonic must not be confused. The process has reached the point where, behind the apparent perfection of unification, several modes of norm production may be distinguished that mean something very different in terms of pluralism. On the one hand, unification is occurring through unilateral transplants from one system to another, particularly in business law but also in other fields, such as the cultural area. Generalisation of this process can lead to one system's hegemonic domination, which would eliminate all diversity, erase history and cause us to forget the inventiveness of different peoples. On the other hand, unification through the innovative process of hybridisation, which combines elements from various legal systems, is being carried out with more or less success by the European courts and the international criminal tribunals and court, for example. This kind of unification can be qualified as pluralist.

But transplants are often rejected and hybrids are sometimes sterile, so both metaphors must be used with caution. Only the process of hybridisation conforms to the hypothesis of ordered pluralism, but it requires conditions for development and review that are rarely satisfied, as the difficulty in defining a unified criminal procedure in the ICC Statute shows. This example of unification through the hybridisation of accusatory and inquisitory procedure will nonetheless allow me to elucidate the conditions in which hybridisation can contribute to ordering pluralism.

## Two Processes of Unification

It is not always easy to see that there are two methods of unification, because language and practice confuse unilateral transplantation, which is most often an attempt to dominate the market of laws, with true hybridisation, which requires reciprocal interaction to be pluralist.

### Transplantation

The term is familiar to comparative scholars, who have long highlighted the imperfections related to the linguistic difficulties and social resistance facing attempts to transplant.[1] But it is enjoying renewed popularity due to the opening of borders stemming from both the liberalisation of economic exchanges that foster economic actors' transnational strategies and the development of new technologies, such as the Internet, which tend to make borders

---

[1] This topic was discussed at the Paris congress on *Les Méthodes du droit comparé*, Société de Législation Comparée, 1900 and, a little over a century later, in Brussels. See Mark van Hoecke (ed), *Methodology and Epistemology of Comparative Law* (Oxford, Hart Publishing, 2004).

disappear. As I have discussed elsewhere, globalisation contributes to competition between legal systems. To be sure, this competition can lead to spontaneous coordination through cross-references and other exchanges, but it most often manifests in the form of transplants, which are either imposed or accepted, sometimes even sought after, to the benefit of a system deemed to be more prestigious.

For example, constraint founded the forms of westernisation of law that marked the 20th century, underscoring the link between legal transplantation and economic and/or military domination. Examples of legal acculturation directly or indirectly related to colonisation abound.[2] A more ambiguous example is the westernisation of Chinese law at the beginning of the 20th century, which was both imposed by western powers, first and foremost European, who set westernisation as a condition to their abandoning the privilege of jurisdiction in the concessions, and desired by Chinese reformers as a way to modernise the law.[3]

But even among western nations, globalisation has exacerbated the phenomena of legal competition, pitting the Roman-Germanic models against the common law and thereby creating the impression of competition between the two, despite their dissimilarities. Such a presentation, which is limited to binary opposition and seems to consider the rest of the world *terra incognita*, is legally and politically objectionable. The University of Ottawa, for example, has produced a five-colour map showing not only the two major western families (common and Roman-Germanic law), but also three other groups composed of customary laws, mixed systems and Muslim laws.[4] At about the same time, however, the CIA reduced the world's diversity to a map in three colours: the two major western families appear distinctly, while the rest of the world's legal systems are represented by a white zone. China and the Islamic countries are thus lumped together with everyone else, and the whole zone looks like so many territories to be annexed by

---

[2] See, eg, N Rouland, *Anthropologie juridique* (Paris, PUF, 1988); *Aux confins du droit* (Paris, Odile Jacob, 1999). See also P Dima Ehongo, 'L'intégration juridique des économies africaines à l'échelle régionale ou mondiale' in M Delmas-Marty (ed), *Critique de l'intégration normative* (Paris, PUF, 2004) (concerning the traps of a hegemonic uniform law in the OHADA treaty).

[3] See generally M Delmas-Marty and PE Will (eds), *La Chine et la Démocratie. Tradition, Droit, Institutions* (Paris, Fayard, 2006).

[4] See Conseil d'État, *L'influence internationale du droit français* (Paris, La Documentation française, 2001), p 147.

law merchants, thus nourishing the fear of a common law conquest or even the 'Americanisation of law'.[5]

More recently, the World Bank's reports *Doing Business* ('Understanding Regulation' in 2004 and 'Removing Obstacles to Growth' in 2005) seem to favour transplanting common law systems, at the risk of confusing the efficiency of economic relations with their legitimacy. To illustrate the superiority of 'good laws', the authors favour quantifiable criteria and value formal positive law to the detriment of social reception.[6] Moreover, the theories of rational choice embraced by the reports are based on the postulate of a national legislature that is autonomous and master of the game, which ignores the complexity of normative and judicial interactions resulting from extraterritorial law, regional norms and possible conflicts between global norms (UN, WTO, ILO[7]).

The American model does, nonetheless, enjoy real prestige.[8] This can be attributed to various, dissimilar factors,[9] such as economic, military and linguistic domination and practices of openness, including the availability of experts, the political encouragement of university exchanges, and the omnipresence of lawyers, who are both buyers and sellers of law.[10] I might also add to this list a conception of law that is better adapted, by its flexibility, to new issues. American law is a driving force with respect to issues as varied as the Internet and biotechnology,[11] and even with regard to climate change: the United States has not ratified the Kyoto Protocol, but it invented the

[5] See M Guénaire, 'La *common law* ou l'avenir d'une justice sans code' in M Guénaire, *Le Débat* (Paris, Gallimard, 2001), p 51; *L'Américanisation du droit* (2001) *Archives de philosophie du droit* no 34.

[6] See C Jamin, 'D'autres fondamentaux systémiques' in G Canivet and MA Frison Roche (eds), *La Mesure de l'efficacité économique du droit* (Paris, LGDJ, 2005).

[7] See MA Moreau, 'L'internationalisation de l'emploi et le débat sur les délocalisations en France: perspectives juridiques' in P Auer, G Besse and D Méda (eds), *Délocalisations, Normes de travail et Politique d'emploi. Vers une mondialisation plus juste?* (Paris, La Découverte, 2005), pp 207–35. See also *Une mondialisation plus juste. Le rôle de l'OIT* (report of the Director General of the ILO) (ILO, 2004).

[8] See H Muir Watt, 'Propos liminaires sur le prestige du droit américain' in *L'Américanisation du droit*, above n 5, pp 29–36.

[9] See EA Farnsworth, 'L'américanisation du droit—mythes et réalités' in *L'Américanisation du droit*, above n 5, pp 21–8 (identifying seven advantages to American law).

[10] See *L'influence internationale du droit français*, above no. 4, pp 43–8; Y Dezalay, *Marchands de droit. La restructuration de l'ordre juridique par les multinationales du droit* (Paris, Fayard, 1992); Y Dezalay and BG Garth, *La Mondialisation des guerres de palais* (Paris, Seuil, 2002).

[11] See Delmas-Marty, *Les Forces imaginantes du droit (I): Le Relatif et l'Universel* (Paris, Seuil, 2004), pp 333, 346.

system of permits for greenhouse gas (GHG) emissions.[12] In addition, the difficult access to its particularly complex federal legal system is compensated by the American Law Institute's practice of publishing restatements (explanations of the law), which contribute to the understanding, and perhaps evolution, of American law.

But whether transplantation results from prestige, constraint or, more likely, a bit of both, its primary fault is its unilateral nature: it constitutes a mode of legal integration limited to transporting a concept, an institution, even a 'turnkey' system from one country to another in the interests of short-term efficiency, without reciprocity and without incorporating the fundamental rights protected by international human rights instruments. Bearing the heavy imprint of a statist, even sovereigntist conception of legal systems, such a process fosters a marketing strategy that appears modern, but which is in fact archaic. Neither marketing nor transplantation take into account the processes of pluralist integration developing at the regional and global levels.[13]

The two maps and the World Bank reports mentioned above overemphasise the division between common and Roman-Germanic law to such an extent that the appearance of regional ensembles developing processes of unification by cross-fertilisation seems insignificant. This highlights the importance of distinguishing unilateral transplantation from hybridisation, which involves reciprocity and exchange.

## Hybridisation

The problem, which partially explains the confusion, is that not all multilaterally negotiated norms entail the reciprocity that characterises hybridisation. In other words, transplantation can also take indirect forms and domination may be spread through regional or global law when the dominant system succeeds in influencing negotiations.

As I have said many times, the working language necessarily plays an important, if not decisive, role by conditioning the concepts: translating '*Etat de droit*' by 'rule of law' implies moving toward a less formal, more procedural system, which may lead to sliding further. In Chinese law, for example, *fa zhi* can refer either to law's

---

[12] See *ibid*, pp 388, 404.
[13] See M Delmas-Marty, 'Marketing juridique ou pluralisme ordonné' in M Guénaire, *Le Débat*, above n 5, pp 57 *ff*.

instrumental function in relation to the state, or to the idea of a state subject to law.[14]

But beyond translation problems, the process of elaborating international norms governs the analysis of whether unification is more or less pluralist. Some of the criticisms expressed by French jurists with respect to European or global shared principles seem to reflect a mistrust of unification's unilateral nature. The failure of the 1999 'Principles of European Trust Law' was thus attributed to the persistent fear 'of a certain unilateralism in the principles, which seek to unify the concept of trust and are perhaps not well enough suited to the issues of civil lawyers'.[15] Similarly, French scholars seem to hold two diametrically opposed views on European contract law: supporters of integration assert that the process was conceived as a hybridisation or legal cross-breeding that is a 'source of enrichment, not impoverishment',[16] while opponents reproach the proposal's authors for sacrificing linguistic diversity, not representing various cultures equally, and not respecting the socio-cultural constraints of each state.[17]

Indeed, by incorporating international norms into its domestic law, Germany, which is less timid than France, is able to hold up German law as a model of integration. Two examples are the 2001 reform incorporating into the German Civil Code the Vienna Convention on the international sale of goods, the Unidroit principles, and the Principles of European Contract Law[18]; and the 2002 adoption of the oddly entitled 'German Code of Crimes against International Law', which was openly conceived as a model for

---

[14] See M Delmas-Marty, 'La construction d'un État de droit en Chine, avancées et résistances' (2002) *Dalloz* 2484. See also E Fronza, E Malarino, C Sotis, 'Principe de précision et justice pénale internationale' in M Delmas-Marty, E Fronza and E Lambert-Abdelgawad, *Les Sources du droit international pénal. L'expérience des tribunaux pénaux internationaux* (Paris, Société de Législation Comparée, 2005) (on the problems caused by having multiple official languages).

[15] D Le Grand de Belleroche, 'L'intégration du concept de trust à l'échelle régionale et mondiale' in Delmas-Marty, *Critique de l'intégration normative*, above n 2, pp 139–78.

[16] JB Racine, 'Pourquoi unifier le droit des contrats en Europe? Plaidoyer en faveur de l'unification' (2003) *Revue du droit de l'Union européenne* 403.

[17] See Y Lequette, 'Quelques remarques à propos du code civil européen' (2002) *Dalloz* 2202.

[18] See C Witz, 'La nouvelle jeunesse du BGB insufflée par la réforme du droit des obligations' (2002) *Dalloz* 3156; L Vogel, 'Recodification civile et renouvellement des sources internes' in *1804–2004. Le Code civil, un passé, un présent, un avenir* (Paris, Dalloz, 2004) p 165.

incorporating the ICC Statute.[19] Though the method seems to foster hybridisation, it can lead to a certain renationalisation: during the process of transposition, the Rome Statute was infused with a number of German dogmatic concepts, such as the principles of guilt and legality. Encouraging other states to follow the German model of incorporation could thus lead indirectly to a certain unilateral domination.

It is not entirely illegitimate, of course, for the first countries to make the effort to incorporate international norms, and who thus have accepted a certain reciprocity that requires modifying their domestic law, to contribute actively thereafter to the process of hybridisation.[20] In this regard, the Conseil d'État's report on the influence of French law underscores 'the insufficient ability to export French solutions',[21] noting that had France adapted Anglo-American trust law to the French system early enough, the French trust could have served as an example elsewhere. In the same way, when the French Commission on criminal justice and human rights (*Justice pénale et droits de l'homme*) was working on reforming the Code of Civil Procedure, it thought it necessary to anticipate the Europeanisation of criminal procedure and, by incorporating advances made in European law, contribute to outlining the common criminal procedure of the future.[22] Though it didn't dare adopt this reform, France eventually adopted the guilty plea, but without adapting it to the French system, such that the Cour de cassation's decisions illustrate the perverse effects on French law, which limits the impact of the plea as well.[23]

[19] See G Werle and S Manacorda, 'L'adaptation des systèmes pénaux au statut de Rome: le paradigme du *Völkerstrafgesetzbuch*' (2004) *Revue de science criminelle* 501; G Werle and F Jessberger, 'International Criminal Justice Is Coming Home: the New German Code of Crimes against International Law' (2002) *Criminal Law Forum* no 13.

[20] The Brazilian law on children and adolescents (Law no 8.069 of 13 July 1990), for example, followed the international example and is often used as an example itself in Latin America for legal reform in this area. See K Martin-Chenut, 'Les politiques criminelles française et brésilienne applicables aux mineurs délinquants: l'interaction avec le droit international des droits de l'homme' (doctoral dissertation), University of Paris I, 2002.

[21] Conseil d'État, *L'Influence internationale du droit français*, above n 4, p 67.

[22] See *La Mise en état des affaires pénales* (Paris, La Documentation française, 1991); M Delmas-Marty (ed), *Procès pénal et Droits de l'homme. Vers une conscience européenne* (Paris, PUF, 1992).

[23] On the Law of 9 March 2005, see J Pradel note on Crim., 18 April 2005 (2005) *Dalloz* 1200; B Pereira (2005) *Dalloz* 2041. For a critique of the law, see C Saas, 'De la composition pénale au plaider-coupable: le pouvoir de sanction du procureur' (2004) *Revue de science criminelle* 827. Cf M Langer, 'From Legal Transplants to

The line between hegemonic unification (by transplantation) and pluralist unification (by hybridisation) is certainly a fine one, but criminal procedure provides a clear example of the difference, as hybridisation is developing in this field at both the regional and global levels.

## Hybridisation and Criminal Procedure

To illustrate the process of hybridisation, I have long taken inspiration from Paul Klee's Bauhaus lectures from the 1930s. Klee explained how to compose a drawing using only circles and straight lines: domination (lines absorbing circles or circles dissolving lines); uninteresting superposition (a row of lines alternating with a row of circles); or composition-fusion, illustrated by a face in which lines and curves of equal value blend harmoniously.

As imaginative as it is, I find the metaphor too static today. Having had the occasion to participate in developing several hybrid criminal procedures (the line very approximately representing the inquisitory conception and the circle the accusatory view), I know that laws are not conceived according to a definitive design by legislator-artists or demiurges. Once again, adjustments and readjustments are necessary, because developing hybrid norms is not immediately definitive. Even though the shared norm is initially unified, its interpretation in international law evolves and its reception in domestic law can provide for implicit national margins (renationalisation) that transform the unification process into harmonisation.

Twice—in 1993 as a member of the Truche commission tasked by the United Nations Security Council with drafting a statute for an international criminal tribunal, and between 1996 and 1999 as coordinator of a project initiated by the European Commission and Parliament called *Corpus juris* for protecting the financial interests of the European Union—I was able to take stock of the limits of too rigid a theorisation. Neither the *Corpus juris*[24] nor the statutes of the international criminal tribunals or court are meant as substitutes for domestic law: they are designed to play a role in a much more

---

Legal Translations: the Globalization of Plea Bargaining and the Americanization Thesis in Criminal Processes' (2004) 45 *Harvard International Law Journal* 1.

[24] M Delmas-Marty (ed), Corpus juris *Introducing Penal Provisions for the Purpose of the Financial Interests of the European Union* (Paris, Economica, 1997); M Delmas-Marty and J Vervaele (eds), *The Implementation of the* Corpus Juris *in the Member States* (Mortsel (Antwerp), Intersentia, Vols I–III, 2000, vol IV, 2002).

complex set of interactions where harmonisation and horizontal cross-references also play a role, demonstrating that hybridisation is a non-linear process and that the result (the hybrid) is not a perfect form like that drawn by an artist, but a composite and unstable one.

### Adjustments: A Non-linear Process

The European example of the *Corpus juris* illustrates the need for adjustments that are not restricted to a linear path from harmonisation to unification, but that oscillate between the two processes. Before elaborating a draft, we undertook comparative research to establish an 'analysis grid'[25] that gave us a common language to designate procedural actors as neutrally as possible: 'prosecuting party', 'accused', and 'judge'. Similarly, the powers governing the procedure were split into eight categories detached from their national contexts: 'reporting of the offence', 'investigation', 'evidence', 'accusation', 'adversariality', 'coercive measures', 'disposal of the case', and 'decision making'.

Using this grid, we were able to constitute a grammar, properly speaking (that is, the structure linking actors and powers) for each system. The accusatory grammar gives most of the powers to private actors, from reporting offences to disposing of cases (through plea bargaining) via obtaining evidence (to the point of excluding hearsay, as a general rule). The inquisitory grammar, however, privileges public actors, particularly the emblematic investigating judge (*juge d'instruction*), who is responsible for both police functions (the investigation, during the preparatory phase, from which the file transmitted to the tribunal is constituted) and judicial duties (deciding on detention).

Such differences would have precluded any attempt to hybridise if harmonisation had not already been both imposed by the European Court of Human Rights (whose judgments enabled us to verify that each model has its weaknesses), and initiated spontaneously, through repeated reforms. Most countries on the Continent have progressively done away with the investigating judge and have given a more active role to the defence: criminal procedure in Italy and Portugal is now partially accusatory, and France has instituted a judge of freedoms (Law of 15 June 2000) and the guilty plea (Law

---

[25] See J Spencer and M Delmas-Marty (eds), *European Criminal Procedures* (Cambridge, CUP, 2002), p 70; M Delmas-Marty (ed), *Procédures pénales d'Europe* (Paris, PUF, 1995) p 60.

of 9 March 2004).[26] The United Kingdom, meanwhile, has introduced a public prosecution service and considerably reduced the ability to exclude indirect evidence (Criminal Justice Act 2003, Prevention of Terrorism Act 2005), as did the United States Supreme Court, though by a different method.[27]

Highlighted by the comparative study, this progressive harmonisation enabled us to construct the hybridisation phase around unified rules primarily governing the conduct of investigations, the rights of the parties and methods of proof. These rules are consistent with the European Convention on Human Rights' three guiding principles governing a new, hybrid 'grammar' called 'contradictory'[28]:

(1) European territoriality, the conceptual foundation for attributing jurisdiction over the entire territory to a European prosecutor—a public prosecution office borrowed from the inquisitorial model;

(2) judicial guarantee, assured during the pre-trial phase by a national or European 'judge of freedoms' (not an investigating judge, but a judge who is sufficiently neutral to moderate between the prosecution and the defence, in the style of the accusatory model); and

(3) 'contradictory' proceedings, a new conception, particularly as regards evidence, combining a written file (from the inquisitorial model) with strict exclusionary rules (from the accusatory model).

Proposed in a European Commission green paper on the European prosecutor and incorporated into the Lisbon Treaty article providing for the institution of a European prosecutor by unanimous vote (Article 86 TFEU), the hybridisation process would require yet another European law to flesh out the various points addressed by the *Corpus juris* (status of the prosecutor, rules of procedure and evidence, and appeal mechanisms).

But it is already clear that the procedure will not be entirely unified. Before it is extended to transnational criminality, the European prosecutor's jurisdiction will be limited by the Constitutional Treaty to the PIF Convention (Protection of the European Communities'

---

[26] See D Charvet, 'Réflexions autour du plaider coupable' (2004) *Dalloz*, Chr. 2517.

[27] See *Crawford v Washington*, 541 US 36 (2004). See also G Giudicelli-Delage (ed), H Matsopoulou (co-ord), *Les Transformations de l'administration de la preuve pénale. Perspectives comparées: Allemagne, Belgique, Canada, Espagne, Etats-Unis, France, Italie, Portugal, Royaume-Uni* (Paris, Société de Législation Comparée, 2005) (introduction and conclusion reprinted in (2005) *Archives de politique criminelle*).

[28] Cf JD Jackson, 'The Effect of Human Rights on Criminal Evidentiary Processes: Towards Convergence, Divergence or Realignment?' (2005) 68 *The Modern Law Review* 737 (suggesting the term 'participatory model').

financial interests, which are of course supranational). In addition, unification will concern only the preparatory phase of the trial, as the European prosecutor will exercise her functions thereafter under the jurisdiction of national tribunals. The precise relationship between national and European institutions will be set out some time in the future in a European law that will undoubtedly have to provide for minimal harmonisation of national rules as well. But the process will not stop with legislation, as readjustments will no doubt be necessary, as is shown by that other procedural hybrid, international criminal justice.

### Readjustments: An Unstable Result

International criminal justice is far ahead of European criminal justice. The *ad hoc* tribunals (ICTY and ICTR) were established more than 10 years ago[29] and have adopted more than 20 modifications to the rules of procedure and evidence. Criticised on the basis of the separation of powers, which should prohibit judges from modifying procedural rules as problems arise, these reforms nonetheless contributed significantly to perfecting a hybrid on which the ICC Statute is partially based. The instability of the first mechanism thus seems to have been necessary to develop the second.

The subject of hybridisation was broached by the judges from the very beginning: 'The general philosophy of the criminal procedure of the International Tribunal aims at maintaining a balance between the accusatory procedure of the common law systems and the inquisitorial procedure of the civil law systems, whilst at the same time ensuring the doing of justice.'[30] But the danger of domination remained strong. Drawing on the existence of rules drawn directly from the common law, such as the guilty plea, most judges tended to base their interpretation on common law principles. In a dissenting opinion[31] that continues to voice a minority view, then President Cassese insisted that '[i]nternational criminal procedure', the product of 'the gradual decanting of national criminal concepts and rules into the international receptacle', does not result from a corpus of uniform law, but from 'combin[ing] and fus[ing]' two different legal systems (common and Roman-Germanic law). He vainly underscored that the 'mechanical importation' of concepts drawn

---

[29] See Symposium, 'The ICTY 10 Years On: The View from Inside' (2004) 2 *Journal of International Criminal Justice* 353.

[30] ICTY, *Delalic et al* case, 4 February 1998, para 20.

[31] ICTY, *Erdemovic* case (Cassese dissent), 7 October 1997, paras 3, 4.

from only one of those systems 'may alter or distort the *specificity*' resulting from the interstate context and lack of autonomous means of coercion.

Over time, things have stabilised, however. Various reforms have strengthened both the equality of arms (accusatory grammar) and the active role of the judge (inquisitory grammar). A typical example of the need for successive readjustments is the institution, in practice at first, then by an amendment (Article 65 *ter*), to the ICTY rules adopted in July 1998 of a pre-trial judge responsible for ensuring the proper application of admissibility rules. This judge thus plays the role of the 'grand jury (or committing magistrate) in the common law system [or of] the *juge d'instruction* in some civil law systems'.[32] In creating a pre-trial chamber, the ICC statute (Article 15, 56, 57 and 58) thus expands and strengthens the ICTs' institution of a pre-trial judge.

The same is true for the sensitive issue of the case file: successive reforms to the general rules of evidence eventually gave judges the power to receive oral or written depositions 'where the interests of justice allow' (ICTY Rules of Procedure and Evidence, Rule 89(f)) and eliminated the prohibition on indirect evidence. The ICC Statute approves this hybrid model in Article 64, which reaffirms that the judges, not the parties, direct the proceedings (particularly with regard to witnesses, Article 64(6)(b)).

On other issues, such as the participation of victims, the ICC Statute (Article 68(3)) goes even further by providing that they may be represented by counsel. This gives them a status similar to the '*parties civiles*' of Roman-Germanic systems, though they are technically only joined parties whose intervention does not require instituting criminal proceedings.

Stabilisation has not yet been achieved in other areas, such as bargaining between prosecution and defence, however. Initially excluded due to the gravity of international crimes, plea-bargaining may become necessary for practical reasons, but its legal regime has yet to be decided upon. While the Statute provides for pleading guilty (Article 64(2)), this is defined (Article 65) more along the lines of the Continental confession than as a guilty plea in the Anglo-American sense, and gives no indication as to possible negotiation between prosecution and defence.

---

[32] ICTY, *Brdanin* case, *Decision on the Motion to Dismiss Indictment*, 5 October 1999, para 13.

Noting the confusing complexity of the current legal landscape and describing criminal law specialists as 'mariners on the ocean without compass, star or landmark',[33] the American comparative law professor Mirjan Damaška states that in different models, plea-bargaining obeys different, and apparently irreconcilable, rules, namely as to the role of the judge and the publicity given to bargaining.[34] He concludes that we must innovate, both because of the hybrid nature of the statute and the pedagogical function proper to international criminal justice. He suggests specific rules to avoid judicial bias and to make bargaining transparent. But he leaves open the question of the judge's role, suggesting either a public hearing of the testimony of the prosecution's principal witnesses, according to the Anglo-American model, or questioning of the accused by the judge, as in the Continental model. I would also be tempted to add that plea bargaining, the only way to avoid or simplify trial in the West, must no doubt be expanded to include the various forms of mediation and reconciliation that exist in other legal traditions and cultures.

But instability is not only technical. It affects the very bases of a hybridisation that is essentially limited to western laws, with the attendant risk that other traditions will be reduced to progressive acculturation, even as the ICC proceeds with cases primarily from Africa. The prosecutor, who announced the opening of an investigation in the Congo in June 2004, has tried to remedy this by explicitly raising the issue of taking into account cultural relativism and alternative forms of justice in the decision to undertake prosecution.[35] The issue must indeed be raised, because the very concept of hybridisation cannot be limited, at the global level, to western models only. The concept of the interests of justice that conditions the decision to pursue a case or not ('prosecution is not in the interests of justice', ICC Statute, Article 53(1)(c)), must take into account various forms of alternative justice (negotiation, mediation, reconciliation).

In the end, hybridisation constitutes more than elaborating norms. It also raises the issue of their interpretation in the case of imprecision

---

[33] Mirjan Damaska, 'Negotiated Justice in International Criminal Courts' (2004) 2 *Journal of International Criminal Justice* 1018, 1019.

[34] See M Langer, 'From Legal Transplants to Legal Translations', above n 23.

[35] See Office of the ICC Prosecutor, 'Interpretation and Scope of 'Interests of Justice' in Art 53 of the Rome Statute', ICC Memorandum, 7 May 2004 (on file with author). See also M Delmas-Marty, 'Interactions between National and International Criminal Law at the ICC' (2006) *Journal of International Criminal Justice* 4.

or silences in the written law. As I mentioned earlier, the ICC Statute provides for the application of the principles and rules of international law, then the 'general principles of law derived by the Court from national laws of legal systems of the world' (Article 21). But it does not indicate how to decide between different national traditions, nor how to adapt these principles to the hybrid nature of the rules. The conditions must therefore be set out for creating the order necessary for unification to be consistent and pluralist.

## Conditions for Creating Order

While the 'benevolence' dear to former Chief Justice Canivet appears to be the key to spontaneous coordination and the national margin of appreciation the key to harmonisation because it accommodates differences, within limits, a common grammar is undoubtedly the key to creating unified, pluralist order: it provides systemic consistency and enables hybridisation to be distinguished from transplantation. But grammar also reveals the supranational nature of unified legal ensembles and the consequent limits of unification, which greatly modifies the nature of interstate relations and elicits strong resistance.

### A Common Grammar

As international criminal justice shows, one of the characteristics of a form conceived by hybridisation is that it distinguishes itself from national forms by progressively establishing its autonomy. That hybridisation goes hand in hand with autonomisation[36] seems to be confirmed in various areas, such as civil[37] as well as criminal procedure, and contract and trust law.[38] Consequently, consistency is not a foregone conclusion and cannot simply be borrowed from a pre-existing system. It must be built using not only technical rules, but guiding or meta- principles that define a common grammar.

[36] See J de Hemptinne, 'Hybridité et autonomie du règlement de procédure et de preuve du TPIY' in M Delmas-Marty, E Fronza and E Lambert-Abdelgawad (eds), *Les Sources du droit international pénal. L'expérience des tribunaux pénaux internationaux* (Paris, Société de Législation Comparée, 2005), pp 135–56.

[37] See P Fouchard, 'Une procédure civile transnationale: quelles fins et quels moyens' (2001) *Revue de droit uniforme* 779; P Fouchard (ed), *Vers un procès civil universel? Les règles transnationales de procédure civile de l'American Law Institute* (Paris, LGDJ, 2001).

[38] L Fin-Langer, 'L'introduction du droit du contrat en Europe' in Delmas-Marty, *Critique de l'intégration normative*, above n 2; D Le Grand de Belleroche, 'L'intégration du concept de trust à l'échelle régionale et mondiale', above n 15.

As I mentioned above, the *Corpus juris* was based on the idea that to be viable, the proposed hybridisation had to be consistent, and consistency was to be drawn from principles found in both the European Convention on Human Rights and comparative law that could guide interpretation as new issues arose. At the global level, the principles set out in international human rights instruments might be considered guiding principles, but as I discussed in Chapter 1 (Coordination through cross-references), the judges of the international criminal tribunals do not consider themselves bound by these instruments, due precisely to the specificity of international criminal justice.

Indeed, these principles are not precise enough to resolve differences between traditional models, namely those between the accusatory and inquisitory models. This is why an autonomous grammar is necessary, as the apparently technical issue of bargaining between prosecution and defence shows. To resolve such differences, the principles framing the solution must be found in the very conception of this hybrid criminal justice. Traditional national and international principles of defence rights (presumption of innocence, right to contradictory debate) are insufficient; the specifics of international criminal justice are what enable the establishment of an implicit principle of transparency, which must govern practice.

Instead of defining the elements composing systemic consistency one at a time as issues arise, developing a grammar adapted to the process of hybridisation requires more systematic work. This work must take place at the intersection of general international law principles, which must be adapted to the interstate nature of the principles of human rights due to the particularly antagonistic relationship between them and criminal justice (which both protects and threatens them), and model principles of national criminal justice (because the purpose is to punish individuals determined to be guilty).

The same need arises in the related area of civil procedure: a draft transnational civil procedure code, begun by Unidroit and the American Law Association in the form of a set of highly technical rules, evolved into a two-part code containing 'principles' and 'rules'. Without using the term 'grammar' with respect to the principles, the commentators clearly indicate that this is their role. The rules were drafted on the American model, while the principles, 'more familiar to civil law jurists',[39] were formulated as generally,

---

[39] P Fouchard, *Vers un procès civil universel?*, above n 37, p 159. See also 'Le procès équitable' in M Delmas-Marty, H Muir Watt and H Ruiz Fabri (eds), *Variations autour d'un droit commun* (Paris, Société de Législation Comparée, 2002).

abstractly and succinctly as possible, which made them 'acceptable, in their method and in their content, to the various countries'.[40]

The relationship between the concepts of common grammar and pluralism is thus that to avoid a unification resulting from the transplantation of a dominant model, a conceptual effort must be made to define common principles that are acceptable to each system composing the new legal form.

This observation is confirmed by a comparison of the hybrid procedure established for the ICTs and the ICC or, with better or worse results, the mixed tribunals (Kosovo, Sierra Leone, Cambodia) and the procedure imposed on the Iraqi Special Tribunal.[41] Instituted by the governor rather than legal action under international law, this tribunal applies a procedure that combines American law and Iraqi criminal procedure; the rules are therefore defined by transplantation, that is, by grafting rather than true hybridisation.

The problem is that the transplant may be rejected, or the entire system paralysed. By grafting American rules drafted according to an accusatory grammar (which entails conducting the procedure, from investigation to trial, as a contradictory debate before a neutral judge) onto an inquisitory system (where the investigation is conducted in the preparatory phase by an investigating judge who compiles a file), a legal and practical impasse may be reached. Not only are foreign counsel totally ignorant of inquisitory procedure imposed on Iraqi judges and prosecutors and Iraqi lawyers required to engage in cross-examination, a practice that is extremely foreign to their legal culture, but the procedure is considerably more cumbersome. In particular, investigations are carried out first by the investigating judge during the preparatory phase, then by the parties, namely in the form of cross-examining witnesses during trial.[42]

Clearly, the American government wanted to avoid legitimating the ICC model,[43] but expressing its rejection of supranational justice in this way may serve as a counter-example and, very indirectly, foster development of this model in the long term. Still, the United States' resistance has the merit of highlighting the limits of unification.

---

[40] G Mecarelli, 'Les principes fondamentaux de procédure civile transnationale et les "nouvelles" règles transnationales' in P Fouchard, *Vers un procès civil universel?*, above n 37, p 159.

[41] See Delmas-Marty, *Le Relatif et l'Universel*, above n 11, pp 231, 240, 398.

[42] See S Zappalà, 'The Iraqi Special Tribunal's Draft Rules of Procedure and Evidence: Neither Fish nor Fowl' (2004) 2 *Journal of International Criminal Justice* 855.

[43] See J Alvarez, 'Trying Hussein: Between Hubris and Hegemony' (2004) 2 *Journal of International Criminal Justice* 319.

## Limits of Unification

The very idea of a common grammar, which conditions the consistency of pluralist unification, in fact requires a significant change in interstate relations, because it requires moving from inter- to supra-state relations.

Beyond political resistance, the legal debate that began with respect to criminal justice took two forms revealing different conceptions of the internationalisation of law: one between sovereigntists and universalists; the other among international, criminal and human rights scholars.

If interstate law is considered to be the foundation of international law, there is no need to seek a common grammar. It is enough to define technical rules to fight impunity and subject 'the principal agents of states, those who originate policies perceived as gravely criminal, . . . to a form of international responsibility'.[44] But from the supra-state perspective, the legitimacy of a justice that is not national but is nonetheless criminal, that is, coupled with heavy sanctions including life imprisonment, calls for a common grammar to provide a consistency sufficient to protect both victims and accused from arbitrariness. Depending on whether the accent is placed on an international responsibility requiring state backup, or on a supranational form of criminal law, hybridisation may be judged useless or necessary: it is useless in the classical interstate area, but necessary to protecting interests that are neither national nor international, but transnational or supranational.

For the debate also includes the interests to be protected. A criminal law analysis of the nature of the crimes prosecuted shows that supranational interests are at stake (the financial interests of the European Union for the *Corpus juris*, crimes 'against humanity' and other violations of values considered universal for the ICTs and the ICC). Similarly, contract law seems to limit global unification to transnational contracts (Unidroit principles or the UN Convention on the international sale of goods), while the European principles of the Lando Commission or the von Bar group extend to all contracts.[45]

---

[44] R Maison, 'Le droit international, les droits de l'homme et les jurisdictions internationals pénales' in G Cohen-Jonathan and JF Flauss (ed), *Droit international, Droits de l'homme et Juridictions internationales* (Brussels, Bruylant, 2004) pp 121–39.

[45] Another scholarly debate exists in private law between international private law specialists and Community (EU) law specialists. Refusing to choose between partially unified community law and international private law, guardian of the historical conception that constructed domestic legal systems by separating them, some jurists,

If the interests are considered national, *inter*, *trans*, or *supra-national*, it would apparently be logical to favour harmonisation for the first two and unification for the others. But this solution must be qualified due to the almost complete absence of a supranational court capable of guaranteeing its application. In practice, domestic law must therefore incorporate the protection of transnational and supranational interests and, conversely, supranational law must preserve national jurisdiction. This is why the principles of subsidiarity and complementarity are so important.

For similar types of interests, different processes must therefore be combined. Even stabilised over time, hybridisation does not lead to unity conceived on the national model of an independent, perfectly autonomous order. It cannot be isolated from either coordination or harmonisation, which are necessary when cases are tried before domestic courts.

It would be tempting to see in this pluralism of fusion the realisation of the Messianic promises of the great western and Chinese classics announcing the marriage of the One and the Many. But fusion continues to be utopian and it would no doubt be imprudent to want to hurry its coming. Long before the 'ten thousand things . . . intertwine[e] their breaths' to create harmony and bring about the Great Peace, more modest work must be done to order legal systems by combining the various processes of interaction according to regional and global organisational levels.

<hr/>

such as JS Bergé, try to make the case for a 'variable-geometry internationality' at the European level (but the idea can also apply at the global level): 'Le drioit d'une communauté de droit: le front européen?' in *Le Droit international privé : esprit et méthode. Mélanges Paul Lagarde*, special edition of the *Revue critique de droit international privé* (Paris, Dalloz, 2004) pp 113–36.

# Part 2
## Organisational Levels

'Clusters of events, even if they are interconnected, do not become organised.'[1] The same may be said of groups of legal events. Even though they are interrelated via the processes of interaction discussed in Part 1, normative and legal clusters do not easily become sufficiently autonomous and stable organisations to constitute a legal order. Order continues to be identified with the state, and legal organisation is generally situated at the national level.

In the early 20th century, however, authors emphasised the role of certain infra- or transnational organisations (professional, religious, even criminal). The Italian jurist Santi Romano gave the name 'legal pluralism' to situations in which the law is not that of a single state and institutional organisations other than the state are taken into account.[2] Publishing in 1918, he could not have suspected that the fragmentation he observed at the infra- or transnational level would develop in the international sphere as well, and simply assumed the unity of the international order.

Beginning in the post-war period (1945), however, and especially since the end of the cold war and the beginning of the current globalisation (1989), internationalisation processes have multiplied and created a dynamic movement of 'organisation', but the movement is incomplete and only rarely creates a genuine 'legal order', namely, a mechanism sufficiently autonomous and stable to be qualified as such. In his defence of the 'unity of international law'[3] at the Hague

[1] D Andler, A Fagot-Largeault and B Saint-Sernin, 'La causalité' in D Andler, A Fagot-Largeault and B Saint-Sernin, *Philosophie des sciences*, vol 2 (Paris, Gallimard, 2002), p 920.
[2] See Santi Romano, *L'Ordre juridique* [*L'ordinamento giuridico*, Pise, 1918, 2d edn 1945] 2nd edn (Paris, Dalloz, 2002).
[3] PM Dupuy, *L'Unité de l'ordre juridique international. Cours général de l'Académie de droit international public* [2000] (Leiden, Martinus Nijhoff, 2003).

Academy, Pierre-Marie Dupuy underscores the problem when, using regional (Community law) and global (global trade law) examples, he refers to what he calls 'the myth of self-sufficient regimes': the vague term 'regime' indicates to me a hesitation at using more precise words such as 'system' or 'order'.

Before they establish an order, the processes of interaction discussed above create, through adjustments and readjustments, formerly unseen forms that require a tailor-made vocabulary. It is probably no accident that use of the term 'area' has multiplied and the word has taken on a functional and even structural meaning, in addition to its geographical one. In Fernand Braudel's historical con-struction, the area had become a 'key to understanding the time of civilisations' but this view 'no longer suffices to explain both the terracing of areas and the ordering of time periods; the science of eras and the science of places must be readjusted like the set of social sciences'.[4]

The remark holds for the legal field as well. Gérard Timsit was the first to distinguish normative order (No) from normative area (Na),[5] explaining that 'this dual approach does not refer to the duality of normative system*s*, but of *the* normative system considered in its two constitutive elements: a normative order properly speaking *(No)*, a hierarchical system of creating norms founded on the existence of a hierarchical relationship or a relationship of order between norms, and a normative area *(Na)*, a system of belonging or of inclusion of norms in a non hierarchical ensemble'.[6]

While in mathematics belonging is considered a relationship of order, order and belonging can nonetheless be separated, as one reflects hierarchy and the other a non-hierarchical principle that Timsit calls inclusion. The problem is that neither of these prin-ciples exists in a pure state in international practices. In this world where independence is giving way to interdependence, fewer and fewer autonomous institutions (interinstitutional), norms (inter-normative) and courts (interjudicial) are developing intersecting relationships, seemingly devoid of order. There is less a piling up or superposition of norms and institutions like so many sedimentary

---

[4] D Roche, 'L'espace et les historiens: pratiques et réflexions' in A Berthoz and R Recht (eds), *Les Espaces de l'homme* (Paris, Odile Jacob, 2005) 309–18 at 310, 312.

[5] See G Timsit, *Thèmes et Systèmes de droit* (Paris, PUF, 'Les voies du droit', 1986).

[6] G Timsit, 'L'ordre juridique comme métaphore' (2001) *Droits* no 33, p 8 (emphasis in original).

layers than an overlapping[7] characterised by the interactions discussed in Part 1.

Here again, history seems transferable to law: 'The area's function is no longer to highlight the weight of immobility and the froth of circumstances, but to enable dynamic questioning into what makes societal change possible and what can slow it down.'[8]

This 'dynamic questioning' is all the more important today as the 'normative areas' negotiated between states generally loath to abandon their sovereignty does not require, or requires very incompletely, creating the executive, legislative and judicial institutions that would stabilise the ensemble. The expression 'variable geometry' (or even 'variable geography' according to which states belong) has thus become common to express the phenomenon's complexity, and especially the observers' perplexity in the face of this variability, and thus instability, that accompanies it.

This is why organisation 'levels' are important: they drive progressive normative and institutional stabilisation and foster, as Europe's Community organisation shows, the eventual transformation of an area into a legal order. But they cannot be built linearly, from the national to the regional or global level. Not only do they separate human rights from the market and pit several models of economic integration against each other, their chronologies vary: regional organisations can anticipate globalisation, as 'testing laboratories', or can react to it to try to change directions or speeds (to speed it up or slow it down).

To keep my presentation linear, however, I will start by discussing the regional level, which is both more familiar, at least with respect to European construction, and more diversified when other regional organisations are included.

---

[7] See C Girard, 'Procès equitable et enchevêtrement des espaces normatifs (réflexions sur la problématique générale)' in H Ruiz Fabri (ed), *Procès équitable et Enchevêtrement des espaces normatifs* (Paris, Société de Législation Comparée, 2003) pp 22–23.

[8] D Roche, Inaugural lecture, Collège de France, 1999.

# 4

# Regional Organisations

I WILL NOT BE able to discuss regionalisation in an exhaustive way, but I would like to make a few points to highlight its extent and the variety of forms it has taken since the 19th century and, more recently, since the UN Charter provided for 'Regional Arrangements' (Ch VIII). While regional human rights instruments are limited to three conventions (the European and American Conventions on Human Rights of 1950 and 1969, respectively, and the African Charter on Human and Peoples' Rights of 1981) and a few declarations unencumbered by any monitoring or review mechanisms (such as the Cairo Declaration on Human Rights in Islam of 1990 and the Arab Charter on Human Rights of 1994), economic integration areas have multiplied over the last 15 years to such an extent that they cover much of the globe.[9] These regional economic areas tend to organise themselves empirically; that is, they have no great foundational agenda, but build themselves up around more concrete and limited purposes that occasionally evolve into a genuine agenda over time. To get from purpose to agenda, certain conditions for stabilisation must be met. After setting these out, I will provide an example of how a bipolar (economic and ethical) criminal justice area has gradually stabilised in Europe.

## From Purpose to Agenda

At the opposite end of the spectrum from a globalisation that would reduce the legal world to almost a single form designed to meet the

---

[9] See J Dutheil de la Rochère, 'Mondialisation et régionalisation' in E Loquin and C Kessedjian (eds), *La Mondialisation du droit* (Paris, Litec, 2000) pp 435–53; J Ténier, *Intégrations régionales et Mondialisation. Complémentarité ou contradiction* (Paris, La Documentation française, 2003); L Burgogue-Larson, 'Le fait regional dans la juridictionnalisation du droit international' in Société française du droit international, *La Juridictionnalisation du droit international* (Paris, Pedone, 2003).

requirements of global trade, regionalisation seems to stay closer to the ground and to its residents. Predetermined by the continents, regional organisations are further shaped by the courses of the great rivers (Rhine, Danube, Niger, Senegal, Mekong) or sea basins (Mediterranean, Caribbean, China, Black, Caspian, even the Arabo-Persian Gulf and the Pacific and Indian Oceans). They are also subject to the caprices of history, which alternates war with reconciliation, conquest with decolonisation. Even if the dreams of great visionaries such as Victor Hugo for the European Union and Simon Bolivar for the South American Community[10] are sometimes invoked as founding myths, they little resemble today's reality as it results from the accidents of geography and history.

As regionalisation is above all movement, typology cannot fully describe regional economic organisations, which coincide only very partially with the rare regional human rights organisations. I will therefore try to show how the founding states' strategies acquire their own dynamic and escape the states' control as institutions become autonomous and develop their own strategies.

### Founding States' Strategies

Unlike federations of states, regional areas are initially characterised by a purpose more limited than a true political agenda: though generally economic (free-trade area, customs area, common market or monetary union), organisational purposes are occasionally ethical (protecting human rights or human and peoples' rights) and sometimes include protecting security (fighting terrorism or transnational crime), health (market for medicines, AIDS prevention) or the environment (protecting biodiversity or combating climate change). These 'thematic partnerships'[11] tend to reflect the interdependence created by globalisation rather than the independence associated with states, and they are highly diverse, as the following examples show.

---

[10] R Bielsa, former Argentine Minister of Foreign Affairs alluded to the 'Bolivarian ideal' of the South American Community of nations (<www.liberacion.press.se/anteriores/anteriores2/041217/notas/turco.htm> accessed 2 November 2008), as did Allan Wagner Tizon, former Secretary General of the Andean Community (<www.comunidadandina.org/prensa/notas/np14-11-05.htm> accessed 2 November 2008).

[11] J Ténier, 'Universalisme et régionalisme: les chemins du partenariat,' *Questions internationales* no 11: *L'ONU à l'épreuve*, January 2005, 72 (discussing 'thematic partnerships').

In North America, NAFTA (Canada, Mexico and the United States) creates a free-trade area for goods and capital. However, the only policies common to the three partners arise from two complementary agreements regarding the environment and labour, but cover neither solidarity (no structural funds) nor immigration (no free circulation of persons, as in the European Union). To the south, however, several organisations have a more political agenda, such as the Andean Community (Bolivia, Colombia, Ecuador, Peru and Venezuela); Caricom, or the Common market of the Caribbean; and especially Mercosur, the common market of the south (Argentina, Brazil, Paraguay, Uruguay, and soon Venezuela, with Bolivia, Chile, Colombia, Ecuador, Peru having associate member status).

It took until 1998 to see Mercosur's social dimension, and 2002 for the loss of parity between the Argentine peso and the United States dollar to open the perspective of coordinated macroeconomic policies. The association of the Andean Community countries with Mercosur in December 2004 may lead, beyond a customs union, to a more social-policy oriented form of integration, potentially reinforced by the presence of states parties to the American Convention on Human Rights (ACHR). In this sense, the South American Community of nations, symbolically launched in December 2004 in the ancient Inca capital of Cuzco, Peru, may bring South American states together in the same way the European Union has in Europe— unless the competing project of a Free Trade Area of the Americas (FTAA-ALCA), supported by the United States, succeeds in imposing the free-trade model underlying NAFTA throughout the Americas.

As for the African continent, colonisation left it extremely fragmented. Unity was thus the goal of the Organization of African Unity, as its name suggests, and the adoption of the African Charter reinforced. But this Organization was never much more than a diplomatic arena, so it was replaced in 2001 by the African Union, the goal of which is to create a unified African economic community by 2025.[12] The proposed six-stage process is slow, due to the existence of numerous institutions: two organisations in the west, one in the centre, one in the south, one for eastern and southern Africa, and another to the north for the Maghreb region, plus

---

[12] See AO Konaré, 'L'Afrique est de retour!' in M Aubry (ed), *Agir pour le Sud maintenant* (Paris, Editions de l'Aube, 2005) pp 22–35 (discussing the projects of the Chairperson of the African Union).

OHADA, comprising 16 French-speaking black African states. But the African project remains modestly focused on free trade and legal security for investments, because solidarity projects are hampered by both a lack of resources (in west and central Africa) and extreme dissymmetry (in 2000, seven states had fewer than 1 million inhabitants while 36 had up to 10 million).

These problems also exist in Asia, namely with regard to the South Asian Association for Regional Cooperation (SAARC), which also evidences the dissymmetry characterising the Indian subcontinent. The SAARC nonetheless strives to achieve goals of both trade and solidarity through fighting poverty and promoting health and education (the decade 2001–2010 is to be devoted to the rights of the child).

Similarly, the Association of Southeast Asian Nations (ASEAN) groups together countries as economically, politically and demographically different as Cambodia, Indonesia, Laos, Singapore, Thailand, and Vietnam. In its report *Vision 2020*, the ASEAN mentions strengthening economic integration, but also indicates its interest in fighting transnational criminality by creating a centre in the Philippines, and announces the goal of reducing poverty and disparities.[13] But it has a tough competitor in the Asia-Pacific Economic Cooperation forum (APEC), a veritable juggernaut initiated by Australia and the United States that includes 21 countries, including Canada, China, Japan and Russia, and whose sole objective is to liberalise trade and investment.

As for organisations in Central Asia, Asia Minor or Eurasia, such as the Economic Cooperation Organization (ECO) established by Iran, Pakistan and Turkey, the Organization of Black Sea Economic Cooperation (BSEC) initiated by Turkey, the Shanghai Cooperation Organization (SCO) linking China, Russia and several Central Asian republics, and co-operation between Gulf states, they tend to focus on security as much as integration. And last but not least, the Organization of the Petroleum Exporting Countries (OPEC), which, without reference to geographical criteria, aims primarily to harmonise oil policies, while the League of Arab States (constituted by reference to the Arab nation) and the faith-based Organization of the Islamic Conference initially fostered co-operation and adopted the human rights texts mentioned above, but

---

[13] See S Boisseau du Rocher, 'L'ASEAN entre crise de la souveraineté nationale et crise de la mondialisation' in *Souveraineté et Mondialisation*, Francophone seminar on Southeast Asia, Singapore, 2001, pp 59 *ff*.

on Iran's initiative proposed creating a common Islamic market in 1997.[14]

There is such variety that it is difficult to foresee whether some of these regional organisations will succeed in adopting an agenda of genuine integration, including interstate solidarity and thus, in the long term, common fiscal policy and citizenship, or if they will be paralysed by competition from powerful models of free trade. Such variety and instability confirm the impossibility of a true typology, especially since, as institutional structures are established, they develop their own dynamic and their 'autonomisation' sometimes transforms the purpose into an agenda.

## Autonomisation of Regional Institutions

Regionalisation begins with meetings among executive representatives, and the first institutions they establish constitute a sort of diplomatic forum. But once the legal personality of regional institutions is recognised and permanent judicial or quasi-judicial bodies having the power to order sanctions begin to appear, a dynamic is created that can lead to granting legislative power and even creating a regional parliament to provide a public sphere for debate and deliberation.

The major innovation, indeed almost a revolution, in the area of human rights was the creation of tribunals to which individuals could petition for redress. There is an undeniable circumscription, if not abandon, of national sovereignty[15] when states can be sanctioned by a regional human rights court. But only a few states have had the experience, as only the European and Inter-American Courts of Human Rights (ECtHR and IACHR) have proved themselves. Since the African Court of human and peoples' rights has only just been created, it is too early to evaluate its impact on application of the African Charter, especially since establishing this court's independence will require the judges to abandon their reserve with regard to the political powers and break through their 'political wall of silence'.[16]

---

[14] See E Beigzadeh and A Nadjafi, 'Les problèmes de régionalisation à géographie variable (le cas de l'Iran),' (2001) *Archives de politique criminelle* 141.

[15] See generally M Delmas-Marty (ed), *Raisonner la raison d'État. Vers une Europe des droits de l'homme* (Paris, PUF, 1989).

[16] JF Flauss, 'Propos conclusifs' in JF Flauss and E Lambert-Abdelgawad (eds), *L'Application nationale de la Charte africaine des droits de l'homme et des peuples* (Brussels, Bruylant, 2004).

In fact, it took years for the ECtHR and the IACHR to affirm their independence. Even sociologists, typically complacent with regard to human rights, which they describe as a showcase for so-called civilised nations, were surprised at the ECtHR's assertiveness. As if caught in their own trap, member states are now sanctioned by a 'civilising body'[17] they created but did not truly believe in and were not wary of. The IACHR has also surpassed state expectations, such as when it held self-granted amnesty laws to be contrary to the American Convention, namely the victims' rights to an effective remedy and due process, and its decision influenced proceedings in domestic courts (the *Pinochet* case in Chile and the reopening of trials in Argentina).[18] The non-ratification of the Convention by Canada and the United States stands, however, as an obstacle to the goal of pan-American harmonisation.

As for organisations promoting economic integration, even though judicialisation is less revolutionary, it is slow and its impact ambiguous. Though the same clause appears in the free trade area of the Americas draft, NAFTA is as yet the only organisation to grant companies the right to sue states with respect to investments,[19] a right that may endanger state social or environmental policies. In other areas, a special arbitration group may be set up to resolve disputes, but in the event of an unfavourable decision, the United States, scorning 'the trade rules established under NAFTA',[20] generally prefers to return to bilateral negotiations. Mercosur, however, provides evidence of a judicialisation that favours supranational interests that become 'communitised' over private interests. While the original treaty established only an *ad hoc* arbitration tribunal, in

[17] M Rask Madsen, 'Make Law not War' (2004) *Actes de la recherché en sciences sociales* 151–52.

[18] See H Ruiz Fabri, G Della Morte, E Lambert-Abdelgawad and K Martin-Chenut (eds), *La Clémence saisie par le droit. Amnistie, grace et prescription en droit international et comparé* (Paris, Société de Législation Comparée, 2007), especially the reports of G Della Morte on amnesty in international law and E Lambert-Abdelgawad and K Martin-Chenut on prescription in international law.

[19] See V Loungnarath, 'Les articulations juridique de l'Accord de libre-échange nord-américain' in MF Labouz (ed), *Intégrations et Identités nord-américaines vues de Montréal* (Brussels, Bruylant, 2001) pp 311 *ff*; Ténier, 'Universalisme et régionalisme' above n 3. See also M Delmas-Marty, *Les Forces imaginantes du droit (1): Le Relatif et l'Universel* (Paris, Seuil, 2004) pp 201–02 (discussing global investment law).

[20] G Gagné, 'L'ALENA et le différend canado-américain sur le bois d'oeuvre: le règne de la loi du plus fort' in *Intégrations et Identités nord-américaines vues de Montréal*, above n 11, p 340. See also K Milanova, 'Systèmes d'information sur les traits d'intégration économique: l'exemple de l'ALENA' (doctoral dissertation, University of Montpellier, 1999).

2003 the member states established a permanent tribunal in Asunción, Paraguay, which held its first session in September 2004. Such judicialisation is the logical extension of the punitive administrative sanctions ordered by supranational institutions acting somewhat similarly to European institutions and has been accompanied by the strengthening of civil and criminal co-operation through various instruments of legal harmonisation: action plans (1999 plan in the areas of drug trafficking, organised crime and crimes against the environment, 2001 plan against international trade-related offences); conventions (2000 convention on money laundering); and even unified codes (draft customs code initiated by the 1994 Ouro Preto Protocol).[21]

Judicialisation is also sometimes accompanied by the creation of regional legislative institutions. In Africa, for example, a parliament was established for the East African community and another was provided for in the OHADA treaty,[22] while in Latin America, a joint parliamentary commission composed of legislators from four states parties presented a proposal for a Mercosur parliament to the heads of the founding states in July 2004 (the Parliament was inaugurated on 7 May 2007).

While such judicial independence and institutional autonomy is necessary for stabilisation, there are other conditions that must be met before regional organisations may be deemed pluralist, that is, to have succeeded in neutralising power struggles.

## Stabilisation Conditions

This quick trip around the world reveals the ambivalence of regional integration, which constitutes both the 'instrument of liberalism by the deconstruction of national regulation and the means of its organization at a higher level, provided there exists a minimum of political will'.[23] Deconstruction and reconstruction are the necessarily unstable results of power struggles that persist despite the existence of cohesion factors. This is why true stabilisation requires political will, which, more than geography, creates the points of convergence essential to stabilisation.

---

[21] See A Alvarez, *Justicia penal y espacio regional en tiempos de reformas e internacionalización* (Buenos Aires, Ad Hoc, 2004).

[22] See P Fouchard (ed), *L'OHADA et les Perspectives de l'arbitrage en Afrique* (Brussels, Bruylant, 2000).

[23] Ténier, 'Universalisme et régionalisme', above n 3, p 221.

*Power Struggles and Cohesion Factors*

Power struggles and cohesion factors are not necessarily antagonistic: the existence of a common, external enemy has always been a powerful cohesion factor, as the examples of the former American and African colonies illustrate. But for cohesion factors to produce stability, power struggles within each region much be neutralised.

In Europe, for example, the principle of equality among member states has been preserved despite numerous disparities because after centuries of war, none of the 'major' powers imposed its hegemony on others. The temptation may exist, but attempting it seems out of the question, as the more powerful countries neutralise each other and European construction acts as a restraint. In fact, the entire European project is founded explicitly on the desire to 'transcend . . . former divisions', 'forge a common destiny' (Preamble, Constitutional Treaty), 'deepen solidarity' and 'create an ever closer union among the peoples of Europe' (Preamble, Lisbon Treaty). The constitutional crisis of 2005 did not seem directed towards this desire, but at the speed with which it is being realised and the rhythm of EU enlargement (see below, 'Speeds of Transformation').

Transcendence is even more difficult when geographical and/or demographical inequalities benefit a single country, such as Brazil in Latin America, India in South Asia, China in the Far East and Russia in Eurasia, or in the face of economic disparities (South Africa and Nigeria in Africa, Japan in Asia), and *a fortiori* when the disparities are both economic and military (United States). Internal imbalances can only be overcome if there are sufficient cohesion factors.

To be sure, cohesion results primarily from the cultural, linguistic and sometimes religious make-up of each region, but it is not stuck in history. Moreover, the process of stabilisation also results from more voluntarist political projects that express, to cite the Constitutional Treaty once more, the desire to 'forge a common destiny'. The factors of cohesion necessary to realising such projects therefore vary depending on whether internal or external cohesion is concerned. Externally, legal personality enables a regional organisation to negotiate with global organisations, such as the WTO, and have an impact on decisions. It also facilitates horizontal, interregional relations (Mercosur/CAN, EU/Mercosur, or EU/Maghreb) and makes coordination between a regional organisation and a country possible (ASEAN/China, or OHADA/France). Internally, solidarity and citizenship enable economic and political integration. Legal integration, however, is more complex, because to foster free trade and the circulation of goods and people, it may deconstruct a national system built on ethical values. It is therefore important that not only intersections, but more voluntarily taken 'itineraries to convergence' exist between ensembles.

### Intersections and Itineraries to Convergence

Intersections abound in regional organisations. For example, Mexico is a member of NAFTA (North American continent), a candidate for the future South American Community of Nations, and a state party to the American Convention on Human Rights, as are other Latin American states but not Canada and the United States. On the European continent, Turkey, which sits at the intersection of Europe and Asia, provides a particularly important example. As I mentioned above, Turkey initiated the Organization of Black Sea Economic Cooperation, which the Yalta Charter of 1998 transformed into a genuine organisation for integration, namely in the area of criminal law (struggle against organised crime, trafficking of drugs, arms and radioactive materials, terrorism and illegal immigration). It is also a member of the ECO, headquartered in Teheran, and the Council of Europe (it not only ratified the ECHR, but also granted individuals the right to petition the ECtHR directly). Turkey is also a candidate for membership of the European Union, with which it formed a customs union in 1996. The scope of the debate sparked by Turkey's candidacy and the importance placed by some on historical and geographical factors indicate not only the political difficulty in imagining the future without limiting it to its past, but also the legal difficulty in solving problems of multiple loyalties.

As each organisation adopts its own legal norms, and sometimes its own courts, conflicts are apt to multiply. Political will is needed to look beyond geographical or historical facts and draw up 'itineraries to convergence', an expression Jacques Ténier used to describe projects aimed at gradually converging economies (for example, the convergence programme for Europe established by the Maastricht Treaty and the African Economic Community project, which provides for progressing from sub-regional fragmentation to continental regionalisation in six steps). Ténier sees such itineraries as allowing for better articulation between the regional and global levels: 'The "region" can gain an autonomy that the International Monetary Fund denies to states under structural adjustment programmes.'[24]

[24] *Ibid.*, p 214.

Conversely, regions can relay global commitments, as in the case of the European Commission's ratification of the Kyoto Protocol on climate change, or the studies realised within the Arab Maghreb Union in the context of the United Nations Convention to Combat Desertification.

But to resolve the conflicts resulting from the simultaneous application of different normative ensembles, convergence must also be understood in a legal sense. Tensions develop as integration progresses around the two poles of economic and, by reference to human rights, ethical integration. In Europe, the partial geographical overlap between the Council of Europe (CoE) and the European Union (all EU member states have ratified the ECHR and are thus member states of the CoE) make these tensions more visible, especially in criminal matters; but through the cross-references between the two European courts discussed above, it also facilitates making economic integration compatible with protecting human rights.

In other regions, however, the lack of geographical overlap creates problems that cannot be solved legally and lead to power struggles when states' commitments to different international organisations conflict. For example, at a 2004 conference on integration with respect to criminal matters in Latin America, I naïvely suggested that Mexico could refuse to comply with clauses in bilateral criminal cooperation treaties with the United States that violate the American Convention on Human Rights. I can still hear the bitter laughter my suggestion aroused—and better understand the importance of Mexico's candidacy to join other parties to the ACHR in the future South American Community of Nations.

Whether resolving tensions or filling gaps between the areas covered by regional human rights instruments and economic integration organisations, itineraries of convergence will not take on their full meaning as 'political' choices, that is, choices of values, until they succeed in laying the groundwork for making various instruments that internationalise law compatible with each other and synchronising them. I would like to leave the topic of synchronisation until later, though, and use the European construction of a criminal justice area between the two poles of economic integration and human rights (including its failures, weaknesses and delays) as an example of how economic integration and human rights can be made compatible.

# Building a Bipolar European Criminal Justice Area

European construction relating to criminal justice is not yet complete, and though the singular—'a' European criminal justice area—is used, it does not mean that national penal systems will disappear. They will be inserted into an area described since the Tampere Summit of 1999 in the glowing terms of an 'area of freedom, security and justice' (Lisbon Treaty, Article 3(2) TEU and 67 TFEU).

In reality, such a pleasing harmony has yet to be found in the criminal field, where progress is slower and less direct than reading the Treaty leads one to believe, as there are currently tensions between the two main European organisations.

## Tensions between the Europe of Human Rights and the Europe of Security

Far from having died down, the quarrels between that old couple security and liberty seem to have flared up again, not only as a consequence of the 11 September attacks in the United States, but due to the dichotomy between the two normative areas overseen by the courts in Strasbourg and Luxembourg.

Europe is one of the rare regions to have simultaneously moved towards economic integration, beginning with the European Union's three founding treaties (ECSC, EEC and Euratom, 1950–1957), and ethical integration (CoE and ECHR, 1950). Integration with respect to criminal justice was not an explicit objective of either system in the beginning, but the issue occasionally arose in the case law of one court or the other. Construction of a kind of European criminal law thus began in each system.

Fifteen years ago, it seemed that the European Convention on Human Rights was the driving force behind the harmonisation of criminal law. To be sure, the Convention has only indirect influence and contains only a few references to criminal law (death penalty and legitimate defence in Article 2 and Protocol 6; criminal procedure in Articles 5 and 6; non-retroactivity of criminal statutes in Article 7; and the rule of *ne bis in idem* in Protocol 4). Its structural constraints are sufficient, however, to require member states to harmonise their criminal justice policies,[25] and at times even unify them (abrogation of the death penalty, for example).

---

[25] See Delmas-Marty (ed), *Raisonner la raison d'État*, above n 7; M Delmas-Marty, *Les Grands systèmes de politique criminelle* (Paris PUF, 1992), pp 357 *ff* and 373 *ff*.

At the same time, the influence of the European Community, then the European Union, began to be felt. Even though neither the Rome Treaty (1957) nor the Maastricht Treaty (1992) grants criminal law powers to Community authorities, the implications of Community law for criminal justice policy have become more and more clear as domestic criminal statutes were held to be incompatible with European treaties because they acted as a restriction on intra-community trade. And because European Community law is directly applicable in domestic courts, various areas of business and white collar criminal law (refusal to sell, illicit pricing practices, door-to-door sales, prohibited forms of advertising, tax and customs law, etc) were decriminalised through the courts, without legislative intervention. Criminalising activity that threatens Community interests (such as fraud with respect to a product's origin or quality), however, requires legislative action at the national level.

The situation completely changed with the 1997 Amsterdam Treaty's 'common actions', and even more so with the 2000 Nice Treaty's 'framework decisions', which can lead to overcriminalisation because national legislatures must transpose them into domestic law without ratifying them as they would a treaty. Indeed, as regards the struggle against terrorism, the sexual exploitation of children and paedophilia, organised crime and the European Arrest Warrant, to name only a few of the examples I have discussed elsewhere,[26] the fear has developed that Europe 'over ideologises security'.[27] And the European Court of Justice crossed a new threshold in 2005 when it held that although, '[a]s a general rule, neither criminal law nor the rules of criminal procedure fall within the Community's competence', this 'finding does not prevent the Community legislature, when the application of effective, proportionate and dissuasive criminal penalties by the competent national authorities is an essential measure for combating serious environmental offences, from taking measures which relate to the criminal law of the Member States which it considers necessary in order to

---

[26] See Delmas-Marty, *Le Relatif et l'Universel*, above n 11, pp 281–307. See also S Manacorda, 'Droit de la Communauté et de l'Union européenne' (2004) *Revue de science criminelle* 969 (discussing the proposals for framework decisions on confiscation, a European Evidence Warrant, and the struggle against drug trafficking).

[27] W Capeller, 'Criminalité du risqué et harmonisation pénale' in M Delmas-Marty, G Giudicelli-Delage and E Lambert-Abdelgawad (eds), *L'Harmonisation des sanctions pénales* (Paris, Société de Législation Comparée, 2003), p 492. See also the debates among Italian scholars regarding European criminal law: A Bernardi, 'L'Européanisation de la science pénale' (2004) *Archives de politique criminelle* 5.

ensure that the rules which it lays down on environmental protection are fully effective.'[28] In other words, in areas such as environmental law that are already 'communitised', the Community can insert criminal penalties into the member states' laws via directives.

The fear of 'overcriminalisation' is further heightened by the increase in European police powers: the Schengen acquis instituted transnational police co-operation, which is reinforced by the 'Schengen information system' (which may be replaced by a European police record) and was further enhanced by the creation of Europol in 1995[29]; the 1999 OLAF regulation created the European Anti-Fraud Office and financial police; and military forces fulfil police functions during civil and military peacekeeping missions.[30]

On the judicial side, however, the fragile apparatus of Eurojust links member state judges having very diverse statuses and powers. Overlaying the pre-existing European Judicial Network, Eurojust facilitates interstate judicial co-operation but does not truly coordinate criminal investigations.[31] And despite the misleading symmetry of their names—Europol/Eurojust—and the national traditions pleading for judicial oversight of police forces, it has not been possible, either in practice or even in theory, to obtain approval for Eurojust to monitor Europol activities, nor for a European prosecutor to supervise OLAF (though this was suggested in the 1997 *Corpus juris* discussed above). As president of the OLAF supervisory committee I raised the issue of police supervision several times with Commissioner Vittorino, who was in charge of Justice and Home Affairs. As aware as our committee was of the issue's importance, he could not overcome member state resistance or the inertia of existing institutions, which naturally did not want to give up their independence. In providing for the creation of a European prosecutor, the Lisbon Treaty could have resolved the issue of monitoring OLAF's investigations, but it seems to limit the prosecutor's jurisdiction—unless the member states decide otherwise—to the PIF

---

[28] Case C-176/03, *Commission v Council of the European Union* (ECJ, 13 September 2005), paras 47–48.

[29] See C Chevallier-Govers, 'De la cooperation à l'intégration policière dans l'Union européenne' (doctoral dissertation, University of Paris II, 1998); 'De la nécessité de créer une police européenne intégrée' (1999) *Revue de science criminelle* 77.

[30] See generally the symposium 'Polices d'Europe, politique étrangère et sécurité commune' (2004) *Revue de science criminelle* 549–631.

[31] See A Weyenbergh, 'L'Humanisation des procedures pénales au sein de l'Union européenne' (2004) *Archives de politique criminelle* 61.

Convention (Lisbon Treaty, Article 86(4) TFEU). Europol's activities are therefore subject to political monitoring only, namely by the European Parliament and, perhaps, national parliaments (Article 88(2) TFEU). These unresolved tensions foster state resistance, which manifested with respect to the European Arrest Warrant. Though all the member states eventually transposed the framework decision (Italy and Germany held out for quite some time), national judges did not hesitate to put the text's escape clauses to good use. In France, for example, the *Cour de cassation* upheld the refusal to execute a warrant issued by a Spanish judge in a case related to Basque terrorism because some of the acts were committed in France.[32] In a more radical move, the German Constitutional Tribunal first suspended application of the law transposing the framework decision while it checked its constitutionality, then declared the law of transposition unconstitutional because it had a disproportionate impact on the right of German citizens not to be extradited and violated the principle of the right to an effective remedy.[33] Eventually, execution of a European Arrest Warrant may end up before the ECtHR.[34]

Itineraries of convergence must therefore be found to transform duality (having one system for economic integration and another devoted to human rights) into bipolarity, which provides structure.

### Itineraries of Convergence Leading towards a Bipolar Criminal Justice Area

A bipolar criminal justice area is one that has not eliminated all tensions between security and respect for human rights, as some are no doubt necessary, but which uses bipolarity to establish an itinerary of convergence and to create a balance between the two poles.

In Europe, the first itineraries have no name. Long and winding, they seek convergence one step at a time: either through national constitutional courts,[35] as the above-mentioned example of the German

---

[32] See Cour de cassation, Criminal chamber, 8 July 2004, reprinted in (2004) *Juris-Classeur Périodique* 395.

[33] See 2 BvR 2236/04, 18 July 2005 (citing Arts 16(2) and 19(4) of the German fundamental law). See also Manacorda, 'Droit de la Communauté et de l'Union européenne', above n 8.

[34] See G Cohen-Jonathan, 'L'adhésion de l'UE à la CESDH' in G Cohen-Jonathan, *Quelle justice pour l'Europe?* (Brussels, Bruylant, 2004) at 68 (discussing petitions to the ECtHR challenging 'common positions on terrorism').

[35] See F Garron, 'L'Interprétation des normes supralégislatives en matière pénale' (2004) *Revue de science criminelle* 793.

tribunal illustrates, or through the European Court of Human Rights. The first route leads only very indirectly to European integration, as the effect of convergence is limited to the country in question. The second is similarly circuitous, as the European Community is not a party to the ECHR and therefore cannot be brought before the ECtHR. Plaintiffs must instead proceed against either a state that granted exequatur to an ECJ decision[36] or transposed a European norm into its domestic law,[37] or all EU member states at once.[38]

Censure has been rare until now due to the caution of the two courts and their avoidance strategies,[39] but conflicts have increased as repressive Community law has developed through framework decisions and conflicts would undoubtedly have increased had the Constitutional Treaty been ratified, due to its provisions for harmonising criminal law. To avoid such a result, the Commission exchanged its all-repressive policy for a 'shield', namely through a framework decision on procedural rights in criminal trials.[40]

The Constitutional Treaty would have opened up more direct routes: Article I-9, for example, provides for recognising the rights, freedoms and principles set out in the Charter of Fundamental Rights constituting Part II of the Treaty, and for the Union's becoming a party to the European Convention on Human Rights.[41] The latter provision would have shortened the current itinerary by providing a direct route to a remedy from the Strasbourg Court in the event Community law was contrary to the ECHR, and could also have contributed to transforming duality into bipolarity. But the Charter's entry into force would establish the shortest route, as it

---

[36] See *Melchers et Co v Germany*, Commission decision of inadmissibility (1990) DR no 64, p 146.

[37] See *Cantoni v France* (1996) 1996-V; *Bosphorus Hava v Ireland* (2005) 2005-VI.

[38] See *Senator Lines v the fifteen member states of the EU*, reprinted in (2000) *Revue universelle des droits de l'homme* 119 (based on the European Court of First Instance's judgment of sanctions); G Cohen-Jonathan, 'L'adhésion de l'Union européenne à la CESDH,' above n 26 at 68 (discussing cancellation of the sanctions); and the ECtHR's decision of inadmissibility reprinted in (2004) *Revue universelle des droits de l'homme* 109.

[39] See inter alia A Bernardi, 'Entre le pyramide et le réseau: les effets de l'européanisation sur le système pénal' (2004) 52 *Revue interdisciplinaire d'études juridiques* 1.

[40] See A Weyembergh, 'L'Harmonisation des procedures pénales au sein de l'Union européenne' above n 23 at 45; S Manacorda, 'Droit de la Communauté et de l'Union européennes' (2004) *Revue de science criminelle* 976.

[41] See G Cohen-Jonathan 'L'adhésion de l'Union européenne à la CESDH,' above n 26.

would allow for a sort of constitutional check of European law: any European provision, particularly criminal provisions, could be checked against the Charter. Had this been possible with respect to the framework decision on terrorism, the vague definitions of certain infractions could have been challenged by reference to the principle of legality and made more precise.

Though the Lisbon Treaty does not incorporate the Charter, it grants the Charter the 'same legal value as the treaties' (Article 6(1) TEU) and maintains the Constitutional Treaty's provision for EU ratification of the ECHR (Article 6(2) TEU). While the Lisbon Treaty's ratification is still uncertain, the European example is nonetheless useful for showing that regionalisation is, in and of itself, neither good nor bad; everything depends on how the regional area is structured. Duality at least allows for gradual balancing if it is transformed into bipolarity. The same can be seen in other regions having a similar structure that have begun to promote criminal law integration (South American and, in the long term, Africa).

Such a balance seems difficult to achieve at the global level, however, as the forms of internationalisation are still too diverse. Though the establishment of the international criminal tribunals gives the impression that integration seems further advanced in the area of criminal law, the lack of a world court of human rights may considerably slow the stabilisation of global organisation.

# 5

# Global Organisation

THE GLOBAL ORDER as we know it was set out in the San Francisco Charter establishing the United Nations in June 1945 and the Universal Declaration of Human Rights, adopted in Paris in 1948. Designed according to principles the drafters thought clear (peace through collective security, human rights that are universal because indivisible) and an architecture they thought simple (General Assembly, Security Council, Economic and Social Council, Trusteeship Council, Secretariat and International Court of Justice),[1] the United Nations has been enriched by the adoption of legal instruments in areas as diverse as human rights, trade, health and the environment. But it has also been upset by the great political upheavals of the latter half of the 20th century, namely decolonisation, the Cold War, the fall of the Soviet empire, globalisation and global terrorism.

The Cold War ideological split among UN member states (which increased from 50 to 191) was transferred to the Universal Declaration's principle of indivisibility of human rights, producing two separate covenants in 1966. Then globalisation splintered internationalisation factors[2] such that the globalisation of law, which

---

[1] See namely JP Cot, A Pellet and M Forteau, *La Charte des Nations unies. Commentaire article par article* (Paris, Economica, 3rd edn 2005); P Moreau-Desfarges, 'L'ONU a soixante ans' in T de Montbrial and P Moreau-Desfarges (eds), *Ramsès 2006* (Paris, Dunod, 2006) pp 31–46; *Questions internationales* no 11 (January 2005): *L'ONU à l'épreuve.*

[2] See generally M Delmas-Marty, *Vers un droit commun de l'humanité* (Paris, Textuel, 1996, 2nd edn 2005); *Trois Défis pour un droit mondial* (Paris, Seuil, 1998 (English version: Naomi Norberg (trans), *Global Law: A Triple Challenge*, Ardsley, NY, Transnational Publishers, 2003); 'La mondialisation du droit: chances et risques' (1999) *Dalloz* 43; AJ Arnaud, *Entre modernité et mondialisation. Leçons d'histoire de la philosophie du droit et de l'Etat* (Paris, LGDJ, 1994, 2nd edn 2004); B Auby, *La Globalisation, le Droit et l'Etat* (Paris, Montchrestien, 2003); MM Salah, *Les Contradictions du droit mondialisé* (Paris, PUF, 2002); E Loquin and C Kessedjian (eds), *La Mondialisation du droit* (Paris, Litec, 2000); CA Morand (ed), *Le Droit saisi par la mondialisation* (Brussels, Bruylant, 2001).

brings domestic legal orders together around human rights and tries to 'civilise' globalisation, conflicts with the law of globalisation, which produces specific, market-related rules and symbolises the return to a natural state.[3] Suddenly it is clear that national sovereignty is threatened more by globalisation than by universalism.

This observation holds true beyond the economic sphere: global terrorism (the 11 September attacks) and the counterattack in the form of a 'war on terror', in both a figurative and a literal sense, have contributed to dissolving the borders between crime and war, internal and external, unilateral and multilateral. The London attacks of 7 July 2005 further highlighted the specificity of global terrorism, which tends to reduce the entire globe to a single area and therefore does not allow for labelling the enemy as either external (as in a foreign war) or internal (as in a civil war). This poses the formidable problem of the enemy who is everywhere. But this is, in fact, a problem of globalisation in general, which encourages thinking of the world as a single area with no exterior.

For example, the 2005 World Summit final document[4] places terrorism and international crime in Chapter III on peace and collective security. Crime, risk, and economic, financial and information flows all create interdependency and lead to the adoption of intergovernmental agreements that tend to weaken nation-state autonomy and foster a model that is more authoritarian than democratic. As Jürgen Habermas has pointed out, an 'internal global policy'[5] is urgently needed, but has not yet been invented.

The term 'globalisation' refers not only to a pre-existing global law, the components of which can be described, but also to a movement that might lead just as easily to an alienating uniformity as to *mondialité*, an 'inextricability from the world' that the poet Édouard Glissant distinguishes from globalisation: 'this unprecedented adventure that we are allowed to live in a world that, for the first time and so concretely, immediately, strikingly, is being conceived all at once as multiple, one and inextricable.'[6] The adventure is indeed unprecedented, including in the legal field, where the law is sometimes organised in a plural, but rarely pluralist, fashion.

---

[3] See J Chevallier, 'Mondialisation du droit ou droit de la mondialisation' in Morand, *Le Droit saisi par la mondialisation*, above n 2, pp 36 *ff*; F Ost, 'Mondialisation, globalisation, universalisation, s'arracher encore et toujours à l'état de nature' in *ibid.*, pp 5 *ff*.

[4] A/Res/60/1, 15 September 2005.

[5] J Habermas, *Une époque de transitions. Écrits politiques 1998–2003* (Paris, Fayard, 2005), pp 124, 163.

[6] E Glissant, *La Cohée du Lamentin* (Paris, Gallimard, 2005), p 15.

It seems that, conversely to the movement of regional organisation described in the preceding chapter, the global organisation imagined in the after-war period has been divided into disparate legal purposes that become globalised according to national or transnational strategies at the whim of states and transnational corporations. The global criminal law area currently forming where universalism and globalisation meet could offer a means to bring them together, but the criminal law example is also a counter-example: it reveals the legal risks and political limits of globalisation when pluralism is not guaranteed. To reset the agenda, the conditions for pluralist stabilisation must be determined.

## From a Global Agenda to Globalised Purposes

The highly diverse events that have left their mark on the last few decades have the following point in common: they foster both fragmentation, which disperses global legal instruments among disparate purposes, and privatisation, which blurs the common agenda for the benefit of private interests.

### Fragmentation

As I have explained in depth elsewhere,[7] fragmentation affects both universal concepts (human rights, humanity as perceived through crimes against humanity and the common heritage of humanity, or the market) and responses to globalisation (law applicable to globalised crime, the flow of intangibles, or global risks). I will therefore limit my discussion here to a few examples of the dispersion of purposes that make for twists and turns between different levels of organisation.

Human rights are emblematic of legal universalism and illustrate both the positive and negative aspects of fragmentation. As envisioned by the drafters of the Universal Declaration, their vertical division into national, regional and global areas should have facilitated pluralist and evolutionary integration.[8] But the non-ratification of regional instruments by certain states (Canada and the United States), the sluggishness of the process (Africa), the persistent lack

---

[7] See generally M Delmas-Marty, *Les Forces imaginantes du droit (I): Le Relatif et l'Universel* (Paris, Seuil, 2004).

[8] See RJ Vincent, *Human Rights and International Relations* (Cambridge, CUP, 1986); J Morsink, *The Universal Declaration of Human Rights. Origins, Drafting and Intent* (Philadelphia, University of Pennsylvania Press, 1999), p 20.

of judicial review (Islamic Declaration and Arab Charter) and, finally and even more radically, the lack of a regional human rights instrument in entire areas of the world (Asia, Middle East, Asia-Pacific), have considerably weakened the original organisation. And the separation of civil and political rights from economic, social and cultural rights effected by the two UN covenants of 1966 has partially paralysed it: by allowing selective ratification of the covenants (the United States has ratified one covenant and China the other), separation destroyed the principle of indivisibility, whereas human rights cannot be recognised as universal (or universalisable) until all parties have accepted that all fundamental rights are equally important. The entire system is therefore threatened: without the Universal Declaration as its guide, the global legal space is open to generalised fragmentation.

In other words, law will be globalised around purposes the most powerful entities—states but also economic actors—will be pleased to identify and legally further. This is how trade law and the WTO's dispute resolution body were so quickly judicialised, while competition is ordered through the more and more extensive extraterritorial application of the law of the United States or the European Union, rather than through the adoption of a *lex economa* applicable to all parties.[9]

Of course, fragmentation does not mean legal rapprochement around each purpose cannot have positive effects. For example, the globalisation of trade, primed by the GATT accords but truly launched with the creation of the WTO in 1994,[10] no doubt contributed to laying the foundations for the rule of law in China[11] and fostered the adoption of common positions in the European Community, which negotiates directly with the WTO in the place of the member states.

In practice, however, the degree of organisation and the capacity for integration of each fragment depend on the legal means states are willing to create and the areas in which they are willing to share sovereignty. Their coolness to sharing sovereignty with respect to global risks (ecological, biotechnological, sanitary or social) explains the

---

[9] See Delmas-Marty, *Le Relatif et l'Universel,* above n 7, pp 106 *ff.*

[10] See H Ruiz Fabri, 'La contribution de l'OMC à la gestion d'un espace public mondial' in E Loquin and C Kessedjian (eds), *La Mondialisation du droit* (Paris, Litec, 2000), pp 347 *ff.*

[11] See L Choukroune, 'L'accession de la République populaire de Chine à l'OMC, instrument de la construction d'un Etat de droit par l'internationalisation' (doctoral dissertation, University of Paris I, 15 December 2004).

fragility of legal areas that are, nonetheless, global: environmental law has no global organisation[12] and health and labour law, governed by the WTO and the ILO respectively, lack supranational judicial review. Combined with the isolation of each sector, this fragility creates a dissymmetry that benefits the better organised area of trade law and may lead to either instituting a *de facto* hierarchy in its favour or leaving contradictions unanswered.

As the Kyoto and WTO mechanisms illustrate (see above, 'Processes of Interaction'), horizontal fragmentation is a source of contradictions, the primary one being the United States' refusal to join the Kyoto Protocol while it is heavily involved in the WTO. But the principle of differentiation between states, which is essential to taking national diversity into account, has created an internal distortion and raised the broader issue of 'the compatibility of the mercantile approach to the atmosphere with the legal regime of the climate . . . a concept of common interest'.[13]

The issue can be transposed to other areas, such as medical research, namely with respect to vaccines and medicines: a globalisation that imposes western standards (International Organization for Standardization (ISO) norms) in the name of a universalism that refuses to take national specificities into account has perverse effects.[14] As for the draft Declaration on Universal Norms on Bioethics adopted in 2005 by UNESCO's International Bioethics Committee, it at least sets out the principles of solidarity and responsibility with respect to the biosphere (Articles 13 and 17) and the sharing of 'benefits resulting from any scientific research and its applications' (Article 15), and mentions the role of transnational practices (Article 21). But it explains neither how to reconcile the universalism of the rights enunciated therein with the principles of cultural diversity and pluralism (Article 12),[15] nor how to coordinate

---

[12] See P Jacquet, J Pisani-Ferry and L Tubiana (eds), *Gouvernance mondiale* (Paris, La Documentation française, 2002), pp 95 *ff* (proposing to add 'the international archipelago's missing islands' by creating a global environmental organisation).

[13] L Boisson de Chazournes, 'Le droit international au chevet de la lutte contre le réchauffement planétaire: éléments d'un régime' in *L'Evolution du droit international. Mélanges Hubert Thierry* (Paris, Pedone, 1998), p 54.

[14] See 'La mondialisation des normes et standards, conséquences pour les soins aux malades' in JP Alix, L Degos and D Jolly (eds), *Normalisation, Mondialisation, Harmonisation. Trois objectifs en contradiction pour soigner les malades* (Paris, Flammarion, 2005).

[15] Cf Comité consultatif national d'éthique, Opinion no 78: *Inégalités dans les accès aux soins et dans la participation à la recherche à l'échelle mondiale, problème éthiques* (18 September 2003).

the various areas governed by UNESCO, the WTO, the WHO and WIPO), nor how to determine the responsibility of private economic operators in the event they violate these principles. But fragmentation is not the only problem. Globalised financial and information flows turn privatisation, which has no shared agenda, into the primary legal response to globalisation.

## Privatisation

'Privatisation' refers, first, to the initial distinction between subjects of public law (states, their representatives and, in France, territorial collectivities, which are all responsible for defending and promoting the general public interest) and subjects of private law (who defend their own interests). But due to new forms of internationalisation, private subjects are gradually entering the international arena, which does not mean the same thing to everyone.

Universalism turns members of civil society into actors: as victims of human rights violations, they can act individually or collectively against a state before regional courts or the UN Human Rights Committee (when the right of petition has been recognised); as perpetrators of crimes against humanity, they can be prosecuted in international criminal tribunals. Though non-governmental organisations (NGOs) play an increasingly important role in international human rights law,[16] civil society's 'legislative' power is limited to the indirect participation of NGOs in elaborating global norms and instituting judicial or quasi-judicial structures.

Meanwhile globalisation is transforming 'private economic powers',[17] namely transnational corporations, into both direct norm producers, as the development of *lex mercatoria* illustrates,[18] and equal partners with states in international agreements in the investment area.[19] As Charles Leben explained during a seminar at the Collège de France on 'Discontinuities and Interactions', there were two steps to this process: after the first attempt to regulate transnational corporations between 1970 and 1985 failed (offensive of the new global economic order and attempt to draft an international code of

---

[16] See Institut international des droits de l'homme, *Les Organisations non gouvernementales et le Droit international des droits de l'homme* (Brussels, Bruylant, 2005).

[17] G Farjat, 'Les pouvoirs privés économiques' in *Souveraineté étatique et Marchés intenationaux à la fin du XXe siècle. Mélanges en l'honneur de Philippe Kahn* (Paris, Litec, 2001), pp 613–61; *Pour un droit économique* (Paris, PUF, 204).

[18] See Delmas-Marty, *Le Relatif et l'Universel*, above n 7, pp 100 *ff.*

[19] See C Leben, *Le Droit international des affaires* 6th edn (Paris, PUF, 2003) pp 54 *ff.*

conduct for technology transfers), a second phase began in the 1980s during which investment law developed and corporations, transnational for the most part, acceded to public international law.[20] This latter development was aided by the appearance of 'state contracts' between states and private investors[21] and, more importantly, the creation of the International Centre for Settlement of Investment Disputes (ICSID) as provided for in the Washington Convention of 1965 concluded under the auspices of the World Bank. By 2002, this convention had been ratified by 184 states, including China, which had long been hostile to this type of arbitration. The number of treaties protecting investments that refer disputes to the ICSID attests to its success. Increasing from a few hundred per year in 1990 to more than 2,000 annually in 2002, these treaties are most often bilateral, but the multilateral NAFTA treaty and the proposed free trade area of the Americas also refer disputes to the ICSID. Arbitration might therefore become the only solution to investment disputes throughout the Americas.

Granting private investors status as subjects of public international law seems to be of the same importance as recognising private persons as subjects of international human rights law.[22] But in fact, it is even more important, as corporations have been given access to justice with respect to all of investment law: any investor domiciled in a state having concluded a treaty with the host state can bring the host state before an international arbitration tribunal, independently of any contract. Victims of human rights violations, on the contrary, may bring suit only in the regions where human rights courts exist and only if the state concerned has accepted the right of individuals to petition the court. In addition, such action does not implicate the individual liability of the person(s) responsible for the violation(s).

This inequality is compounded by the fact that human rights violations are committed not only by states, but more and more often by transnational corporations to which human rights mechanisms do not apply. To try to remedy this situation, in August 2003 the Sub-Commission on Human Rights proposed a set of 'Norms on

[20] See C Leben, 'Entreprises multinationales et droit international économique' (2005) *Revue de science criminelle* 777.

[21] See P Weil, *Ecrits de droit international* (Paris, PUF, 2000), pp 203 *ff*; C Leben, 'Retour sur la notion de contrat d'Etat et sur le droit applicable à celui-ci' in *Mélanges Hubert Thierry* above n 13, pp 247–80.

[22] See C Leben, 'Entreprises multinationals et droit international économique', above n 20.

the Responsibilities of Transnational Corporations and Other Business Enterprises with Regard to Human Rights'. While the proposal is modest in that it does not provide for judicial review, the Human Rights Commission was wary and treated it as a simple 'preliminary draft' with no legal value.[23] Support from the High Commissioner on Human Rights and the appointment of an independent expert, however, allowed the process to continue[24] and a decision on a new draft is expected in June 2008.

At this stage, evolution by fragmentation and privatisation of the legal area is not likely to establish a more equal balance between the market and human rights. Instead, it seems to herald increased disorder as the result of globalisation. But criminal law, situated where merchant and non-merchant values meet and are theoretically applicable to even the most powerful political and economic actors, might help avoid both fragmentation and privatisation.

## A Global Criminal Law Area in Formation

I have already mentioned the paradox of criminal law, which is on the front lines of globalisation even though the right to punish has, at least since the modern era, been considered the emblem of state sovereignty and limited by the principle of territoriality. Of course, the obstacle of sovereignty has not been totally removed, which no doubt explains why, despite unprecedented criminalisation, the global criminal law area is still only 'in formation'.

Criminalisation seems to be imposed by the universalism of values, which leads to punishing the 'worst' international crimes. Even though the foundation remains vague and the concept imprecise, it is explained by the limitative list of crimes subject to a supranational criminal justice validated by the establishment of the International Criminal Court, the first true permanent world court. Nonetheless, globalisation was initially associated with deregulation and self-regulation mechanisms (soft law, codes of conduct). But it is now also the subject of criminalisation: to 'level the playing field'[25] criminal penalties are more effective than are administrative or civil

---

[23] See Delmas-Marty, *Le Relatif et l'Universel*, above n 7, p 187.

[24] See Report of the UN High Commissioner on Human Rights, Doc.E/CN.4/2005/91, 15 February 2005. See also E Decaux, 'La responsabilité des sociétés transnationales en matière de droits de l'homme' (2005) *Revue de science criminelle* 789.

[25] See Delmas-Marty, *Le Relatif et l'Universel*, above n 7, p 253.

penalties. It is therefore not surprising that liberalism entails a return to criminal law, as if combining globalisation and universalism inevitably fosters the globalisation of criminal law, despite the risk of 'overcriminalisation'[26] which, in the area of terrorism, has led to weakening fundamental principles without guaranteeing a pluralist vision.

This risk is even more worrisome since European protective devices are not directly transposable to the global level. As I explained in the preceding chapter, stabilisation is facilitated in Europe by the bipolar construction and balancing carried out by the two European courts, and pluralism is part of the process, which precludes any attempts at unilateral hegemony. Such attempts exist at the global level, however: the lack of a human rights court fosters strategies that are not always consistent, vacillating between a conqueror's unilateralism that leads to the efficient but hardly legitimate extension of domestic criminal law and an ambitious multilateralism that bases its legitimacy on international law but is not very effective in overcoming the sovereignty of the most powerful states.

## Unilateral Strategies

Unilateral strategies are hard to understand because they are not always coordinated: while globalisation seems to rhyme with decriminalisation in France and Italy, the United States Congress deployed the inverse strategy of overcriminalisation when it adopted the Sarbanes–Oxley Act (SOX). To restore investor confidence after the Enron debacle in 2002, SOX doubled the pre-existing penalties for submitting fraudulent statements to the Securities and Exchange Commission (SEC) (up to 20 years' imprisonment in some cases, and/or fines of one million dollars), created new offences and extended criminal liability to all persons implicated in the fraudulent declaration. The effects of this criminalisation are felt throughout the world, as all companies listed on the United States stock exchange must comply with the new rules. In fact, Royal Dutch Shell almost provided the first case after it knowingly inflated its hydrocarbon reserve estimate.[27]

---

[26] Y Cartuyvels, 'Le droit pénal et l'Etat: des frontières « naturelles » en question' in M Hanzelin and R Roth (eds), *Le Droit pénal à l'épreuve de l'internationalisation* (Paris/Brussels, LGDJ/Bruylant, 2003), pp 3 *ff.*

[27] See N Norberg, 'Entreprises multinationales et lois extraterritoriales: l'interaction entre le droit américain et le droit international' (2005) *Revue de science criminelle* 739.

But the strategy of unilateral expansion can also be based on protecting universal values. Royal Dutch Petroleum, a subsidiary of Royal Dutch Shell, was sued in the United States for human rights violations related to its operations in Nigeria.[28] The suit is based on the Alien Tort Statute (ATS) of 1789, which grants the federal district courts jurisdiction over tort suits brought by aliens seeking damages for violations of the law of nations or treaties of the United States. Even though the ATS grants strictly civil jurisdiction, the penalties may be quite severe.

The ATS was rediscovered in the late 1970s, when it began serving as a basis for suing former officials of foreign governments for human rights violations perpetrated in their home countries (primarily former Latin American dictatorships).[29] As economic globalisation progressed in the mid-1990s, the ATS began forming the basis for lawsuits against transnational corporations. The case against Unocal,[30] the American sister company of Total-Fina-Elf, progressed the furthest through the courts. Accused of benefiting from the forced labour of Burmese villagers during the construction of a pipeline, Unocal was sued under the ATS for complicity in forced labour, murder and rape. At the same time, Total's directors were prosecuted in France for false imprisonment[31] (*séquestration*) (both cases were settled out of court[32]), which shows that unilateral strategies are not limited to American law. Nor do they necessarily preclude pluralism: while SOX transplants American law to most transnational corporations, the ATS extends international law and its application by American courts.

In the criminal context, adopting the 'Norms on the Responsibilities of Transnational Corporations and Other Business Enterprises with Regard to Human Rights' could provide a basis for incorporating

[28] See *Wiwa v Royal Dutch Petroleum Company and Shell Transport and Trading Company, PLC*, 226 F 3d 88 (2nd Cir 2000). See also Norberg, 'Entreprises multinationales et lois extraterritoriales', above n 27; 'The Supreme Court Affirms the Filartiga Paradigm' (2006) 4 *Journal of International Criminal Justice* 387.

[29] See Norberg, above notes 27 and 28.

[30] *Doe I v Unocal Corp*, 963 F Supp 880 (CD Cal 1997); *Doe v Unocal Corp.*, 395 F 3d 978 (9th Cir 2003) (vacated and rehearing, en banc, granted by *Doe v Unocal Corp*, 395 F 3d 978 (9th Cir 2003)).

[31] See W Bourdon, 'Entreprises multinationals, lois extraterritoriales et droit international des droits de l'homme' (2005) *Revue de science criminelle* 747.

[32] See L Girion, 'Unocal to Settle Rights Claim', *Los Angeles Times*, 14 December 2004, p A1; Pascal Ceaux and Jacques Follorou, 'Total va indemniser ses accusateurs', *Le Monde* (Paris, 30 November 2005). The case settled in June 2009. See Ed Pilkington, 'Shell pays out $15.5m over Saro-Wiwa killing' *The Guardian* (London, 9 June 2009).

international law that is more in line with the legality principle (the ATS is quite vague): judges might be encouraged to incorporate these principles when interpreting domestic criminal statutes in a transnational context, whether it concerns labour, environmental or corporate law. In the case of Total, for example, the *partie civile* suggested interpreting the French Penal Code's definition of false imprisonment in light of the international definition of forced labour, particularly as used by the ILO. Internationalising domestic law in this way can introduce a little pluralism into unilateral strategies and thereby increase their legitimacy. Conversely, multilateral strategies do not automatically guarantee pluralism.

## Multilateral Strategies

Many international conventions providing for the rapprochement of domestic criminal law systems in various areas linked to globalisation, such as bribery, money laundering, organised crime and terrorism, have been drafted on the initiative of the United States and generally result in transplanting the American model.[33] Significantly, the OECD working group tasked with implementing the 1997 Convention on Combating Bribery of Foreign Public Officials in International Business Transactions uses the oxymoron 'collective unilateralism' to describe how its collective peer evaluation system, which is based on the unilateral commitment of each state and grants a national margin of appreciation through the concept of functional equivalence, results in overall harmonisation, even of states not party to the Convention.[34]

As for criminalisation related to the 'worst' international crimes, beginning with crimes 'against humanity', its legitimacy stems from the universalism of the underlying values, but without a domestic support, neither effectiveness (real application of the law) nor efficaciousness (applying the law makes a difference) are assured. This is why the principle of complementarity (ICC Statute, Articles 1 and 17) in fact provides that the ICC's jurisdiction is subsidiary to that of the states, and why the ICC's duty to investigate and prosecute is qualified by the clause granting the prosecutor the power to forgo prosecution in the 'interests of justice' (Article 53). To determine these interests, the prosecutor takes into account 'all the

---

[33] See Delmas-Marty, *Le Relatif et l'Universel*, above n 7.

[34] See M Pieth, 'Introduction' in *OECD Convention on Combating Bribery of Foreign Officials in International Business Transactions, International Commentary* (Paris, OECD, 2005).

circumstances', including not only the 'gravity of the crime, the interests of the victims and the age or infirmity of the alleged perpetrators', but also, apparently, practical issues such as the feasibility of an investigation, the possibility of making arrests, and the impact of proceedings on the local situation. And in applying these criteria, the prosecutor recognises the need to reconcile universalism and pluralism by taking into consideration the national context and, perhaps, alternative reconciliation procedures.

Conflicts between unilateral and multilateral strategies can therefore be overcome by combining legitimacy and efficaciousness. Unilateral strategies, which tend to be related to globalisation, cannot be limited to the sole criterion of their formal validity (efficaciousness), but must incorporate international norms to found their legitimacy. Conversely, multilateral strategies, which are generally based on universalism, cannot be upheld solely on the basis of their legitimacy (symbolic and axiological validity): they must be made effective through co-operation and strengthening domestic justice systems. In the long term, the two strategies might join forces to contribute to a pluralist complementarity encompassing the entire global criminal justice area.

To achieve a new balance between universalism and globalisation, global criminal law must no doubt be conceived as an 'area', rather than as an autonomous and closed 'system'. But unlike the bipolar area developing in Europe, the global area is multipolar: open to a whole set of interactions that are both vertical (between international criminal law and domestic criminal law) and horizontal (between international criminal, humanitarian, and human rights law, as well as general international law). Indeed, it is interesting to note that in the memorandum I mentioned earlier on the 'interests of justice', the ICC Prosecutor's Office seems to position itself in just such a multipolar area to interpret the Statute: it recognises the autonomy of international criminal law (referring to the Statute's *travaux préparatoires* and the ICTs' case law on the concept of gravity), expresses an openness towards national systems out of concern for respecting legal diversity in evaluating the interests of the victims and the pertinence of alternative procedures, and refers to international human rights law (citing ICC Statute Article 23(3) and IACHR case law on impunity and the victim's right to due process). In the end, the ICC is the only court that can take a position on the possible supremacy of human rights law over criminal law, even if it is international (the ICTs have always accepted interactions while refusing any hierarchy favouring human rights[35]). In addition, this law of a universal nature arouses strong political opposition that limits legal interaction, as illustrated by the Security Council's reticence with respect to the Darfur Commission's report,[36] which eventually led the Council, as the Commission recommended, to refer the crimes to the ICC in application of Chapter VII of the UN Charter (to re-establish peace).

While it may thus contribute to resolving such crises,[37] the criminal justice area that is currently taking shape will not, by itself, stabilise the global legal area. At best, through reference to underlying values, it might found an ethic of globalisation[38] and show how to organise interactions at different levels to achieve pluralist stabilisation.

## Conditions for Pluralist Stabilisation

The point is not to return to the original agenda for global organisation, but to reformulate it in light of today's complexity, making it sufficiently pluralist and evolutionary to be acceptable by everyone. Achieving pluralist stabilisation of the processes of internationalising law at the global level will require vertically organising the regional and global levels and overcoming fragmentation and privatisation to reconcile universalism and globalisation at the horizontal level.

### Vertical Stabilisation

The apparently logical order (from the national to the regional to the global level) is not always respected: interregional relations can modify the course of integration and, depending on the domain, the initiative may be national, global or regional. For example, when the Kyoto Protocol was stalled at the global level, European Community

---

[35] See *Crimes internationaux et Juridictions internationales* (Paris, PUF, 2002), pp 144–88; M Delmas-Marty, H Muir Watt and H Ruiz Fabri (eds), *Variations autour d'un droit commun* (Paris, Société de Législation Comparée, 2002), pp 245–65; M Delmas-Marty, E Fronza and E Lambert-Abdelgawad (eds), *Les Sources du droit international pénal. L'expérience des tribunaux pénaux internationaux* (Paris, Société de Législation Comparée, 2005).

[36] See International Commission of Inquiry on Darfur, *Report to the Secretary General* (New York, United Nations, 2005); symposium, 'The Commission of Inquiry on Darfur and its Follow-Up: A Critical View' (2005) 3 *Journal of International Criminal Justice* 539.

[37] See P Alston, 'The Darfur Commission as a Model for Future Responses to Crisis Situations' (2005) 3 *Journal of International Criminal Justice* 600.

[38] See M Delmas-Marty, 'Le droit pénal comme éthique de la mondialisation' (2004) *Revue de science criminelle* 1.

ratification got it started again at the regional level. Early imposition of the Protocol on the member states via a European directive then contributed to Russian ratification, which brought the Protocol into force globally.

Whatever the discontinuities, the global legal area seems to be gradually stabilising in accordance with the ideal model described by Pascal Lamy in his essay, *La Démocratie-monde*. Though he notes that regionalism is not natural and 'geography does not determine history',[39] the WTO Director-General and former European trade commissioner considers that regional constructions may constitute an initial form of what he calls *alternational* democracy. In fact, they 'constitute reusable materials on the global scene; the convergence they bring about among their members produces common positions; these regional groups are the first site of synthesis where states learn to determine collective preferences, test the choices made together, compromise, and reduce distrust'. The positions taken will then be clarified and consolidated during discussion of global issues at the global level.

But convergence must exist, common positions must be arrived at and collective preferences must reflect genuine consensus. In other words, stabilisation implies that regional ensembles are playing the role of 'globalisation laboratories'[40] that has occasionally been ascribed to European construction. But Europe obviously holds no monopoly: at best, its age enables it to clarify the substantive and procedural conditions, as well as the practical methods for achieving stabilising well beyond Europe.

A first condition stems from the status of the regional organisation at the global level, that is, from the share of sovereignty the member states delegate to it in global negotiations. To play the role described above, the regional organisation must be represented, as the European Community was at the WTO by the trade commissioner. But representation in other areas is more problematic, as the struggle with respect to GMOs among the organisations responsible for health, trade and the environment shows. But above all, the highly diverse situations in the different regions must be taken into account, as reticence to delegating sovereignty is still strong.

[39] P Lamy, *La Démocratie-monde. Pour une autre gouvernance globale* (Paris, Seuil/La République des idées, 2004) pp 69–70.

[40] See M Delmas-Marty, 'L'espace judiciaire européen: laboratoire de la mondialisation' (2000) *Dalloz* 421; P Lamy, *La Démocratie-monde* above n 39, pp 35 *ff*; J Dutheil de la Rochère, 'Mondialisation et régionalisation' in Loquin and Kessedjian, *La Mondialisation du droit* above n 10, pp 435–53.

In addition, for convergence to exist, regional construction must be based on solidarity, which is not the case in all the examples discussed above (particularly in free trade areas, such as NAFTA and APEC) but, inversely, may arise outside official networks (the Chinese diaspora in Southeast Asia, for example). It seems that despite practical difficulties, common positions are gradually being adopted at the WTO[41] on behalf of regional organisations other than the EU, such as Mercosur, the ASEAN, the Caricom, and the ACP (Africa, Caribbean and Pacific Group of States), and occasionally *ad hoc* groups such as the Cairns Group, which groups together various states threatened by agricultural subsidies. The idea of a common position refers to the preparatory work that each regional organisation is supposed to carry out, and which it does do in a certain number of cases.[42] But to be entirely efficacious, this work needs to be both political, so that value choices are made on the basis of expressed and hierarchically ordered collective preferences, and legal, by harmonisation and sometimes hybridisation of shared norms.

But even satisfying all these conditions is not enough to constitute a new, overall agenda. On the contrary, the partially integrated and well-ordered regional level may now diverge from the global level, which has been described as 'chaotic, decentralised, and opaque for the most part'.[43] For the two levels to converge, fragmentation and privatisation must be overcome by horizontal stabilisation.

## Horizontal Stabilisation

As long as globalisation is synonymous with adopting norms unrelated to the universalism of values, global integration will be chaotic. I will not discuss here what Lamy calls the 'flaws of inter-national governance', which he believes is too often nothing more than 'gesticulations of a declamatory governance',[44] nor the necessary reforms of institutions such as the UN Security Council,[45] the WTO, the ILO and global financial institutions,[46] which I include in

---

[41] See the WTO website: www.wto.org.

[42] See J Ténier, *Intégrations régionales et Mondialisation. Complémentarité ou contradiction* (Paris, La Documentation française, 2003), p 200.

[43] A Lepiney, 'Européanisation et mondialisation du droit: convergences et divergences' in Morand, *Le Droit saisi par la mondialisation* above n 2, p 161.

[44] Lamy, *La Démocratie-monde*, above n 39, p 22.

[45] See High Level Panel on Threats, Challenges and Change, *A More Secure World, Our Shared Responsibility*, UN, 2 December 2004.

[46] See Lamy, *La Démocratie-monde*, above n 39, pp 28 *ff.*

my discussion of the increased power of national and international judges in *La Refondation des Pouvoirs*.[47] But in the more strictly normative perspective of 'ordering pluralism', I will, however, try to indicate the direction to take to re-establish an agenda for global organisation other than the hegemonic choice of the most powerful country.

If the compass constituted by the Universal Declaration of Human Rights was broken by separating rights into two categories, it should be possible to fix it by reuniting them and developing their use by judicialising remedies, and the Human Rights Council created in 2006 should be able to contribute. However, this Council is far from a world human rights court: organising negotiations and defining 'the mandate, means of organization, functions, size, composition and work methods' was left to the General Assembly, which had to take into account resistance on the part of numerous countries, from the United States to China via Russia, the Muslim countries and Israel.

Nonetheless, without modifying any texts, judges can recognise certain fundamental rights as *jus cogens* norms, that is, imperative rules of general international law applicable to all states regardless of their status as parties to any given treaty. Given the International Court of Justice's caution in this regard, the regional human rights courts are the pioneers, combining both horizontal and vertical stabilisation.[48] With respect to *jus cogens*, the IACHR's 2003 advisory opinion concerning the *Legal status and rights of undocumented workers*[49] put it on the front lines. Strongly supported by the Latin American states, the Court, in the words of Mexican judge (now President) Sergio García Ramírez, wants 'to help move mountains'. In its unanimous opinion concerning issues raised by Mexico and the United States, the Court audaciously set out the bases for a universal status of undocumented workers, recognising namely that the principle of equality before the law and the prohibition of discrimination guaranteed by Article 26 of the International Covenant on Civil and Political Rights are *jus cogens* norms. By thus incorporating

---

[47] M Delmas-Marty, *Les forces imaginantes du droit (III). La Refondation des Pouvoirs* (Paris, Seuil, 2007).

[48] As I discussed in the section on the 'judicial dialogue on the death penalty' in *Le Relatif et l'Universel* (above n 7), cross-references among courts began in 1989 with the European Court of Human Rights and were picked up in 1999 by the Inter-American Court before moving to the ICJ and a few national supreme courts.

[49] Inter-American Court of Human Rights Advisory Opinion OC-18 (17 September 2003) reprinted in (2004) *Revue générale de droit international public* 235.

a global text into its decision, the Court replaced the missing global level with the regional level. Unfortunately, this is simply an advisory opinion and undocumented workers are still faced with the 'mountain', not likely to be moved any time soon, comprising the legal argument of immigration status and the economic argument of conflicts of interests between countries of immigration and emigration (which exists in Europe as well).

Collective preferences might offer another way to reunite rights by identifying 'global public goods'. After the universalist concept of a shared 'heritage of humanity'[50] was rejected, the World Bank began promoting 'global public goods and services'[51] in the context of financing. The criteria defining such goods and services are therefore economic: non-rivalry in consumption and non-excludability of potential consumers. These criteria explain the variability of a concept that may protect goods as diverse as health, drinking water, the ozone layer, and access to information via Internet, but they do not apply in all areas of conflict, beginning with that of employment.

To reconcile universalism and globalisation by emphasising both the complexity of the world, which is already globalised, and the attachment to the universalist agenda of the UDHR, a new instrument is no doubt needed, such as the Universal Declaration of Interdependence[52] proposed in 2005 by the International Collegium at the 60th anniversary of the UN Charter. The idea behind this Declaration is that interdependence has become a fact bringing both opportunities and risks. Through the intensity of exchanges, interdependence bears witness to a community of life on a global scale; but through the globalisation of various natural and man-made threats, it transforms humanity into an 'involuntary community of risks',[53] in the words of Jürgen Habermas. What is needed is to consciously transform this circumstantial interdependence into a global agenda built on the principle of inter-solidarity, a principle that would legally bind states and international organisations as well as private, individual or organisational actors who hold global power (economic, scientific, media, religious, cultural, etc.). As the Declaration states, 'Implementing this principle involves:

---

[50] Delmas-Marty, *Le Relatif et l'Universel*, above n 7, pp 92, 123, 149, 203, 385, 400–01.

[51] B Campbell, 'Le bien commun comme réponse à la pauvreté' in O Delas and C Deblock (eds), *Le Bien commun comme réponse politique à la mondialisation* (Brussels, Bruylant, 2003).

[52] See *Libération* (24 October 2005), p 36.

[53] J Habermas, *Le Bicentenaire d'une idée kantienne* (Paris, Cerf, 1996).

- the reaffirmation of the fundamental rights of individuals of the present as well as future generations in a global democratic society that respects public order at both national and supranational levels;
- the recognition that the exercise of power on a global scale—whether it be economic, scientific, religious, cultural, or even that of the media—implies the corollary of global responsibility for all the effects of this exercise of power;
- the encouragement of sovereign states to recognize the necessity of combining supranational public order with a defense of the common values and interests to which their commitment is indispensable;
- the development of institutions representing regional international communities, while at the same time reinforcing both the world community and global civil society—all this with the goal of articulating a common policy for the regulation of global forces, the prevention of global risks, and the suppression of global crime.'

Accountability at the global level would clearly be necessary and requires: a more precise definition of common interests which, by reference to human rights and global public goods, could provide the basis for the concept of international crime; a pluralist application adapted to the practical conditions specific to each national and regional normative level; and favouring processes of interaction and harmonisation. This implicitly includes the concept of a national margin of appreciation, which preserves pluralism while ordering it.

But it is not enough to arrange differences in a specific area presumed static. The rhythms of each state and region and, more broadly, the speeds of transformation that vary from one area to another, must be taken into account. Ordering pluralism therefore also requires synchronisation.

# Part 3
## Speeds of Transformation

One of the distinguishing features of the processes of internationalising law is that they are evolutionary. It therefore seems impossible to avoid discussing normative time and speeds of transformation, the end result of all evolutionary processes. In studying ordered pluralism, I therefore favour a sort of legal kinetics combining the energy produced by diverse processes of organisation and their variations depending on the organisational level, with movement, in its two dimensions of direction and speed.

Movement is initially perceived through changes in direction. In noting differences between imperceptible variations and abrupt directional changes, Henri Bergson distinguished among the latter those that are *indissociable* and those that are *complementary*. The former are related by their common origin, while the latter have different origins but 'coordinate with each other to maintain and even perfect an organ's functioning under more complicated conditions.'[1] To avoid using only an organic metaphor, I have borrowed from René Thom and his genesis of forms (which he thought common to all sciences, physical, biological, sociological and human) to represent shifts in criminal justice policy (criminalisation/decriminalisation, nationalisation/privatisation, etc).[2] Today, this would require pinpointing bifurcations or, to use Thom's terminology, catastrophes of bifurcation, of which the terrorist attacks of 11 September 2001 are a remarkable example.

---

[1] H Bergson, *L'Evolution créatrice, Oeuvres* (Paris, PUF, 2nd edn 1963) p 551.
[2] See R Thom, *Stabilité structurelle et Morphogénèse* (Interéditions, 1977); M Delmas-Marty, *Modèles et Mouvements de politique criminelle* (Paris, Economica, 1983) p 153; M Delmas-Marty, *Grands Systèmes de politique criminelle* (Paris, Seuil, 1992).

Whether they are continuous or discontinuous, directional changes are always associated with the progression from past to present to future. In his book on legal time, for example, François Ost alternates memory and forgiveness in the past with promise and calling into question in the future.[3] And Zaki Laïdi has shown how globalisation replaces historical time with global time, an eternal present that he believes leads to a cult of the present.[4] To add to this discussion (including my earlier contribution to it[5]) of chronology and directional changes, I will now turn to the apparently unprecedented issue of speeds.

'Speed is power itself', according to Paul Virilio, who adds that 'power means, above all, *dromocratic* power—*dromos* from the Greek, meaning race—and all societies are competitive societies.'[6] And there are indeed speed contests taking place between national and international normative ensembles, and even between various sectors of regional and global law. What interests me here, however, are the differences in speeds or, more precisely, the rhythms: as I noted earlier, when describing the 'common nature of nations',[7] the 18th-century philosopher Giambattista Vico emphasised the differences in rhythms: isomorphism is not synchrony. Rhythms contribute to the adjustments and readjustments of today's legal bricolage. Adjusting to achieve greater justice and greater precision does not mean 'searching for lost time', but trying to find an opportune time (*kairos* in Greek, in the literal sense of 'mix'). Ordering pluralism, as well, is the art of blending rhythms and combining speeds as precisely as possible—here again, adjusting—to the energy and inertia specific to each society. Just as the global normative area has not eliminated the national area nor impeded the development of regional areas, global time has not supplanted the historical time of states or regions.

When evolution is too slow, it stagnates and, in losing the race, the ensemble in question loses its normative autonomy. For example, if the European Union's constitutional agenda fails, certain policy

---

[3] See F Ost, *Le Temps du droit* (Paris, Odile Jacob, 1999).

[4] See Z Laïdi, *Le Sacre du présent* (Paris, Flammarion, 2000).

[5] See generally M Delmas-Marty, *Les Forces imaginantes du droit (I): Le Relatif et l'Universel* (Paris, Seuil, 2004).

[6] See P Virilio, *Cybermonde, la politique du pire. Entretien avec Philippe Petit* (Paris, Textuel, 1996).

[7] G Vico, *Principes d'une science nouvelle relative à la nature commune des nations* [*Principi di scienza nuova d'intorno alla commune natura delle nazioni, 1744*], A Pons (trans), (Paris, Fayard, 2001).

choices may be made for member states at the global level. However, if change occurs too quickly, it creates distortions not only in terms of competition in the same market but, worse, in terms of splitting up various sectors of human and social activity: trade law cannot forever outrun environmental, labour or health law, or human rights law more generally, without destroying systemic balance. But wisdom is also called 'temperance', and what I would like to develop here, by pointing out the primary instruments that slow or accelerate evolution and transformation, is the art of combining different rhythms harmoniously. Virilio was not afraid of arousing Egyptologists' indignation when he liberally reinterpreted Tuttenkamen's likeness, placing a whip (rather than a flyswatter) in one hand to spur his war chariot and a hook in the other to slow it down or stop it.[8]

Finding the most well-adapted brakes and accelerators for our societal chariots would prove the wisdom of good governance. Indeed, it is probably no accident that Temperance sits next to Justice in the allegory of Sienna's Palazzo Pubblico, because the contemporary period is characterised not only by an 'acceleration of legal time'[9] in each normative area and the strange association between virtual areas and real time,[10] but also by variations in speeds among different areas. As long as law resists internationalisation, these variations are part of the diversity of peoples and their legal systems, but as interdependence imposes more and more normative and judicial interactions (see above), they produce perverse effects that must be taken into account before any attempt is made at organisation.

A first hypothesis is that in responding to this 'asynchrony' from one area to another, ordering pluralism should not require making legal times agree, as uniformity would reduce pluralism. Instead, rhythms should be 'synchronized', in the sense of making them compatible or rendering them harmonious (though they would no doubt always be at least partially different). But if synchronicity, like harmony, should not be confused with uniformity, other possibilities offered by the concept of 'polychrony' must be explored, namely the

---

[8]  See Virilio, *Cybermonde, la politique du pire* above n 6, p 16.
[9]  For a deeper analysis, see P Gérard, F Ost and M van de Kerchove (eds), *L'Accélération du temps juridique* (Brussels, Facultés Universitaires Saint-Louis, 2000), esp M Vogliotti, 'Faut-il récupérer *aidos* pour délier Sisyphe? A propos du temps clos et instable de la justice pénale italienne' in *id.*, pp 661–710.
[10]  See Delmas-Marty, *Le Relatif et l'Universel* above n 5.

use, in a single legal area, of different speeds for different states. This leads to a second hypothesis: that polychrony is the means to facilitate synchronisation, just as harmonisation is largely based on the concept of a national margin of appreciation. This concept introduces variations into the area and even calls for varying rhythms of transformation, because it would be absurd and counter-productive to impose the same rhythm, or tempo, on every state.

To get from asynchrony (different areas, different speeds) to polychrony (one area, several speeds), the conditions for pluralist synchronisation will have to be discerned.

# 6
# Asynchrony

VARIATIONS IN SPEED from one organisational level to another make it hard to manage differences from one area to another. For example, when the Kyoto Protocol on climate change went into effect, it was reported that American transnational corporations, subject to global as well as to American law, favoured ratification: differences in national and international norms create unacceptable financial distortions, and '[such corporations] cannot manage a system with two speeds, one for the United States and another elsewhere'.[11]

Compounding the problem is the fact that speeds also vary from one legal sector to another. For example, the rhythm of transformation is not the same for environmental law as for trade law: they are not synchronised. I will therefore discuss the multiplicity of time scales before moving on to illustrating it by comparing the speed with which human rights instruments evolve to that of trade law. This example will allow me to set out conditions for a pluralist synchronisation.

## Multiple Time Scales

I will begin with scales that measure differences between the organisational levels of normative areas,[12] that is, differences between the national, regional and global tempos.

### Time Scales and Organisational Levels

In *Le Gai Savoir*, Nietzsche asserts that tempo has 'as much importance for the forces driving peoples' development as it does for

---

[11] P Radanne, 'Les pays finiront par plier à un gouvernement mondial du climat', *Le Monde* (Paris, 16 February 2005).

[12] See G Soulier, *L'Europe. Histoire, Civilisation, Institutions* (Paris, Armand Colin, 1994) (distinguishing, in line with Fernand Braudel's grammar of civilisations, between 'founding time' and 'organisational time').

music'.[13] He adds that humanity needs both a slow tempo, the 'imitation of a tortoise that constitutes the norm', and a gay, rapid one, which he attributes to impatient spirits, artists, poets and deserters, warning that this exception must not become the rule. The slow pace must be preserved, along with something Nietzsche calls virtuous silliness: 'We need those who imperturbably beat the measure of the slow spirit so that the believers of the great overall faith stay together and continue to dance their dance.'[14] But the dance is not certain to continue for long, because the slow pace may not remain the norm. As Nietzsche foresaw over a century ago, '[the image of] things will move and change perhaps more, and more quickly, from now on than ever before'.[15] In the legal field, this is both true and more complex, because everything is happening as if the ball was being tossed from one level to another to try to overcome obstacles.

For example, the internationalisation of the law on bribery,[16] that is, the extension of domestic criminal law to acts committed abroad, began at the national level with the American Foreign Corrupt Practices Act of 1977, adopted in response to the Lockheed scandal. It then took more than 30 years for a global instrument to be adopted. Since there was no chance other states would spontaneously adopt similar legislation, a solution at the global level had to be found to avoid the law's negative effects being felt by American corporations only. The United States thus pressured the UN for an international convention on the corruption of foreign officials, but the combined inertia of developing and developed nations stalled progress on the 1979 draft. Fifteen years later, the United States was able to get the OECD to start the ball rolling again and a recommendation was adopted in 1994. This stimulated activity at the regional level, resulting in the Inter-American convention of 1994, then the European Union and Council of Europe conventions of 1997 and 1999, respectively, followed by the African convention of 2003. In the meantime, internationalisation was imposed at the quasi-global level through the binding OECD convention of 1997. Only thereafter did this extension of domestic law reach the truly global level, indirectly through the UN Convention against

---

[13] F Nietzsche, *Le Gai Savoir* (P Woting, trans) 2nd edn (Paris, GF-Flammarion, 2000), p 69.

[14] *Ibid.*, pp 123–4.

[15] *Ibid.*, p 69.

[16] See M Delmas-Marty, *Les Forces imaginantes du droit (I): Le Relatif et l'Universel* (Paris, Seuil, 2004), pp 246–64.

Transnational Organized Crime of 2000 (Palermo Convention) and directly through the UN Convention against Corruption of 2003.

In this case, the national, regional, quasi-global and global dynamics operated complementarily or, as Bergson meant the term, in a coordinated way: 'to maintain and even perfect the functioning of an organ in more complicated conditions.' But other examples indicate that neutralisation or even impasses from one level to another may result from increasingly complicated conditions, such as those caused by the United States' refusal to ratify the Rome Statute establishing the ICC (and its bilateral sanctions imposed to dissuade other states from doing so) and the Kyoto Protocol. In such cases, regions may act as relays, as the EU's anticipatory role and the NAFTA states' role of accompaniment show. But the global level can also anticipate the regional level: the ICC instituted a global prosecutor while the European Union refused to institute a European prosecutor in the Nice Treaty (2000) and conditioned the creation of one via the Lisbon Treaty (2007) on the unanimous approval of the now 27 member states.

Terrorism provides even more examples of law's chaotic movement. Despite the convention produced by the League of Nations in 1937, internationalising the struggle against terrorism was long stymied by relativism, as terrorism is closely related to attacks on national security. At the global level, mutual aid has made progress only slowly and with respect to specific forms of terrorism, since the impossibility of agreeing on a comprehensive definition of terrorism foreclosed granting jurisdiction to the ICC. Even at the European level and despite the crime's being depoliticised in 1977, conventions designed to facilitate the extradition of terrorists contained the so-called 'French' clause enabling states to refuse extradition in the event the request appears politically based. It took the shock of the events of 11 September 2001 and the UN resolutions of September and October of that year for the European Union to adopt the 2002 framework decisions on terrorism and the European arrest warrant, thereby 'Europeanising' the struggle against terrorism.[17]

The various national, regional and global instruments are complementary with each other and seem to converge to accelerate the movement and herald the adoption of a comprehensive definition.[18]

---

[17] On these different episodes, see *ibid.*, pp 285–307.

[18] See the report of the UN Secretary-General, *In Larger Freedom. Towards Security, Development and Human Rights for All*, September 2005 (www.un.org/largerfreedom/ last accessed 3 November 2008). See also United Nations, 2005 World Summit Outcome, Final Document, A/Res/60/1, 15 September 2005.

But other recent episodes indicate that the rapid tempo adopted since 11 September to combat a terrorism considered global is countered by the slow tempo of human rights principles, as if certain sectors resist acceleration more than others.

## Time Scales and Regulatory Sectors

Is there a tempo for universalism and another for globalisation? Fostered by great crises (the Second World War and the conflicts in the former Yugoslavia and Rwanda, for example), legal universalism has nonetheless progressed very slowly, as well as discontinuously, hindered if not stymied by national sovereignty, while economic globalisation steams ahead at full throttle. Facilitated by new technologies and flows of intangibles that know no borders, globalisation has advanced since the end of the Cold War without directly challenging national sovereignty or arousing state resistance. On the contrary, states have hastened to render their legal systems attractive on the 'market of laws' and concluded bi- and multilateral investment agreements (see Chapter 5).

But the difference between the slow tempo of universalism and the quick tempo of globalisation is actually more qualified than my description makes it seem, because legal sectors cannot be closeted in one category or another. Should international terrorism be assimilated to a crime against humanity or considered simply a globalised crime? Similar questions arise with respect to environmental law: 'If there were a hit parade of multilateral treaties, there is little doubt the Kyoto Protocol, which entered into force February 16, 2005, would top the list.'[19] To be sure, between its signature in 1997 and entry into force, 'climatic diplomacy advanced with surprising speed', but it would be an exaggeration to consider this success as a triumph of legal universalism indicating our recognition of the environment as a 'global public good'. In fact, the 'surprising' speed results above all from the interdependency created by the globalisation of risks, which brings us back to the beginning of *Le Relatif et l'Universel*: the incompleteness of ideas compounded by the way things are.

To try to move forward, the issue must be discussed in more concrete terms while observing how different timescales operate in one of the most important races, namely that between human rights law and trade law.

---

[19]  H Kempf, 'Kyoto, an I', *Le Monde* (Paris, 16 February 2005).

# The Race Between Human Rights Law and Trade Law

Both processes of internationalisation began at the same time, in the period immediately following the Second World War. Free trade was validated by the 1947 General Agreement on Tariffs and Trade (GATT) and the protection of human rights by the 1948 Universal Declaration of Human Rights. The take-up was slow on both sides, however. While the financial (International Bank for Reconstruction and Development, IBRD) and monetary (International Monetary Fund, IMF) pillars were instituted,[20] states renounced creating the International Trade Organization (ITO) provided for in the Havana Charter, which never entered into force. The world trade pillar was thus built up little by little on the foundations of the GATT, which was temporary. As for human rights, the Declaration is not binding and fundamental rights, the universalism of which implies indivisibility, have been weakened by being split up into the two binding covenants of 1966, as well as by the lack of genuine judicial review, but the evolution that followed was quite different at the global and European levels.

## The Race at the Global Level

After the end of the Cold War, and especially after the creation of the WTO and its Dispute Resolution Body (DRB) in 1994, asynchrony became preoccupying at the global level as the gap widened between human rights law, which remained sluggish, and trade law, which clearly accelerated.

With respect to human rights, the slow pace is not due to a legal void: under the auspices of the Council (formerly the Commission) on Human Rights, and even the Human Rights Committee for the roughly 100 states having accepted its jurisdiction, several procedures exist for verifying general and thematic violations.[21] However, despite the Committee's effort to judicialise its procedures and indicate to states the measures they need to take, the lack of real sanctions weakens this type of monitoring, which cannot be called 'judicial review'. This weakness has not been compensated for by the

---

[20]   See G Burdeau, 'Le FMI et la surveillance de l'espace monétaire et financier mondial' in E Loquin and C Kessedjian (eds), *La Mondialisation du droit* (Paris, Litec, 2000) 262–75.

[21]   See Delmas-Marty, *Le Relatif et l'Universel*, above n 6, pp 198 *ff.*

existence of a High Commissioner of Human Rights since 1993 or the 'contradictory and discouraging' case law of the ICJ, which too often goes against the current, 'alternating its undoubtedly excessive caution in concrete cases with slicing the air with a sword, which is all the more spectacular as the results are nil'.[22] Even the transformation of the Commission on Human Rights into a more independent Council will have little chance, without true judicial review, of accelerating a process that state resistance seems to be able to freeze in its tracks.

In stark contrast, since the Marrakech agreement's creation of the WTO, the global trade law area has come into full bloom and is advancing full speed ahead: it continues to acquire new members (China joined in 2001 and Russia is currently a candidate) as it steams ahead (contrary to predictions) thanks to the quasi-judicial DRB. This body began operations in 1995 and treated close to 30 cases in extremely diverse areas. Analysing it as both the 'birth of a court' and the 'consolidation of a law', Hélène Ruiz Fabri attributed this success to two causes confirmed by the report: 'One is that the procedure takes place within strictly defined time periods (whether they are too long or too short is another matter); the other is that the procedure is initiated unilaterally and cannot be blocked.'[23]

In other words, speed results from the institution of accelerators (time periods) and the elimination of brakes. States can, of course, take retaliatory measures based on classical private justice principles; but like compensation, retaliatory measures are temporary and subject to multilateral supervision, which ensures equivalence between the measures taken and the prejudice suffered and thereby reduces the possibility that the most powerful states will overevaluate and hinder free trade.[24] This change in speeds from the GATT to the OMC was no doubt accepted for economic, political and legal reasons related to the end of the Cold War.

[22] E Decaux, 'La CIJ et les droits de l'homme', in *Studi di diritto internazionale in onore di Gaetano Arangio-Ruiz* (Naples, Editoriale scientifica, 2004), pp 921–66.

[23] H Ruiz Fabri, 'Le règlement des différends auprès de l'OMC: naissance d'une juridiction, consolidation d'un droit' in *Souveraineté étatique et Marchés internationaux à la fin du XXe siècle. Mélanges en l'honneur de Philippe Kahn* (Paris, Litec, 2001), pp 303–34; 'La juridictionnalisation du règlement des litiges économiques entre Etats' (2003) *Revue française d'arbitrage* 881. See also V Tomkiewicz, 'L'organe d'appel de l'Organisation mondiale du commerce' (doctoral dissertation, University of Paris I, 2004).

[24] In the banana case, for example, the United States' estimated damages of USD 520 million were reduced to 191.4 million, while Canada's estimated damages in the hormone-fed beef case were reduced from CAD 75 million to 11.3 million.

From an economic point of view, stabilising the international trade system contributes to more efficient management as transaction costs are lowered and reciprocity strategies improving the treatment of new problems are more easily implemented.[25] Politically, the partially diplomatic nature of the cyclical negotiation process (trade rounds) produces agreement networks as distinct yet interdependent instruments are added and superposed.[26] Moreover, this process does not place states in conflict with private economic actors, whose interests are so similar that states often seem like their spokespersons.[27] The international trade apparatus is therefore better tolerated than the human rights apparatus which, by virtue of higher principles of a universal nature, places victims and states in direct conflict.

From his comparison of these two processes, Thomas Cottier has deduced two different legal cultures, 'the one [being] top down, the other [being] mainly bottom up',[28] and reached the conclusion that the human rights culture would prohibit the gradual regulation process and the inductive method partially responsible for trade law's success. One can see why the gap is widening between trade and human rights law, but this is not inevitable: at the regional level, particularly in Europe, the race is being run differently, with an inverse speed ratio.

### The European Level

The gap between human rights and trade law opened up immediately after the war: the failure of the political construction undertaken under the auspices of the Council of Europe (Treaty of London, 1949) led to the creation, in the 1950s, of the European Coal and Steel Community (ECSC), followed by the EEC and Euratom. As with the WTO, this two-fold process combined geographic expansion with acceleration, but in the case of Europe, acceleration occurred in 'small steps' as successive reforms led to the Constitutional Treaty signed in Rome in 2004 by 25 member states.

---

[25] See CA Michalet, 'Les metamorphoses de la mondialisation: une approche économique' in Loquin and Kessedjian, *La Mondialisation du droit* above n 10, pp 11–42.

[26] See PM Eisenmann, 'Le système normatif de l'OMC' in Société française pour le droit international, *La Réorganisation mondiale des échanges* (Paris, Pedone, 1996), pp 53–73 at 60.

[27] See Delmas-Marty, *Le Relatif et l'Universel*, above n 6.

[28] T Cottier, 'Trade and Human Rights: a Relationship to Discover' (2002) *Journal of International Economic Law* 111, 119.

That Treaty was rejected and its replacement, the 2007 Lisbon Treaty, has not yet been ratified, but for a half century at least, European Community construction has constituted 'a break with prior experiments'[29] in two ways. First, economics were given priority over politics; second, a global, immediate approach was favoured over a sectoral, progressive approach. At the same time, a formidable legal instrument serving to both stabilise and accelerate was created: seconded by national courts due to the direct applicability of Community law and the technique of interlocutory appeals, the ECJ and the Court of First Instance have contributed, by establishing principles such as the primacy of European law and non-discrimination among member states, to accelerating the shift from horizontal co-operation (cross references) to vertical integration (harmonisation and unification).

In contrast, however, the Council of Europe floundered. While adoption of the ECHR in 1950 led to the immediate establishment of a remedial apparatus in the form of the Commission and Court of Human Rights, 'Sleeping Beauty',[30] as Lord Lester of Herne Hill has called the ECHR, took her time waking up. Though the Convention was first signed by the United Kingdom (in 1951), it was not directly applicable in the UK until the Human Rights Act 1998 came into force in October 2000. And though France actively participated in drafting the Convention, it waited 25 years to ratify it (1974), then another seven to recognise individuals' right to petition the Commission and, once Protocol 11 of 1998 entered into force, the Court itself.

In the beginning, this remedial apparatus suffered many handicaps, both political (such as lack of ratification) and economic (insufficient budget and judicial pay) as well as legal. Former first president of the *Cour de cassation* Guy Canivet recalls that interlocutory appeals to the ECJ created a spirit of co-operation, whereas a 'climate of distrust and even conflict' reigned with respect to the ECtHR, which national judges perceived as signalling disapproval and questioning their authority when it ruled that the Convention had been violated.[31] But bit by bit, through a mix of 'audacity and

---

[29] D Simon, *Le Système juridique communautaire* (Paris, PUF, 1997), p 18.
[30] Lord Lester of Herne Hill, 'La tradition de *common law*' in C Teitgen-Colly (ed), *Cinquantième anniversaire de la Convention européenne de sauvegarde des droits de l'homme* (Brussels, Bruylant, 2002), p 29.
[31] See G Canivet, 'Rapport' in *La Réforme de la Cour européenne des droits de l'homme* (Brussels, Bruylant, 2003), pp 71–5.

restraint',[32] both the Commission and the Court overcame most of these handicaps and the human rights legal area has both outdistanced the economic legal area geographically (15 original member states to the EC's six have now grown to 47, compared to the EU's 27) and outstripped it in terms of speed: having decided its first case in 1960 and 836 more in the 38 years between then and the 1998 reform, the post-reform ECtHR decided almost as many (691) between 1998 and 2000 and continued to accelerate such that in 2001, it decided 888 cases while the ECJ decided only 240.[33] (Seeing these figures as 'preoccupying and even clearly excessive',[34] the Court's president has pushed for a procedural form, which will occur when Protocol 14 enters into force.)

What explains the different speeds of transformation at the regional and global level? The remedial apparatus is no doubt the key, and it almost never saw the light of day! When Pierre-Henri Teitgen presented the draft convention (which had been adopted in commission by a very slim margin of one) to the Council of Europe's Parliamentary Assembly, not only the British but even the French representative Robert Schuman expressed strong reservations, believing it was useless to raise the issue of human rights when the United Nations was already addressing it. The convention was thus struck from the Committee of Ministers' agenda; but fortunately, it was reintroduced *in extremis* and adopted by a large majority (64 to one, with 21 abstentions).[35] The incident may serve as a lesson in modesty, as it shows the large part chance plays in transforming human society: a bifurcation as important as the right to petition, which enables an individual to obtain a judgment against a state for violating human rights, hangs on the presence and obstinacy of a handful of people who were no doubt taken for naïve dreamers. In any case, once the road was taken, though acceleration was slow, it was continuous, and therefore fostered a flexible relationship between politics and law.

---

[32] JP Costa, 'Propos introductif' in Teitgen-Colly, *Cinquantième anniversaire de la Convention européenne de sauvegarde des droits de l'homme* above n 20, p 168.

[33] See L Wildhaber, 'Un avenir constitutionnel pour la CEDH?' (2002) 14 *Revue universelle des droits de l'homme* 1.

[34] L Wildhaber, 'Table ronde' in Teitgen-Colly, *Cinquantième anniversaire de la Convention européenne de sauvegarde des droits de l'homme* above n 20, p 317.

[35] See E du Réau, 'La genèse de la CESDH' in Teitgen-Colly, *Cinquantième anniversaire de la Convention européenne de sauvegarde des droits de l'homme* above n 20, pp 48 *ff*; C Russo, 'Le rôle de Pierre-Henri Teitgen' in *ibid.*, pp 59 *ff*.

Politically speaking, the European human rights system's 'force of attraction'[36] has been reinforced since 1974, when France's ratification caught the human rights area up to the economic area: all 15 members of the EEC had now ratified the ECHR, so the two systems could be linked. Beginning with Greece, Spain and Portugal, ratification of the ECHR, including the right of individuals to petition the Commission and the Court, became a condition for entry into the Community. The 'club of democracies' thus became a 'school of democracies',[37] which contributed to the human rights area's acceleration.

But there are also legal reasons for acceleration: as case law develops, reasoning changes. Earlier I described the ECtHR's reasoning as deductive, as opposed to the inductive reasoning that has facilitated trade law's rise to prominence. However, the ECtHR has altered its reasoning to adapt to national diversity, namely by inventing the 'national margin of appreciation'. Combining flexibility and creativity in its interpretation, the Court has created new, autonomous categories such as 'criminal matter', which broadens the concept of criminal law to include any law that provides for sanctions determined to be punitive according to criteria developed by the Court. Since autonomisation and acceleration go hand in hand, the ECtHR's increased independence has enabled the European human rights area to catch up to the trade area. Indeed, it may even have passed it and be pointing the way, considering the references to the ECHR in the Maastricht and Amsterdam Treaties, the adoption of the Nice Charter of Fundamental Rights (which is largely similar to the ECHR), and the Constitutional and Lisbon treaties' references to EU ratification of the ECHR.

The Council of Europe does not seem to be comforted by this, however; rather, it is beginning to fear 'losing its specificity'[38] in the area of human rights to the EU. The issue is therefore not simply catching up to win the race, but synchronisation, so I will now discuss the conditions for achieving synchronisation at the global level.

### Conditions for Achieving Synchronisation

The above example suggests that synchronisation requires a flexible arrangement: leaving some give in the process of normative integra-

---

[36] C Teitgen-Colly, 'Le rayonnement de la CESDH' in *ibid.*, p 71.
[37] *Ibid.*, p 74.
[38] *Le Monde* (Paris, 3 March 2005).

tion facilitates synchronisation (changes in speed), while rigidity causes the system to lock up.

## Relationships Between Powers

In Europe, there is a fairly flexible arrangement among the political, legal and economic powers that has avoided any blockages until now. Though the future of the EU is uncertain (as will be that of human rights within the EU until the Charter of Fundamental Rights is made legally binding), synchronisation is a lasting effect of the bipolar legal construction made possible by political and economic choices that caused the normative areas to partially overlap (because all EU member states have ratified the ECHR).

At first glance, it doesn't seem that the European experiment can be repeated at the global level, as the overlap of economic and human rights areas that facilitated European legal integration seems impossible to achieve (comparing states' haste to join the WTO with their reticence to ratify the UN Covenants and other human rights instruments, including the Rome Treaty establishing the ICC, ought to convince anyone of that). For example, while Croatia's insufficient co-operation with the ICTY until October 2005 caused negotiations regarding its entry into the EU to be put off,[39] the barriers have since been lifted. But the *ad hoc* tribunals, which have only specific, limited jurisdiction, must not be confused with the ICC, which is a permanent court meant to have worldwide jurisdiction, and the current political context precludes conditioning entry into the WTO on ratification of the Rome Treaty. On the contrary, the United States has put the brakes on international criminal justice by concluding bilateral agreements subjecting partner states to sanctions, in application of the American Service Members' Protection Act.[40]

Nevertheless, developments with respect to the Sudan indicate how legal arguments can avoid entirely locking up the system. Addressing the issue of whether or not the Security Council ought to refer the matter to the ICC, the Darfur Commission showed in its report that the legal conditions for doing so were met.[41] Though the Commission concluded this was not a case of genocide, it did find that crimes of war and crimes against humanity, which are just as

---

[39] See T Ferenczi, 'La fuite d'un chef de guerre entrave l'adhésion de la Croatie à l'UE', *Le Monde* (Paris, 16 March 2005).

[40] See Delmas-Marty, *Le Relatif et l'Universel*, above n 6, pp 197–8.

[41] See International Commission of Inquiry on Darfur, *Report to the Secretary General* (New York, United Nations, 2005).

serious, had been committed (paragraph 642). It also found that other crimes seemed to have been committed on a large scale (thousands of murders, rapes, and villages and homes destroyed, with close to 2 million persons displaced) and indicated that both government representatives and rebels were responsible. The Commission also noted, with respect to complementarity, that the Sudan is neither willing nor able to investigate or prosecute (paragraph 568).

Since the Sudan is not a party to the ICC Treaty and did not ask the ICC to take jurisdiction, the only option was for the Security Council to refer the case. The Commission (followed by the High Commission for Human Rights) therefore laid out several legal arguments supporting referral: the crimes threaten international peace and security; investigation and prosecution of persons in positions of authority controlling the state apparatus are close to impossible in the Sudan, whereas the ICC's authority might convince state leaders and rebel chiefs to submit to such procedures; and the ICC's international make-up and rules of procedure and evidence make it the only tribunal that can guarantee a fair trial. In addition, the ICC could intervene immediately without any extra cost to the international community, while creating an ad hoc tribunal takes time and significant resources.

After two months of tense discussions, the Security Council showed that evolution is possible by referring the matter to the ICC: adopted by a vote of 11 members in favour with four members abstaining (Algeria, Brazil, China and the United States), Resolution 1593 legitimises the ICC.[42] While politics, namely the United States' open hostility and China's reservations, seemed likely to block the resolution's adoption, legal arguments played a decisive role, especially since the President of the United States had himself qualified the events as genocide. I do not consider this a triumph of law, however. For one thing, the resolution includes a legally disputable exemption clause applicable to citizens of states participating in operations in the Sudan and designed to protect leaders and military personnel from prosecution for any international crimes they may commit.[43] For

[42] See C Tréan, 'L'ONU saisit la CPI des crimes commis au Darfour', *Le Monde* (Paris, 2 April 2005); symposium, 'The Commission of Inquiry on Darfur and its Follow-Up: A Critical View' (2005) 3 *Journal of International Criminal Justice* 539.

[43] See L Condorelli and A Ciampi, 'Comments on the Security Council Referral of the Situation in Darfur to the ICC' (2005) 3 *Journal of International Criminal Justice* 590, esp 'Immunity from ICC Jurisdiction for Nationals of Non-Party States', pp 594–7.

another, even if the prosecutor now has the Commission's report and list of suspects, he has no means of direct constraint and, instead of co-operating, the Sudanese authorities have tried to show that, contrary to the Commission's report, they are willing and able to prosecute the crimes themselves.

International criminal law may therefore contribute to synchronisation by introducing a bit of give into the relationship between politics and law, but it is a very modest contribution with limited effect when opposed by the most powerful countries. Resistance is weaker, however, with respect to the economy–law link. For example, China's drive to enter the WTO set off a wave of reforms going well beyond business law (law of corporations, contracts, intellectual property, insurance, antitrust, foreign trade, etc.) to reach general principles imposed by the accession protocol, such as transparency, uniform application of laws and effective review of administrative acts.[44] Entry into the WTO can thus contribute to strengthening the rule of law and the indirect synchronisation of trade and human rights law.

This indirect effect is of course stronger when normative integration 'wakes up' national judges who learn to use new international instruments even when they are not binding (that is, soft law). As I mentioned earlier, if a version of the UN Norms on Transnational Corporations were adopted, these norms could be invoked before domestic judges who could incorporate them when interpreting domestic law. The relationship between normative levels is therefore important.

## The Relationship between Levels

I have discussed several situations in which things seemed stalled at the global level and momentum was regained at the national, regional, or inter-regional level. In the area of corruption as well as climate change, for example, the relationship between the global and regional—and even infra-national (despite the United States'

---

[44] See M Delmas-Marty, 'La construction d'un Etat de droit en Chine, avancées et résistances' (2002) *Dalloz* 2484; 'La construction d'un Etat de droit dans le contexte de la mondialisation' in M Delmas-Marty and PE Will (eds), *La Chine et la Démocratie, Tradition, Droit, Institutions* (Paris, Fayard, 2006). See also L Choukroune, 'L'Accession de la Chine à l'OMC et la réforme légale: vers un Etat de droit par l'internationalisation sans démocratie?' in *ibid.*; 'L'Accession de la République populaire de Chine à l'OMC, instrument de la construction d'un Etat de droit par l'internationalisation' (doctoral dissertation, University of Paris I, 15 December 2004).

rejection of the Kyoto Protocol, several constituent states have limited greenhouse gas emissions)—organisations has contributed to indirect synchronisation at the global level by avoiding a political stalemate. In addition, the process I have described of normative integration through cross-referencing and judicial dialogue should enable more direct synchronisation in the long term to accompany the autonomisation of national and international review bodies. All that is needed is for judges to more systematically incorporate the legal reasoning of different normative areas, that is, to practise internormativity (between trade agreements and instruments of the ILO, environmental law, or human rights, for example).

But the temptation might arise to try to impose the same rhythm on every state. I therefore suggest that to be pluralist, synchronisation must respect a national margin of appreciation to preserve the national tempo. In other words, synchronisation may lead to a certain polychrony.

# 7
# Polychrony

I USE THE TERM 'polychrony', which is not usually used in the legal field, to describe the phenomenon of legal mechanisms in a single area evolving at different speeds, as is suggested by the frequently heard reference to a 'multi-speed' Europe. Distinct from asynchrony (different speeds in different areas), polychrony should enable the integration process to continue without 'the slowest wagon dictating the speed of the convoy',[1] as former Chancellor Kohl put it. Polychrony might even avoid the convoy's being completely stalled, if the phrase means that a group of wagons can start up after a halt such as the one called by the failure of certain countries to ratify the Constitutional Treaty.

But Europe's current difficulties in this regard must not obscure analogous phenomena at the global level, since the goal is to take into account the variety of national situations to avoid imposing a rhythm on a state that it cannot maintain. This is the basis for the principle of 'common but differentiated responsibilities' found in Article 3 of the United Nations Framework Convention on Climate Change (UNFCCC) and implemented by the Kyoto Protocol, which divides states into categories depending on their level of development. In short, differentiating commitments over time is a way to reconcile legal expansion (increasing size of the normative area) and integration (deeper penetration of the normative order). But stated this way, the correlation is no doubt too simplistic to account for the variety of instruments that do not always clearly separate differentiation with respect to normative time from other forms of differentiation.

A little over a decade ago, the European University Institute in Florence organised a round table in anticipation of the Amsterdam Treaty, which was about to establish time-based differentiation

---

[1] P Lamy, 'L'Europe à quelques-uns? Les coopérations renforcées' in Mouvement européen, *La Lettre des Européens*, special number (2 November 1996), p 131 (citing former Chancellor Kohl).

under the name 'enhanced co-operation'. The discussion was based on Claus-Dieter Ehlermann's working document placing the various methods of differentiation into three categories: 'multi-speed', 'variable geometry', and 'pick and choose'.[2] Underscoring the need to avoid confusing them, as was the general tendency, Ehlermann graded the three categories according to whether they favoured a primarily national conception or accompanied an integration process that could be inter- or supranational. The 'pick and choose' method (the so-called Thatcher method) was the most poorly integrated because it enabled each state to pick and choose measures and thereby maintain a traditionally intergovernmental international approach. The 'variable geometry' method (horizontal or vertical integration) is more open and, depending on the mechanism's degree of integration, can foster passage from the international to the supranational sphere (so-called Delors method). Lastly, the 'multi-speed' or so-called Willy Brandt method (also employed by Joschka Fischer) seems the most restrictive: the rules to be integrated are decided at the supranational level, and only the rhythm (integration speed) may vary.

In practice, these categories often overlap. In Europe, for example, differentiation appeared in the Schengen acquis, which combines variable geometry with multiple speeds. Such differentiation became entrenched with the Amsterdam and Nice treaties under the name of 'enhanced co-operation'. At the global level, the UNFCCC and Kyoto Protocol set the rules on greenhouse gas emissions and, to a certain extent, determine the integration speed for each category of states.

Before I try to systematise the conditions enabling polychrony to be an instrument of the legal order, I will use these two examples to illustrate the variety of practices.

## The European Example of 'Enhanced Co-operation'

In the words of Jean Monnet, Europe was built in 'small steps'; but in a Europe limited to economic integration, the six founding countries advanced in step, at the same rhythm. This rhythm was broken by enlargement (to nine member states in 1973, then 10 in 1981,

---

[2] CD Ehlermann, 'Increased Differentiation or Stronger Uniformity' (1995) European University Institute Working Paper 95/21; 'Différenciation, flexibilité, cooperation renforcée: les nouvelles dispositions du traité d'Amsterdam' (1997) *Revue du Marché unique européen* 53.

12 in 1987, 15 in 1995 and 25 in 2004) and deeper involvement in common policies.

After France twice used its veto power (in 1963 and 1967), General de Gaulle's retirement in 1969 cleared the way for President Georges Pompidou to accept the United Kingdom's entry into the European Economic Community (EEC). This Community grew to include the Scandinavian countries and the former Communist countries of Eastern and Central Europe, the primary goal of which was to expand the market. Their interests differed from those of the founding countries, which were closer to the United States. Increased differences led inevitably either to stalemate or to differentiation, namely with respect to time.

The first projects designed to reconcile enlargement and deepening involvement in common policies and corresponding to a multi-speed Europe appeared in haphazard order, both internally and externally to the Community framework, before being included in and limited by the European treaties themselves.

## The First Projects

The Schengen acquis (1985–1990) was the first such project. Though external to the treaties, the acquis 'does not compete with the EU, but constitutes one of its ' "laborator[ies]"': in fact, only EU member states may become parties to the convention'.[3] In 1985, five states concluded an agreement in Schengen aimed at phasing out border controls. Complemented by the application convention of 1990, which must be seen as a result of the 1986 Single European Act and the fall of the Berlin wall in 1989, the Schengen apparatus includes mechanisms designed to strengthen integration with respect to security and offer other states the opportunity to join.

The explicit goal is to replace internal border controls with a common legal apparatus comprising, namely, the Schengen Information System (SIS) and so-called judicial and police 'co-operation' measures that entail a certain amount of integration (the rule *ne bis in idem* has been extended to prosecutions and convictions occurring in other Schengen states, for example).[4] The implicit goal for

[3] J Pradel and G Corstens, *Droit penal européen* (Paris, Dalloz, 2nd edn 2002), p 47.
[4] See S Manacorda, '*Judicial activism* dans le cadre de l'espace de liberté, de justice et de sécurité de l'Union européenne' (2005) *Revue de science criminelle* 940 (discussing the ECJ's decisions in joined cases C-187/01 and C-385/01 *Gözütok* and *Miraglia* [2003] and case C-469/03 [2005]).

Schengen states, however, is to accelerate integration, which is now
not only multi-speed, but also of variable geometry. While only five
states ratified the initial agreement in 1985, eight ratified the 1990
application convention, with two more joining in 1997 and another
three by 2001, such that the Schengen area included 13 of the then
15 EU member states (the UK and Ireland opting out). But within
the Schengen area, the degree of integration may vary: France has
refused to grant foreign police officers the right to arrest suspects
during joint cross-border police operations while Germany recognises such a right.[5] Acceleration then became anticipation, however:
the Schengen acquis was incorporated into the EU with the
Amsterdam Treaty, then imposed on candidate states and annexed
to the Lisbon Treaty by a protocol (Protocol no 19, Article 2 concerning admission of new members). In addition, a portion of the
apparatus is meant to be extended to all EU member states (the rule
of *ne bis in idem* was included in a proposed framework decision,
though the proposal failed for unknown reasons[6]).

The first group of states can thus be considered a sort of avant-
garde, but without the permanent meaning attached to such expres-
sions by politicians such as the former German minister of foreign
affairs[7] and French president.[8] Just as Karl Lamers and Wolfgang
Schäuble had underscored in their 1994 report, Joschka Fischer
made clear that the only way to reconcile 'enlargement and deepening' was to allow differentiation. But he separated 'enhanced co-
operation' from the creation of an avant-garde group or 'centre of
gravity'. First, enhanced co-operation would be extended to areas
such as protecting the environment, fighting crime, immigration
and asylum policy, and external security policy. Then a 'centre of
gravity' comprising a few states constituting a 'permanent avant-
garde' would be created by a new treaty, which would be open to
candidates wishing to join the core group of a future federation to
be formed in a third phase.

---

[5] See Conseil d'État, decision of 25 November 2004 in *Rapport public 2005*,
Etudes et documents du Conseil d'Etat no 56 (Paris, La Documentation française,
2005), p 173.

[6] See Conseil d'État, decision of 29 April 2004 (approving the proposal but underscoring its incompleteness in the case of *lis pendens*) in *Rapport public*, above n 5. On
the failure of the proposal for unknown reasons, see S Manacorda, '*Judicial activism*',
above n 4.

[7] See J Fischer, speech at Humboldt University, Berlin, 12 May 2000.

[8] See *Le Monde* (Paris, 28 June 2000) (reporting J Chirac's 27 June 2000 speech at
the Bundestag).

The problem is that Fischer scrambled his message by putting the Schengen acquis and the Economic and Monetary Union (EMU) model on the same plane, as examples of enhanced co-operation. The EMU (organised by the 1992 Maastricht Treaty) neither corresponds to the same group of states nor has the same meaning, since certain states excluded themselves from it, just as they later refused to join the euro area. Unlike the Schengen acquis, which is a transition mechanism designed to accelerate integration and create a kind of centrifugal force of attraction to pull other states in (opt in), the EMU's derogatory clauses create an opt-out dynamic that slows integration down.

The ambiguities and even contradictions of these initial multi-speed projects should have encouraged the legislator to clarify the concept of enhanced co-operation when incorporating it into later texts. In this regard the texts are disappointing, because the concept was entrenched without becoming any clearer.

### Entrenchment

The Amsterdam Treaty incorporated the Schengen apparatus into the acquis communautaire and introduced enhanced co-operation. The goal was to avoid a British veto by allowing countries who want to 'go further faster', in Jacques Chirac's words, to co-operate more closely within the Union framework.

Enhanced co-operation appeared quite novel and was sometimes presented as a revolution compared to the Community vision of unity. States such as the United Kingdom, which despite having requested flexibility, feared it would accelerate the integration process, therefore subjected it to restrictions, including 'critical mass' (at least half the states) and 'last resort' (the impossibility of obtaining a decision by all member states must be shown). In addition, the second pillar (common foreign and security policy, CFSP) was excluded and a suspensive veto granted to states opting out of a particular co-operation programme. And of course, the acquis communautaire had to be respected. Unable to establish a list of issues that could or could not be the subject of enhanced co-operation, the drafters set out very strict conditions requiring, inter alia, that enhanced co-operation not affect the Commission's policies, actions or programmes, constitute a barrier to trade between member states, or distort competition between them (see the '10 commandments' in Treaty on European Union (TEU) Article 43, as well as Treaty on the European Community Article 11 and TEU Article 40, related to specific pillars).

But the Amsterdam mechanism was never applied and, in anticipation of enlargement, was simplified by the 2000 Nice Treaty,
which eliminates the veto, sets 'critical mass' at eight states no matter what the total number of member states, and eases certain financial conditions. In addition, it extends enhanced co-operation to the
CFSP pillar, to the exclusion of defence and military activities.
However, the Nice Treaty preserves the 'last resort' requirement
and, above all, precludes any anticipatory effect by providing that
none of the acts and decisions necessary to implement enhanced co-
operation will form part of the Union acquis, which means that,
unlike the Schengen apparatus, they will not be imposed on new
members.

It is uncertain whether enhanced co-operation, loosely framed and
with a severely limited impact on the EU's future, has any attractive
pull that would advance the EU.[9] It is therefore understandable that,
despite the fact that the Nice Treaty makes it 'legally easier to initi-
ate enhanced co-operation from within, rather than externally to, the
Treaty's institutional framework',[10] political leaders, namely French
and German, want to preserve the possibility for the 'avant-garde',
'pioneer group', or 'centre of gravity' to advance by other means,
including taking initiatives outside the EU framework. In this
regard, the Constitutional Treaty (CT), which maintained enhanced
co-operation, clarified nothing: 'neither fish nor fowl',[11] enhanced
co-operation lost its function of avant-garde anticipation and simply
served to replace the major hurdle of a unanimous vote with a qual-
ified-majority vote. This is particular true since, like the Nice Treaty,
Article I-44-4 explicitly precludes considering 'acts adopted in the
framework of enhanced co-operation' as acquis communautaire that
must be accepted by new member states (see also Lisbon Treaty,
Article 20 (4) TEU).

In fact, the CT as a whole would have weakened differentiation
mechanisms that are anticipatory or transitional integration 'accelerators' and strengthened derogatory and permanent mechanisms that
act as integration 'brakes'. For example, the CT would have enabled
member states to suspend legislative procedures that violate the

[9] See J Rideau, *Droit institutionnel de l'Union et des Communautés européennes*
(Paris, LGDJ, 4th edn, 2002) p 98; D Vernet, 'Conséquences d'un non français', *Le
Monde* (Paris, 10–11 April 2005).

[10] P Ponzano, 'Après l'échec du sommet de Bruxelles: Constitution européenne ou
coopérations renforcées' (2003) *Revue du droit de l'Union européenne* 549, 552.

[11] H Bribosia, 'Les coopérations renforcées au lendemain du traité de Nice' (2001)
*Revue du droit de l'Union européenne* 111.

proportionality and subsidiarity principles (the protocol on the application of these principles simplifies the procedure with regard to the area of freedom, security and justice). Combined with the refusal to consider enhanced co-operation as acquis, these mechanisms should have reassured those who feared the rigidity of a text supposedly 'cast in stone'. In any case, they raised once again the issue of whether or not the goal is to accelerate integration or simply to slow down the disintegration programmed by the Nice Treaty.[12]

The Lisbon Treaty, on the other hand, facilitates enhanced co-operation among nine or more member states (Articles 20 TEU and 326 to 334 TFEU).

The terminology used above indicates that differentiating over time would bring Europe closer to an 'à la carte' system than to true polychrony, unlike the 'differentiated responsibilities' with respect to climate change being instituted at the global level.

## The Global Example of 'Differentiated Responsibilities'

A result of decolonisation and the break-up of the Soviet Union, enlargement at the global level preceded normative integration. To say that expanding the normative area (enlargement) and integrating the order (deepening) call for time-based differentiation (polychrony) means suggesting that multi-speed ensembles be largely used. This idea is only beginning to be embraced, however, extremely cautiously and only in certain sectors of international law, no doubt for fear the fledgling world order will disintegrate.

The concept of 'development' (law of and right to development) could have led to multi-speed normative integration, but the issue is not solely legal. From the 1960s to 1980s when the international law of development became recognised as such, the predominant issues concerned political tensions and economic inequalities, which law obviously cannot resolve on its own, especially since even the poorest states rejected double standards and a 'two-speed international law' that violates the principle of sovereign equality.

---

[12] See F de la Serre, 'Les coopérations renforcées, quel avenir? Elargissement et différenciation: de la cooperation renforcée à l'avant-garde' in P Tronquoy (ed), *L'Europe en perspective* (Paris, La Documentation française, 2000) 298; G Soulier, 'Quand disparaît la Communauté, reste le droit communautaire' in *Les Dynamiques du droit européen en début de siècle. Etudes en l'honneur de Jean-Claude Gautron* (Paris, Pedone, 2004) 513 *ff.*

The idea of a multi-speed normative ensemble thus first appeared in the apparently more neutral area of environmental law. First expressed in concepts such as 'pioneer investors' in the area of managing the sea bottom, the idea was taken up in the 1992 Earth Summit Declaration (Rio Declaration), then in the UNFCCC and the Kyoto Protocol under the name of 'common but differentiated responsibilities'. Now, climate policies pose formidable problems not only for scientists, but also for economists due to 'irreversibility, lengthy time periods and extreme uncertainty'.[13] I will not discuss the irreversibility/uncertainty pair, which is the basis for the precautionary principle (an anticipatory principle[14]), but will review the response to the problem of 'lengthy time periods' contained in the legal mechanism instituted by the 1992 UNFCCC and the 1997 Kyoto Protocol (entry into force, 15 February 2005), which combines territorially differentiated normative integration (variable geometry) with different time tracks (multiple speeds).

To give 'sustainable development' some kind of common meaning, past disparities and responsibilities of the more developed countries had to be taken into account while still aiming to guarantee the well-being of future generations and protecting the ecosystem (defined in UNFCCC Article 2 on biological diversity). Without detailing the law, I will note the main components of a multi-speed legal regime based, unlike European enhanced co-operation, on a schedule and acceleration mechanisms that will help maintain Kyoto's gains in the post-Kyoto world.

### The Kyoto Schedule

The UNFCCC preamble notes that 'the largest share of historical and current global emissions of greenhouse gases has originated in developed countries, that per capita emissions in developing countries are still relatively low and that the share of global emissions originating in developing countries will grow to meet their social and development needs'. But noting this fact does not mean analyses must remain limited to binary opposition between developed and developing nations.

Paradoxically, the 1992 UNFCCC may have been helped by the extreme diversity of national interests: 'states split into several

[13] R Guesnerie, 'L'Evaluation économique des politiques climatiques' in E Bard (ed), L'Homme face au climat (Paris, Odile Jacob, 2004).

[14] See M Delmas-Marty, Les Forces imaginantes du droit (I): Le Relatif et l'Universel (Paris, Seuil, 2004), pp 368–74.

groups that, surprisingly, did not fall along the traditional North/South divide but illustrated . . . the importance they ascribed to specific and sectoral interests.'[15] Most OECD countries were favourable to limiting greenhouse gas emissions, but the United States refused to be subject to such a limitation; the oil-producing states had their reservations as well, though this was evidently for other reasons; and many developing nations were reluctant to give up certain energy sources. But insular countries and those with low coastlines, apt to feel the worst effects of rising oceans, wished to have their specific interests recognised, as did states subject to drought and desertification or high urban pollution, and those with fragile ecosystems, namely in mountainous regions. The list appearing at Article 8(a)–(i) of the Convention illustrates the variety of national interests and avoids binary opposition, which often leads to a political stalemate and, therefore, the failure of legal solutions.

This diversity provides the basis for the Convention's novel mechanism. Borrowing the principle of 'common but differentiated responsibilities' (UNFCCC, Article 4) from the Rio Declaration, the Convention seeks to achieve a common goal through practices that differ across space and time, as outlined in the first schedule appearing in Article 4. Entitled 'Commitments', this article sets out the general commitments of all states parties (such as, *inter alia*, publishing inventories, promoting research and transferring technologies), then adds the specific obligation for developed countries and those transitioning to a market economy to reduce their emissions to their 1990 levels (Article 4(2)).

The Kyoto Protocol provides a more detailed schedule for developed countries, which are presented as the 'avant-garde in the struggle against climate change': for the 2008–2012 period, each of these state's authorised emissions are determined according to quotas set by reference to their 1990 emissions (5 per cent below 1990 levels, Article 3(1)).[16] Transitioning countries are granted some latitude, however, as their emissions are limited to historic levels that may be other than 1990 levels (UNFCCC and Kyoto Protocol, Article 3(5)).

To go beyond Kyoto, however, acceleration mechanisms will have to take over when the schedule reaches its end.

---

[15] L Boisson de Chazournes, 'Le droit international au chevet de la lutte contre le réchauffement planétaire: elements d'un régime' in *L'Evolution du droit international. Mélanges Hubert Thierry* (Paris, Pedone, 1998), p 54.

[16] The EU's environmental minister's goal is even more ambitious: 15–20% by 2020. See *Liberation*, 12–13 March 2005.

*Acceleration Mechanisms to Go Beyond Kyoto*

Russia's ratification on 18 November 2004 enabled the Kyoto Protocol to enter into force on 16 February 2005. But negotiating a schedule to go beyond 2012 has proved difficult. In 2004, the United States continued its resistance and developing countries refused to negotiate regarding post-2012 engagements. Progress since then has been limited and the final conference will take place in December 2009. Various other mechanisms may, however, facilitate the Protocol's implementation and foster a certain degree of acceleration.

The Protocol itself, for example, provides for a certain number of market mechanisms: emissions permit exchanges,[17] which are the basis of the mechanism, authorise countries having reached their emissions-reduction goals to sell their surplus 'pollution rights' to others; 'joint applications' enable countries to obtain emissions credits for investing in other countries of the same category in ways that enable the country of investment to reduce its greenhouse gas emissions, such as modernising a factory (France/Romania agreement, for example); and the 'clean development' mechanism allows states to provide technical assistance in exchange for emissions credits, provided the assistance agreement is between one industrialised and one non-industrialised state party (France/Argentina, for example). In addition, market mechanisms exist outside the international framework, including in countries that are not parties to the Kyoto Protocol. In the United States, after voluntary exchange programmes developed[18] and some constituent states committed to reducing emissions, the Environmental Protection Agency was held responsible for regulating certain greenhouse gas emissions and, in June 2009, the House of Representatives approved an emissions control bill.[19]

Changing organisational levels (legally joining space and time) therefore seems to be a way to foster acceleration, which can come

---

[17] See M Delmas-Marty, 'Aspects juridiques' in Bard, *L'Homme face au climat* above n 13; B Le Bars, 'La Nature juridique des quotas d'émission de gaz à effet de serre après l'ordonnance du 15 avril 2004: réflexions sur l'adaptabilité du droit des biens' (2004) *Juris-classeur périodique* 148 (discussing the 15 April 2004 French decree creating an emission quota exchange programme).

[18] See Delmas-Marty, *Le Relatif et l'Universel* above n 14, p 388.

[19] See H Kempt, 'Sept Etats nord-américains décident de réduire les émissions de CO2' *Le Monde* (Paris, 23 December 2005); *Massachusetts v EPA*, 594 US 497 (2007); JM Broder, 'House passes bill to address threat of Climate Change', *New York Times* (New York, 26 June 2009).

from the infra-national (constituent states of the United States) or regional level. When only some of the states participating in external market mechanisms are parties to the Protocol (Canada and Mexico in the NAFTA context), the acceleration effect is only indirect; but the effect is direct when all the states participating in a programme that anticipates the global schedule are parties to the Protocol, as is the case with the EU.

The liveliness of the debate[20] on the European Directive of 13 October 2003 anticipating the Kyoto Protocol by instituting an emissions exchange system as of 2005 illustrates the difficulties in winning a bet that requires that Europe succeed in avoiding free-riders who threaten the conditions for producing collective goods by reaping the collective benefits without making the essential effort.[21] The solution today consists of monitoring procedures and sanctions, but in the long term, it will require inventing win-win solutions in tandem with developing countries that are both generous and effective.

One such solution is to differentiate integration speeds in areas other than environmental law, namely trade law. This issue was raised from both a historical and a prospective perspective in 2004 by the WTO Dispute Resolution Body in the *India v European Communities* case concerning the 'conditions for granting preferential tariffs to developing countries'.[22] It is a way of raising at the global level the issue raised several times in the European context of the possibility of building 'legal' reasoning in such a context.

## Polychrony and Legal Orders

During the discussions on enhanced co-operation, then European Commissioner Pascal Lamy raised the issue of such co-operation's compatibility with European legal construction. Fearing that too much flexibility would strengthen judicial review of the Commission, he openly suggested that it would be better to limit the use to areas not governed by law.[23]

---

[20] See, eg, B Collomb and G Dollé, 'Kyoto? Oui! La directive européenne? Non!' *Le Monde* (Paris, 11 December 2004). See also the response by Y Jadot and P Quirion, 'Kyoto? Oui! Le leadership européen? Maintenant!' *Le Monde* (Paris, 21 December 2004).

[21] See R Guesnerie, 'L'Evaluation économique des politiques climatiques', above n 13.

[22] H Ruiz Fabri, 'Chronique' (2004) *Journal de droit international* 1036 (citing WTO, *India v European Communities,* 7 April 2004).

[23] See P Lamy, 'L'Europe à quelques-uns?' above n 1, p 119.

But there are more and more of these areas and it has since become clear that such a limitation is impossible: polychrony, like variable geometry, has been entrenched by legal instruments. Far from being reserved for isolated cases, practices seem to extend to using multi-speed mechanisms other than in relation to European construction or climate change law. They therefore need a legal framework.

### Extension of Practices to All Normative Organisational Levels

When the variety of interests in certain areas calls for time-based differentiation at the regional level, organisations other than the EU express interest in 'enhanced co-operation', including organisations such as NAFTA, which has only three partners.[24] Time-based differentiation is also developing at the global level beyond environmental law and the Kyoto Protocol's 'common but differentiated responsibilities'.

In trade law, for example, the 'enabling clause' provides for granting preferential tariffs, and thus 'differential treatment', to developing countries. As the DRB outlined in its *India v European Communities* decision, the states parties to the GATT of 1947 declared one of their objectives to be to 'raise the standard of living', through the GATT's 'universally applied' commitments, regardless of a party's stage of economic development. But a 1971 decision authorised derogating from obligations contained in GATT Article one and granting preferential tariffs to developing countries for a 10-year period, and in 1979, the 'enabling clause' made this authorisation permanent and enlarged its scope to include additional preferential measures.

When the WTO was created in 1994, the member states confirmed the importance of the enabling clause by incorporating it into the new agreement. The relationship between trade and development (particularly due to the enabling clause) was presented as an essential element of the WTO's programme (which was recognised at the ministerial conference in Doha in 2001[25]). Of course, this is still an exception (especially from the perspective of evidence law), but member states are 'encouraged' to use the exception and to deviate from article one to grant 'differentiated and more favorable

---

[24] See E Leser, 'Etats-Unis, Mexique et Canada signent un accord de coopération renforcée', *Le Monde* (Paris, 25 March 2005).
[25] See Ministerial decision of 14 November 2001, *Implementation-related issues and concerns*, WT/MIN (01)/17, paras 12.1 and 12.2.

treatment' to developing countries. The DRB has thus tried to legally frame the use of this clause to prevent states from granting preferences to some developing countries while denying them to others (as India wanted the European Communities to do, thus its challenge to preferences granted to other states, namely Pakistan), as such practices would constitute an indirect return to bilateral negotiations, which are more sensitive to hegemonic tendencies.

Political, cultural and economic differences between parties no doubt justifies the extension and diversification of multi-speed practices that I call 'polychrony'. But to avoid abuse, they also require a new type of legal framework.

### Need for a Legal Framework

Theoretically, polychrony fosters pluralism by not imposing the same rhythm on every state. In practice, when 'multi-speed' becomes synonymous with 'à la carte', it can also lead to disorder and arbitrariness. To avoid these perverse effects, the legal framework must govern both enabling conditions and anticipation.

After the Amsterdam Treaty took effect, legal commentators examined the dynamics and risks created by the flexibility they feared might mean disintegration[26] and tried to systematise the conditions and effects related to the new treaty's various legal instruments. In an article published in 2000 that many authors later elaborated on, Alexander Stubb suggested distinguishing two types of 'à la carte' menus: 'enabling clauses', which define the prerequisites without specifying the effects (enhanced co-operation provisions); and 'pre-defined flexibility', which determines the effects without reiterating the conditions (provisions incorporating the Schengen apparatus into the acquis communautaire).[27] But he presents these as alternatives whereas, if the goal is ordering pluralism, conditions and effects should not alternate but combine and mutually reinforce each other. In other words, to contribute to integration (and perhaps pave the way for enlargement), the legal framework should both define enabling clauses as objectively as possible and prescribe their effects.

---

[26] See H Wallace, 'Flexibility: a Tool of Integration or a Restraint for Disintegration? In K Neunreither and A Wiener (eds), *European Integration after Amsterdam. Institutional Dynamics and Prospects for Democracy* (Oxford, OUP, 2000) pp 175–91.

[27] A Stubb, 'Negotiating Flexible Integration in the Amsterdam Treaty,' in Neunreither and Wiener, *European Integration after Amsterdam*, above n 26, pp 153–74.

Enabling clauses in fact allow for legally as well as politically supervising differentiation. But the types of differentiation must be distinguished—either anticipatory (such as enhanced co-operation under the European treaties), or derogatory (namely opt-out clauses in European treaties and differential treatment within the WTO, such as preferential tariffs)—and objective criteria articulated to allow for rationalising the simultaneous use of different time tracks. The Constitutional Treaty therefore set out conditions in minute detail, incorporating portions of prior instruments and reiterating that enhanced co-operation 'shall aim to further the objectives of the Union, protect its interests and reinforce its integration process' and is open to all member states (Article I-44) (see also Lisbon Treaty, Article 20 TFEU).

Similarly, the 1971 GATT decision on differential treatment stated that the enabling clause was decided 'to facilitate and promote the trade of developing countries and not to raise barriers or create undue difficulties for the trade of any other contracting parties'. In citing this phrase in 2004, the DRB recalled that member states are encouraged to use the exception and to deviate from Article 1 to grant 'differentiated and more favourable treatment' to developing countries. But this deviation with respect to time is encouraged only to the extent that it complies with a series of conditions set out in the enabling clause and satisfying objective criteria. In fact, the DRB's decision calls the European regime with respect to medicines into question not because it differentiates between 12 developing countries and thereby discriminates among them, but because it does not enumerate 'clear, objective criteria' applicable to other countries in the same category affected by the same phenomenon and does not provide a procedure for evaluating the effectiveness of such preferential treatment.

In addition to these cases, the discussions at the WTO's tenth anniversary should help systematise the method. In a working document presented in March 2005, the authors conclude that the 'nothing is agreed until everything is agreed'[28] approach must be abandoned, and suggest establishing two time tracks. One would be for certain areas: 'In fact it would be logical for the new and complex subject areas at early stages of development (like investment or

---

[28] R Howse and S Esserman, 'The Appellate Body, the WTO Dispute Settlement System and the Politics of Multilateralism, First Draft,' working paper presented at the *WTO at 10, the Dispute Settlement System in Action* colloquium (Stresa, 11–13 March 2005).

competition) to be negotiated under longer deadlines than a subject like industrial tariffs.' The other would be for certain states, because a multilateral base does not involve consensus: 'Plurilateral agreements for certain subjects would enable those countries seeking to engage in more ambitious liberalization to proceed and avoid a situation where a small group of countries holds all progress.'

Criticising the ghetto approach, which consists of treating developing countries 'as a bloc—excusing them from obligations but thereby diminishing their legitimate claims to influence the rules', the authors suggest taking a multi-speed approach: 'There is no need to have a single deadline for negotiating all issues; rather groups of issues could proceed together in different time tracks.' They believe this would allow developing countries to participate in the debate and make commitments according to their means and abilities, rather than excluding them on the pretext of their difficulty in integrating at the same speed. This is acceptable if it means preparing the shift from a derogation strategy to an anticipation strategy, as well as thinking about effects and perhaps even developing a schedule.

Until now, effects have been dealt with primarily in the area of climate change, with the legal instrument's effects being predetermined and set out in a schedule that must be renegotiated over time (for the 2012–2020 period, for example). Another possibility is to determine effects *post hoc* by an explicit integration clause (as when the Schengen apparatus was integrated into the acquis communautaire by the Amsterdam Treaty). But this legal technique is ambiguous, as is the refusal (in both the Constitutional and Lisbon treaties) to consider acts adopted in the framework of enhanced co-operation as an acquis to be accepted by new members. The idea is not only to protect states that are as yet unable or unwilling to integrate; but also to maintain the interest of those who do not want to integrate at all and fear being pulled into a process developing without them. The danger is that initiatives may be taken externally to the treaty, leading to the disintegration of the European Union and reintegration into another ensemble, as slow and complex as that would be.

As necessary as work on (multi-speed) normative time is, it must not be isolated from thinking about order (variable geometry) and space (several levels). This no doubt conditions polychrony's ability to further the pluralist synchronisation of the various normative ensembles. In short, even if practices sometimes blend, the movements between processes of organisation, levels of organisation and speeds of evolution have remained separate. 'Ordering pluralism' therefore involves moving from dissociation to correlation and finding the legal mechanisms that, in the presence of chaotic movements (integration/ disintegration, internationalisation/renationalisation), can effect a balance apt to lead to transforming the very concept of legal order.

# Conclusion
## In the Land of Organised Clouds?

STUDYING THE INTERNATIONALISATION of law as movement, focusing on processes of interaction, organisational levels and speeds of transformation rather than their results, borders on calling into question the concept of legal order, perhaps even destroying the intuition that a legal order even exists and resists law's internationalisation and globalisation. In this regard, I am once again following Bachelard, who wrote that '[i]ntuitions are very useful: their purpose is to be destroyed'.[1] But I have not forgotten that his *Philosophie du non* (The Philosophy of No) does not result from a simple desire to negate. 'It does not negate just anything, any time, in any old way,' but includes, or envelopes what it negates. For example, 'non-Euclidean geometry envelopes Euclidean geometry, non-Newtonian physics envelops Newtonian physics, wave mechanics envelops relative mechanics.'[2]

From this perspective, it would seem that the Euclidean ('modern') view of the legal order—identified with the state and represented as a system of norms and institutions at once hierarchical, territorial and synchronised—is now enveloped by a non-Euclidean (so-called 'postmodern') conception. With the proliferation, diversification and dispersion of sources,[3] the state has been challenged in its principal forms: the centralised state has been weakened by the decentralisation of sources and the public-sphere state by their privatisation; but above all, the nation-state, which expresses the sovereignty of a community comprised of entwined interests and

---

[1] G Bachelard, *La Philosophie du non* 8th edn (Paris, PUF, 1981), p 139.
[2] *Ibid.*, p 137.
[3] See M Delmas-Marty, *Pour un droit commun* (Paris, Seuil, 1994) pp 53 *ff* (English version: N Norberg (trans), *Towards a Truly Common Law* (Cambridge, CUP, 2002) pp 31 *ff*); *Les Forces imaginantes du droit (I): Le Relatif et l'Universel* (Paris, Seuil, 2004) pp 171 *ff*. See also C Thibierge, 'Sources du droit, sources de droit: cartographie des sources' in *Mélanges Jestaz* (Paris, Dalloz, 2006).

identical aspirations, has seen this sovereignty eroded by law's inter-nationalisation. Not only is the state 'no longer the sole captain on board',[4] but we're beginning to wonder whether there is a captain and if so, who?

In the preceding chapters I have shown that interactions lead not only to integration, but to the disintegration of the legal order; changing levels between various areas—national, regional and global—produces contraction as well as expansion; and changing speeds can either facilitate gradual synchronisation or desynchronise rhythms between trade law and human rights law. In other words, each of the three axes (normative order,[5] space and time) charac-terises a potential dynamic, a setting in motion, and dissociating them produces apparently contradictory, non-linear, disorganised movements. Like clouds on a windy day, new legal ensembles seem to disperse as soon as they've formed, even before we've discerned their shapes.

To get from disorder to order, to 'organise the clouds', the legal ensembles taking shape must be made a little more stable and sustainable, though excessive stability reduces sustainability. In addition to traditional instruments that produce stability through normative and institutional hierarchy, there are several mechanisms that contribute more to legal ensembles' equilibrium than to their stabilisation, and perhaps therefore to their sustainability. The issue then is, what would a land of 'organised clouds' look like?

The mystery of the one and the many will not be solved by the hegemonic practices omnipresent today, which impose legal trans-plantations that cannot be called pluralist, nor by so-called ultra-liberal practices, which are increasingly common and consist of juxtaposing presumably self-regulating autonomous systems. As for the hypothesis of ordered pluralism set out in the introduction, it would no doubt require a transformation, literally speaking, as it involves replacing the simple conception of the legal order with a complex or even 'hypercomplex' conception.

---

[4] J Chevallier, *L'Etat postmoderne* 2nd edn (Paris, LGDJ, 2004) p 205. See also AJ Arnaud, *Entre modernité et mondialisation. Leçons d'histoire de la philosophie du droit et de l'Etat* 2nd edn (Paris, LGDJ 1994, 2004), pp 265–300.

[5] On the distinction between normative order and normative area, see G Timsit, *Les Noms de la loi* (Paris, PUF, 1986).

# Disorganised Movement: Like the Clouds

The cloud metaphor seems particularly well suited to the European legal ensemble, which is constantly changing shape: who could possibly trace the outlines of the Europe created by superposing the Community and Union treaties as revised by the Nice Treaty? Depending on one's personal experience and centres of interest, one is familiar with various fragments, but the complete outline eludes us all.

The Constitutional Treaty had the indisputable merit of providing the means to unify the legal framework. However, it would have eliminated neither variable geometry nor multiple speeds, as its preamble asserted that Europe is 'united in diversity'.[6] Its drafters may therefore be reproached for having given up too easily on teaching complexity as was expected of them, opting instead for the slightly demagogic discourse of simplification. Complexity seems inherent in any attempt to combine the one and the many and the CT should have more explicitly provided the means to organise these unstable, volatile—in a word, cloudlike—ensembles. Despite its failures, or perhaps thanks to them, Europe constitutes an extraordinary laboratory for studying the internationalisation of law: it illustrates, even sometimes caricatures, the disorder caused by interactions within the legal order and changes in organisational levels and time.

## Interactions: Integration/Disintegration

Integrating external norms begins with horizontal interactions: non-hierarchical cross-references. As old as it is, this practice is both developing, thanks to new technologies that facilitate access to the law, and being updated to include not only foreign law but also the law of international ensembles. These cross-references seem to constitute the primordial fluctuations by which legal matter begins to extend beyond the national sphere into a global area comprised, essentially, of black holes of unknown composition and characteristics, in terms of energy or inertia. If I had to write a short treatise on legal cosmogony, I would start with these cross-references because they very likely contribute to transforming normative masses into normative areas in the structural sense used above. This comparison is not really pertinent, however,

---

[6] The Lisbon Treaty deleted this motto, though some member states declared in an annex that it continues to be one of the symbols expressing the sense of community of the people in the European Union and their allegiance to it.

since, unless I go back to the big bang, my study would be limited to today's horizontal interactions and their occasional verticalisation, from coordination to subordination.

As I discussed above, international co-operation between European states seemed to lead inexorably to the European Union via principles such as mutual recognition and the approximation of national laws based on common supranational norms (see the list of offences in the European Arrest Warrant framework decision). This type of harmonisation, which constitutes an initial verticalisation of interactions, can be taken a step further to unification by hybridisation in areas where no national margin of appreciation is recognised (as in a portion of the draft *Corpus juris*). But at the global level, harmonisation and unification are limited to just a few areas, such as international criminal justice.

Horizontal interactions are also frequent among non-state actors, both private (such as transnational corporations) and public (international organisations or courts). Cross-references to case law both within and across regions (between the European Courts of Human Rights and of Justice or the European and Inter-American Courts of Human Rights) are just one example. Even the WTO has joined the game and integrated certain rules of environmental law,[7] and the recent debates on reforming the WTO lead me to think that the issue of integrating fundamental rights will soon be raised. Their recognition as universal standards could lead the DRB to impose both a social clause and a human rights clause on member states,[8] which could encourage interactions between the WTO and both the UN Human Rights Committee and the ILO.[9] Such exchanges and interactions remain horizontal, however, as verticalisation requires establishing a hierarchy that favours imperative norms (*jus cogens*) or

---

[7] See V Tomkiewicz, 'L'organe d'appel de l'Organisation mondiale du commerce' (doctoral dissertation, University of Paris I, 2004) pp 503–42.

[8] See EU Petersmann, 'Comments and Points for Discussion' in *Trade Negotiations and Dispute Settlement: What Balance Between Political Governance and Judicialization?*, working paper presented at *WTO at 10, the Dispute Settlement System in Action* colloquium (Stresa, 11–13 March 2005). Cf L Choukroune, 'L'Accession de la Chine à l'OMC et la réforme légale: vers un Etat de droit par l'internationalisation sans démocratie?' in M Delmas-Marty and PE Will (eds), *La Chine et la Démocratie, Tradition, Droit, Institutions* (Paris, Fayard, 2006); 'L'Accession de la République populaire de Chine à l'OMC, instrument de la construction d'un Etat de droit par l'internationalisation' (doctoral dissertation, University of Paris I, 15 December 2004).

[9] See P Auer, G Besse and D Méda (eds), *Délocalisations, Normes de travail et Politique d'emploi. Vers une mondialisation plus juste?* (Paris, La Découverte, 2005).

concepts such as global public goods, both of which are still subject to debate.

But this type of interaction can also develop between different normative levels. As the 'dialogue of judges on the death penalty' shows, horizontal, non-hierarchical exchanges are multiplying between national courts (Supreme Courts of Canada, South Africa and the United States, for example), regional courts (ECtHR and IACHR) and global judicial or quasi-judicial bodies (ICJ and UN Human Rights Committee). Similarly, cross-references are developing among national courts (the House of Lords' innovative decisions regarding former officials' immunity in the *Pinochet* case have been cited frequently[10]), regional human rights courts, international criminal tribunals and the ICJ.

These cross-references depend, however, on judges' goodwill, or benevolence as former First President Canivet calls it. Without hierarchy, the movement is incomplete. While too rapid and too rigid a verticalisation might be rejected and result in disintegration, horizontal interactions do not suffice for normative integration. At best, through mutual information, they may facilitate changing levels.

## Changing Levels: Expansion/Contraction

The word 'internationalisation' very explicitly refers to a change from the national to the international level, but the movement is not linear and is as disorganised as integration is. And through premature, poorly prepared or poorly controlled expansion, international organisations can cause a contrary movement of contraction, as the debate on Europe shows.

While internationalisation implies institutional and normative autonomy in relation to member states, it also requires that power struggles be neutralised and cohesion factors strengthened, as they alone make it possible to follow itineraries of convergence. Moreover, the trajectories of these itineraries must be discussed in advance: one of the misunderstandings created by the Constitutional Treaty stems from the fact that the principle bifurcations were taken without consultation, namely during successive enlargements (the

---

[10] See also, on the petition of Rigoberta Menchu and other plaintiffs for crimes committed in Guatemala, the decision of the Spanish Tribunal Constitucional, Second Chamber, of 26 September 2005 overturning the Supreme Tribunal's ruling conditioning the exercise of universal jurisdiction on the presence of Spanish victims. The Constitutional Tribunal refers explicitly to several decisions, namely German and Belgian, as well as of the ICJ.

largest one occurring with the Nice Treaty). Along with prior treaties, the Nice Treaty contributed to setting the 'institutional', if not 'constitutional', framework for the EU, which is almost as difficult to modify as a constitutional treaty. Even if the CT improved on a few points, such as organising powers (first part) or incorporating prior treaties (third part), the option of ratification by referendum chosen by most countries, including France, permitted only a binary response, which is ill-suited to the complexity of the issues raised.

So that contraction does not lead to disintegration of the European area, the major issue must be raised of inserting the Charter on Fundamental Rights into the EU's legal framework independently of the Constitutional Treaty.[11] Precisely because these rights are indivisible (the Charter 'reunites' them in six chapters linking economic, social and cultural rights with civil and political rights), they could either form the subject of an agreement or be rejected entirely. But the Charter's significance lies less in defining the contents of each of these rights, the scope of which will partially depend on the use made of the Charter, than in signalling the value choices made at the regional level that condition building a legal order.

If the Charter were inserted into a binding legal framework, instead of a simple 'normative area' of free trade characterised by a market without internal borders, Europe would constitute a true 'legal order' between the two poles 'market' and 'human rights'. This order would not be completely autonomous—it would be added on to national legal orders that will not disappear—but the collective preferences expressed in the Charter would render it internally consistent. Until now, despite the expression 'Community order', the law of the European communities and the EU is not itself consistent; its fragmentation was in fact underscored by the Maastricht Treaty's creation of three subject-matter pillars. With or without the CT, however, adopting the Charter would entrench the *de facto* bipolarity (market/human rights) that has developed within the EU through cross-references between the courts in Strasbourg and Luxembourg. And bipolarity would be further reinforced by the EU's ratification of the European Convention on Human Rights, which is provided for in both the Constitutional and the Lisbon treaties. Such entrenchment of a bipolar order would be a first in the international area.

At the global level, establishment of a bipolar order does not seem so close at hand, especially since expanding involves changing the

---

[11] The Charter would be binding after the Lisbon Treaty ratification.

order's essence as well as its scale. Expansion over the entire planet leads to inclusion without exclusion, a normative organisation without external enemies—at least no humanly identifiable enemies—unless we consider ourselves, as well as natural and man-made disasters to which we might contribute, as enemies.

But beyond the ontological question and from a solely legal point of view, such expansion requires a specific structure. Interdependence makes globalisation more than simply a piling up of independent and competing national, regional and global organisations. These organisations need legal links, which in turn require new regulatory instruments, particularly since different normative levels must be combined and different rhythms synchronised as changes in speed create further disorder.

## Changing Speeds: Synchronisation/Desynchronisation

Polychrony—different speeds within a single area, such as the Schengen, Kyoto and WTO areas—may seem to generate diversity and protect both pluralism and orderliness. But to do so, it must be implemented according to objective criteria (enabling clause) and its effects must be set out either in advance (Kyoto schedule), progressively, through a moving carpet effect (an automatic mechanism that advances constantly), or *post hoc*, through an irreversible ratchet effect (incorporation of the Schengen apparatus into the acquis communautaire).[12]

Without a legal framework, a multi-speed area conceived as an avant-garde that each state may join if it wants and if it can (opt in clause) risks becoming an 'à la carte' area in which each state may opt out of certain obligations. Instead of anticipating integration, time-based differentiation then acts as a brake and can even foster disintegration, the danger of which is increased by asynchrony between trade and human rights. Comparing the gradual balancing of these two areas in Europe to the growing divide between them at the global level reveals that better synchronisation requires revising the relationships between levels, as well as between legal powers and political and economic powers. But to be flexible enough to be compatible with national sovereignty, these relationships require a new kind of legal mechanism that allows for readjusting to achieve balance: to put the clouds in order, so to speak.

---

[12] See D Simon, *Le Système juridique communautaire* (Paris, PUF, 1997), p 18.

## Balancing Mechanisms: Putting the Clouds in Order

Like 'bricolage', though more neutral, the term 'balancing' evokes oscillation in the exercise of power, be it executive (European or global governance), legislative (the fuzzy), or judicial (the weak and the soft). It brings to mind the billiard-player's gesture described by Barthes[13] and suggests a new conception of legal mechanisms. As if, to resist the world's great disorder without taking refuge in falsely reassuring uniformity, the 'insurrection of the imagination' I mentioned in the introduction had to be encouraged: 'tremulous thought . . . is neither fear nor weakness, nor is it irresolution (think globally, act locally), but the assurance that it is possible to approach this chaos, to last and grow in this unforeseeability, to go against these certainties cemented into their intolerances, to "throb with the very throbbing of the world" that is to finally be discovered.'[14]

In the legal field as well, we need this assurance to approach chaos and respond to the unforeseeability of a law that is internationalising according to variable geometry at multiple speeds and producing unstable forms. We will also need 'tremulous thought' to resist the 'stiffening up of thinking about systems and the angry fits of systems of thought'.[15] This is why it is so important to learn to use the new instruments that have appeared in the legal sphere: regulatory concepts like subsidiarity and complementarity for flexible integration through adjustments and readjustments between the national and international levels; fine-tuning techniques, such as the national margin of appreciation and variability indicators to avoid excessive flexibility which, in the guise of differentiation, can lead to disintegration; and evaluation and monitoring mechanisms to try to reduce the risk of arbitrariness.

### Regulatory Concepts: Adjustment and Readjustment

To adjust the national to the regional or global level, positive law had to invent new mechanisms to leave some give between the supranational norm and its incorporation at the national level. It is well known that the hierarchical principle of the primacy of international law constitutes a frontal attack on state sovereignty. Indeed, neither

---

[13] See R Barthes, *Le Neutre. Cours au Collège de France (1977–1978)* (Paris, Seuil, 2002), p 174 and text above accompanying ch 2 n 8.
[14] E Glissant, *La Cohée du Lamentin* (Paris, Gallimard, 2005) p 25.
[15] *Ibid.*, p 128.

the Constitutional nor the Lisbon Treaty treats it as a principle, but refers to it only discreetly: 'The Constitution and law adopted by the institutions of the Union in exercising competences conferred on it shall have primacy over the law of the Member States' (Article I-6 CT). As if to excuse this audacity, a declaration was annexed to the Constitutional Treaty noting that 'Article I-6 reflects the case law of the ECJ and Court of First Instance'. The Lisbon Treaty is even more shy: a declaration annexed to the treaty merely recalls 'that, in accordance with well settled case law of the Court of Justice of the European Union, the Treaties and the law adopted by the Union on the basis of the Treaties have primacy over the law of Member States, under the conditions laid down by the said case law'.

The 'principles' of subsidiarity and proportionality, however, were given prominent display in the first part of the Lisbon Treaty under the title devoted to 'Common provisions' (Article 5 (3) TEU): 'Under the principle of subsidiarity, in areas which do not fall within its exclusive competence, the Union shall act only if and in so far as the objectives of the proposed action cannot be sufficiently achieved by the Member States.' Applicable only in the area of shared competences, subsidiarity is paired with proportionality: 'Under the principle of proportionality, the content and form of Union action shall not exceed what is necessary to achieve the objectives of the Treaties.' But as research into the origin of the term has shown, subsidiarity is not limited to the purely formal distribution of competences.[16] As Denys Simon has written, it is a 'regulatory concept'[17] that serves to both justify and limit Community action. In other words, subsidiarity functions as a dimmer switch increasing integration if the member states do not attain Union objectives and decreasing it if they do. Because it requires constant comparison of actions envisaged by European legislative acts with EU objectives, it has a more political than legal function. However, the review procedure instituted by the Lisbon Treaty to ensure EU compliance with the principles of subsidiarity and proportionality, which includes not only the political re-examination by legislative authorities but also a right to petition the ECJ for violation of the subsidiarity principle, calls for adjustment to determine the width of the margin left to the member states.

[16] See P Carozza, 'Subsidiarity as a Structural Principle of International Human Rights Law' (2003) 97 *American Journal of International Law* 38.
[17] D Simon, *Le Système juridique communautaire* above n 11, p 78. See also J Clam and G Martin, *Les Transformations de la régulation juridique* (Paris, LGDJ, 1998).

The same is true for the complementarity principle in the ICC Statute. The ICC has only complementary, or subsidiary, jurisdiction to try alleged perpetrators of international crimes. That is, it can take jurisdiction only when the state otherwise competent cannot or will not exercise jurisdiction (ICC Statute, Article 17). This too is a balancing mechanism, which can be used in a very flexible way when a third-party state examines the possibility of exercising universal jurisdiction. In the case brought in Germany against former American Secretary of Defense Donald Rumsfeld under the German Code of International Crimes, for example, the German federal prosecutor refused to take the case because the United States had opened an investigation into the 'situation' in Iraq. As I mentioned above, however, the Spanish Constitutional Tribunal considered that Guatemala was not able to try the case brought by Rigoberta Menchu and others.[18] As for the ICC, when determining whether or not to exercise jurisdiction, it looks to see not only whether an investigation has been opened, but whether or not the suspects are actually being sought. Indeed, in preparing the report on Darfur that enabled the Security Council to refer the case to the ICC, the Inquiry Commission presided by Antonio Cassese examined not only the existence of a national criminal justice system, but also its effectiveness and legitimacy in terms of independence, impartiality and due process. Complementarity is therefore not only a formal principle for assigning jurisdiction; it is also a 'regulatory concept' leading indirectly to a certain harmonisation, that is, to states' aligning their criminal justice systems with international norms.

In this regard, complementarity is similar to principles designed to effect integration more directly, such as 'functional equivalence'. Explained in the commentary on the OECD Convention on the corruption of foreign agents in international commercial transactions, this term refers to achieving the goal of fighting corruption 'without requiring uniformity or changes in fundamental principles of a Party's legal system'. The OECD working group on bribery combines a general appreciation of the functional effectiveness of texts and practices with more formal tests of internal consistency.[19] The issue is still open, however, with regard to whether the evaluation should include tests of external consistency, that is, legitimacy criteria measuring

---

[18]  See above n 10, point II no 6. See also *Le Monde* (Paris, 7 October 2005).

[19]  See Delmas-Marty, *Le Relatif et l'Universel*, above n 3, pp 253 *ff*.

respect for fundamental rights: assuming they were effective, would torture or the death penalty be acceptable?

A final 'regulatory concept' is the principle of mutual recognition, which was introduced at the Tampere summit and incorporated into the Nice Treaty with respect to the 'area of freedom, security and justice'. The idea is that mutual trust between countries subscribing to the same values can provide a basis for mutual recognition of judicial decisions and, if necessary, approximation of laws. But the practical applications, such as the European Arrest Warrant framework decision, have been called into question by several constitutional courts,[20] as if the European legislature had overestimated the efficacy criterion to the detriment of common values and fundamental rights.

These examples show that it is not enough to develop instruments designed to accelerate integration (such as, in Europe, third-pillar framework decisions and now first-pillar directives[21]); braking instruments are also needed to protect fundamental rights at the supranational level. The problem is that until the Charter on Fundamental Rights can be directly invoked, the European Union will have no brakes. Given how slowly appeals to the ECtHR progress, it is no wonder national judges want to replace this system and its faulty brakes.

In short, assuming they also adapt to changes in speed, regulatory concepts introduce the flexibility needed to adjust to international norms. But too much flexibility can create imbalances and a risk of arbitrariness. Fine-tuning techniques then become useful.

## Fine-tuning Techniques

The term might come as a surprise. Norms are theoretically created according to a hierarchical principle such that adjustment and fine-tuning are a single operation: incorporation of the international norm by the national receiver. But only techniques like the national margin of appreciation and indicators of variability provide for pluralist fine-tuning of all movements.

[20] See S Manacorda, '*Judicial activism*, dans le cadre de l'espace de liberté, de justice et de sécurité de l'Union européenne' (2005) *Revue de science criminelle* 940 (discussing decisions by the Polish Constitutional Court (27 March 2005, declaring the text contrary to the Constitution but suspending the decision's application), the Belgian Court of Arbitration (13 July 2005, requesting a preliminary ruling from the ECJ[)], and the Bundesver-fassungsgericht (18 July 2005, finding unconstitutional and invalidating the German law transposing the European Arrest Warrant)[)].

[21] See case C-176/03 [13 September 2005]. See also above text accompanying ch 1 n 9 and ch 4 n 20.

Unlike the judicial margin of appreciation, which weakens the hierarchical principle without questioning the continuity between superior and inferior norms, the national margin of appreciation enables partial integration, understood as the simple approximation of national norms: harmonisation without unification. In the European treaties still in force, this is the difference between regulations, binding in their entirety, and directives,[22] which are binding as to the result to be achieved but which 'leave to the national authorities the choice of form and methods'. It is unfortunate the term 'national margin of appreciation' was not explicitly used, both to give full voice to the clause's underlying premise and to avoid the confusion that arose with respect to directives and regulations.

In fact, the national margin of appreciation, invented by the ECtHR as a jurisdictional self-limitation, may be used in other international contexts, such as the OHADA,[23] WTO,[24] and the Kyoto area, but it requires a change in logic. Whether explicit or implicit, legislative (in a broad sense) or jurisprudential, the national margin of appreciation seems to preclude the disjunction proper to binary reasoning. It replaces conformity, according to which any difference, no matter how small, results in a judgment of non-conformity, with compatibility, which allows differences from one country to another. It involves reasoning according to fuzzy logic or, more broadly, gradation logics; integration can be measured in degrees, so partial integration is possible.[25] But not all differences are acceptable: the margin also marks a boundary not to be crossed. This requires setting a compatibility threshold, which reintroduces a binary disjunction, though it can vary across space and time. Only if fine tuning obeys explicit variability indicators[26] will such variability avoid becoming arbitrariness.

[22] The same difference appeared in the Constitutional Treaty (Art I-33) as European laws and framework laws.

[23] See P Dima Ehongo, 'L'intégration juridique des économies africaines à l'échelle régionale ou mondiale' in M Delmas-Marty (ed), *Critique de l'intégration normative* (Paris, PUF, 2004).

[24] See H Ruiz Fabri and P Monnier, 'A propos des mesures sanitaires et phytosanitaires' (2004) *Journal du droit international* 1025 (discussing Japan—Measures Affecting the Importation of Apples, Appellate Body Report, WT/DS245/AB/R, adopted 26 November 2003).

[25] See M Delmas-Marty and ML Izorche, 'Marge nationale d'appréciation et internationalisation du droit' (2000) *Revue international de droit comparé* 753 (English version: (2001) 46 *McGill Law Journal* 923).

[26] See M Delmas-Marty, *Le Flou du droit* (Paris, PUF, 1986; 'Quadrige' 2004).

So far, only the ECHR has tried to set out variability indicators. Systematised, fine-tuning techniques could be extended to various 'regulatory concepts'. But the very notion of fine tuning cannot be entirely controlled by the norm's transmitter. As Jean-François Coste and I underscored with respect to fuzzy logic, switching from binary to gradation logics, which involve a more complex decision-making process based on compatibility thresholds, transfers power to the norm's receiver.[27] Evaluation and review mechanisms are therefore essential.

*Evaluation and Review Mechanisms*

If the national margin of appreciation is determined by variability indicators, it can join regulatory concepts to vary normative intensity to adapt as smoothly as possible to observable data, somewhat like light-sensitive glasses darken or lighten depending on the ambient light. But such a mechanism's complexity can lead to perverse results: either excessive integration, when the international legislature exceeds its powers and does not respect the subsidiarity principle (an oft-heard reproach in Europe); or, conversely, insufficient integration, when the national authorities, on the pretext of transposing the international norm, renationalise it (as is the case with international criminal law).

Peer evaluation is one response to this problem. In the struggle against transnational corruption and money laundering,[28] for example, peer evaluation has resulted in the elaboration of variability indicators that can facilitate judicial review in domestic courts. But more binding mechanisms are not only possible, they are undoubtedly necessary, as is shown, independently of ICJ review (which is limited by the states parties' discretion), by the development of international review mechanisms, from arbitration (ICSID) to dispute resolution (WTO) to judicial review (ECtHR, IACHR, ECJ, ICC, etc.). However, the current dissymmetry must be corrected: existing mechanisms serve primarily to ensure proper adjustment of the national to the international level, whereas a mechanism such as the Lisbon Treaty provides is needed to review the use of subsidiarity in both directions.

---

[27] See JF Coste and M Delmas-Marty, *Le Genre humain* (Paris, Seuil, 1998) pp 135–54. See also ML Mathieu-Izorche, 'La marge nationale d'appréciation, enjeu de savoir et de pouvoir, ou jeu de construction?'(2006) *Revue de science criminelle* 25.
[28] See Delmas-Marty, *Le Relatif et l'Universel* above n 3, pp 258 *ff*.

But to truly generate diversity, economic and social indicators will have to be integrated with respect to both place (inter-national diversity) and time (evolving compatibility threshold). The ECtHR began to do this with respect to criminal prosecution of adult homo-sexuality,[29] for example: despite the fact that the cases concerned a moral issue and there was no legal common denominator among member states, the Court found that social attitudes were converging towards greater tolerance, in light of which the Court narrowed the national margin almost to the point of extinction. But without more rigorous analyses, the variety of variability indicators weakens legal pluralism, which contributes to an implicit social pluralism that seems to reduce judicial objectivity.[30]

In sum, legal balancing mechanisms provide for accompanying normative integration, but they only very imperfectly control its correlation to other movements. With respect to both expansion (enlargement) and synchronisation (acceleration and braking), a new legal order must be built.

## Models of Transformation: In The Land of Orderly Clouds

I first used the metaphor of orderly clouds with respect to a common, pluralist law after a visit to China where, as an obedient tourist, I looked at the clouds engraved in the stone steps to the Forbidden City and the Summer Palace. These clouds obeyed the imperial command for immutable order, and I had to explain in an after-word[31] that I wanted to illustrate not this static view of order, but on the contrary, an unstable and changing vision based more on Karl Popper's paradigms contrasting clouds and clocks, or the work of Henri Atlan on complex systems, between crystal and smoke.[32] The Forbidden City's motionless clouds have the merit of underscoring the plurality of possible models for a future world legal order and encourage us to seek a new relationship, needed now more than ever, between law and politics.

[29] See *Dudgeon v United Kingdom* Series A no 45 (1981). See also *Norris v Ireland*, Series A no 142 (1988).

[30] See A Lajoie, *Jugements de valeur* (Paris, PUF, 1997). See also F Tulkens and L Donnay, 'L'usage de la marge d'appréciation par la Cour européenne des droits de l'homme. Paravent juridique superflu ou mécanisme indispensable par nature?' (2006) *Revue de science criminelle* 3.

[31] See Delmas-Marty, *Pour un droit commun*, above n 3, pp 283–4.

[32] H Atlan, *Entre le cristal et la fumée* (Paris, Seuil, 1989).

## Multiple Models

The representations most commonly used in domestic legal orders today are based on the pyramid and network paradigms popularised by François Ost and Michel van de Kerchove. The pyramid is organised vertically according to a hierarchical relationship (subordination), while the network is constructed through interactions that may or may not be hierarchical. The 'dialectic' theory these author's develop leads them to conclude that 'contemporary law constantly oscillates between the potential universality of networks and very locally anchored pyramids', and that this oscillation translates 'a modest and preliminary ethic of complex societies in the network age'. [33] In fact, both paradigms also illustrate a shift from a simple (closed and stable) to a complex (open, unstable and polymorphous) structure. Transposing these paradigms to the study of the internationalisation of law, that is, to the phenomena accompanying the expansion of the national legal area to a regional or global partially integrated area, produces even more diversified representations of the legal order.

Expanding according to a pyramidal model leads to a fusional order conceived as a simple structure organised according to hierarchical principles. It is doubly simple, in fact, because the legal order (in terms of the process of producing norms) is predetermined by the hierarchical principle and because consistency is guaranteed by a sort of 'natural' correlation between normative integration, organisational levels and speeds of transformation. Apparently satisfying the condition of legal certainty that foreseeability of norms requires, this is a politically formidable model: it openly contradicts state sovereignty and, on the pretext of fostering the emergence of a global order, risks legitimating hegemonic integration.

Expanding according to a network model, however, seems easier to accept in terms of sovereignty; but it is ambiguous in that it can lead to two types of legal orders depending on whether expansion favours horizontal interactions (international or transnational, organised between public or private actors) or combines them with vertical interactions (through harmonisation or hybridisation).

The first variation would be organised only through horizontal interactions. It would be complex in that the structure is interactive:

---

[33] See F Ost and M van de Kerchove, *De la pyramide au réseau? Pour une théorie dialectique du droit* (Brussels, Facultés universitaires Saint-Louis, 2002).

its movements would spontaneously correlate with each other.[34] It would therefore be a self-regulated order, as ultraliberalism claims to be, bearing the risk of giving preference to more subtle forms of hegemony benefiting private economic powers. But a truly pluralist order is 'hypercomplex': it must combine horizontal and vertical interactions and correlate this variable-geometry integration with other movements occurring at several levels and several speeds.

Hypercomplexity reveals the limits of 'legal' reasoning. To be sure, as the first 50 years of European construction illustrate, it can absorb a certain amount of complexity,[35] but it does so without guaranteeing political legitimacy.[36] The temptation for jurists is to revel in this delicious complexity while citizens reject a system they discovered late and do not understand well. This may be what is happening today to the legal Europe we were so proud of: it has been caught up, and sometimes trampled, by politics. We must therefore go beyond models to find a flexible relationship between law and politics that will make the future European and world orders at least sustainable, if not entirely stable.

### Beyond Models

The principle choices are political, since modelling the legal order will not put an end to the discussion of which model to choose because reason must obey science. Indeed, science tends to describe what is and reason is at its service. But law is 'normative': it says what must be and therefore calls for willpower, or even voluntarism. This is why the legal reasoning in the major human rights texts seems to sometimes contradict reality, as if protesting against it, proclaiming, for example, that '[a]ll human beings are born free and equal in rights' (UDHR, Article 1) when empirical evidence does not support this conclusion.

The gap between the descriptive and the normative can be crossed only by a leap into the unknown, a wager on the future, an attempt to abolish chance: before concluding in the *Coup de dés* (roll of the dice) that 'every thought rolls the dice', Mallarmé announces that a roll of the dice 'NEVER abolishes chance'. But he qualifies that

---

[34] See A Fisher-Lescano and G Teubner, 'The Vain Search for Legal Unity in the Fragmentation of Global Law' (2004) 25 *Michigan Journal of International Law* 999.

[35] See G Soulier, 'Quand disparaît la Communauté, reste le droit communautaire' in *Les Dynamiques du droit européen en début de siècle. Etudes en l'honneur de Jean-Claude Gautron* (Paris, Pedone, 2004).

[36] See JL Quermonne *et al*, *L'Union européenne en quête d'institutions légitimes et efficaces* (Paris, La Documentation française, 1999).

statement, adding 'EXCEPT PERHAPS at the altitude . . . of A CONSTELLATION' and finally evoking a 'total count taking shape'. Because the total legal order taking shape also involves rolling the dice, it cannot be left to jurists alone, nor remain closeted in the law. In other words, because it takes willpower, transforming the national legal order into a supranational, or 'alternational'[37] order requires returning to politics.

The road to take is thus becoming clear. To avoid leaving the movements of law's internationalisation in total disarray, unforeseeable and uncontrollable, actors must be reintroduced and powers redistributed. Then will come the most difficult task: determining whether legal and other symbolic systems share common values. Only then will it be possible to dream of a day when blowing as one, these values organise, without immobilising, the clouds.

---

[37] P Lamy, *La démocratie-monde, Pour une autre gouvernance globale* (Paris, Seuil, pp 69–70). See also P Lamy, A Pellet and M Delmas-Marty, 'Les voies d'un ordre mondial', *Le Débat* No 142 (November–December 2006).

# Index